Shakespeare in Perspective
Volume One

SHAKESPEARE IN PERSPECTIVE
Volume One

Edited by Roger Sales

ARIEL BOOKS

BRITISH BROADCASTING CORPORATION

REFERENCE NUMBERS
A reference number follows each Shakespearean quotation in
this book, all of which are taken from the BBC edition of the
plays. The first digit refers to the relevant act in the play, the
second to the scene and the final digits are the line numbers,
eg 1.3.81–7
Act 1. Scene 3. Lines 81 to 87

Acknowledgement is due to the following:

Extract from *Hamlet* from DOCTOR ZHIVAGO by Boris
Pasternak, translated by Max Hayward and Manya Harari.
Reprinted by permission of William Collins Sons and Co Ltd.

Extract from *Musée des Beaux Arts* from COLLECTED SHORTER
POEMS 1927–1957 by W H Auden.
Reprinted by permission of Faber and Faber Ltd. and
Random House Inc., New York.

First published 1982. Reprinted 1984
Published by the British Broadcasting Corporation
35 Marylebone High Street, London WIM 4AA

Printed in England by Mackays of Chatham Ltd

Set in Ehrhardt by Phoenix Photosetting

ISBN O 563 16505 7

CONTENTS

INTRODUCTION
Roger Sales

These radio and television talks were all given as curtain raisers to the plays transmitted in the first three years of the BBC TV Shakespeare. They were intended to provide informative, entertaining programme notes particularly for those members of the audience who were experiencing Shakespeare for the first time. The radio talks, called *Prefaces to Shakespeare*, were given by a cast of distinguished actors and actresses, who had a professional knowledge of the play they introduced as well as a more personal love for it. The television talks, called *Shakespeare in Perspective*, were given by well-known writers and broadcasters, who approached the plays both as period pieces and in terms of their relevance for a modern television audience. Instead of being palmed off with an impersonal programme note, listeners and viewers had the privilege of being taken on a brisk, unpretentious and highly subjective guided tour by somebody who was not just knowledgeable about Shakespeare, but also excited and thus enthusiastic about him. Our guides spoke from the heart as well as the head.

It would be fondly foolish to pretend that nothing has been lost in putting these talks onto the printed page. The radio programmes were written largely for the ear. The guide's own voice was an integral part of the tour, as were the equally distinctive voices of the actors and actresses on the recordings used. It is one thing to read the Nurse's famous speech in *Romeo and Juliet*, quite another to listen to a recording of Dame Edith Evans's interpretation of it. Similarly, there is no way that the perfect harmony between the visual and the verbal that occurred in so many of the television programmes can be recaptured on the printed page, even with carefully selected and laid out illustrations. Although all the contributors to this volume want Shakespeare to be experienced as performance, they would certainly not discourage anybody from sitting in the armchair and reading some of the plays. Armchair theatre is better than no theatre at all. These talks were, individually, richer and more varied when given as performances for either radio or television, but they can still be read for sheer pleasure.

There are, nevertheless, gains to balance out the inevitable losses as the talks raise general issues as well as particular curtains. They are collected together here not as a conventional tie-in, but because they tie together to form an exciting, and in many ways, unique introduction to Shakespeare. They can still be treated as one-off programme notes on individual plays, but taken as a whole they offer perspectives on Shakespeare which challenge many traditional assumptions and approaches. There is a very strong emphasis in the radio talks on the need to rescue Shakespeare from the classroom or study and put him back in the theatre where he belongs. We are actively encouraged to think in terms of production and performance. For those bored by orthodox criticism, these talks often offer a view straight from the boards. They are written from what Dame Peggy Ashcroft describes as a 'dangerously subjective' point of view. Our guides deal with their own experiences, likes and dislikes as a way of communicating what a particular play means to them. Although they sometimes consider other reactions as a way of clarifying their own, they do not offer a bland summary of received wisdom and opinion. They want to engage an audience in a play and so deal, refreshingly and engagingly, with their own personal reactions to it. Hearts and prejudices are worn, as they should be, on the sleeve. I suspect that this kind of personal perspective is only dangerous to those who don't have the courage to air their own convictions about Shakespeare. Expertise and specialist knowledge are worn, again as they should be, very lightly. The talks are informal as well as informed.

We do not just find out about individual plays. There are, for instance, plenty of general insights to the actor's craft. Donald Sinden explains how to stand and deliver Shakespearean half-lines, whilst Michael Hordern tells us how he looks for a line or phrase early on in a play on which to base his characterisation. Ian Richardson says something about how he researched the part of Richard II by watching films of the present Queen's coronation in 1953. Timothy West acknowledges that his interpretation of Shylock was partially based on a long conversation he had with a rabbi. We also find out about twentieth century stage history, as our guides tell us about the famous productions in which they have appeared. When taken together, these individual reminiscences and anecdotes provide a lively introduction to most of recent waves of Shakespearean interpretation. Similarly, although the talks are not addressed specifically to Shakespeare's life, the incidental details and speculations tie together to form a biographical outline. We are told about acting techniques, stage history and Shakespeare's life. We learn, above all, that the play itself is the most important thing. That may seem a simple, perhaps even simplistic, point to make until you consider how conventional Shakespearean criticism tends to place barriers between the individual and his perceptions of the play as performance. What Janet Suzman describes as the lumpy porridge of criticism can be addictive. You go back for more and more helpings of this thick, grey substance instead of going to the theatre or watching productions on television.

Although the radio talks, particularly the ones on the English and Roman history plays, do deal with Shakespeare's England, this becomes more of a focal point in the television scripts. Shakespeare can, of course, be dragged kicking and screaming into the twentieth century for the hell of it. He does not become our contemporary, however, just because his characters are crammed into jackboots and pinstripes. It is only when we appreciate his relationship to his own contemporaries that we are in a position to talk about him as our contemporary as well. As the title suggests, the *Shakespeare in Perspective* programmes operate this kind of double focus. The producer, Victor Poole, wanted to demystify Shakespeare and so chose guides who could offer personal appreciations rather than impersonal criticisms. He felt that only other writers, or those who worked creatively in the same areas as Shakespeare, could rise to this challenge. The talks offer not just a general interplay between the modern and Shakespearean, but also the specialised perspectives of modern writers on perhaps the greatest writer ever. Both the radio and television talks stress the importance of a creative, imaginative and appreciative approach to Shakespeare. They complement each other in the sense that, whilst the controlling perspective may be broadly similar, the actors and writers map out different routes for their guided tours.

The initial emphasis on Shakespeare's relationship with his own contemporaries means that these television talks contain a wealth of historical detail and speculation about Elizabethan and Jacobean England. We learn about love and marriage, feasting and fun, law and order, religion and magic, kingship and government, war and peace, domestic life and images of a wider world. Taken together, such individual threads may be woven into the varied tapestry of Elizabethan and Jacobean England. The presenters draw attention to the ways in which Shakespeare's world differed from our own, although they are also keen to isolate fundamental similarities. They often do this by identifying with some of the characters. Clive James reckons that he has a smack, or flash, of Hamlet about him. Wolf Mankowitz conducts a cross examination of Anglo-Saxon attitudes towards Jews. If the presenters do not all openly identify at this personal level, they do at least identify some of the characters or types for us. George Melly appears to have been rubbed up the wrong way in the showers at school by Hotspur. Anna Raeburn can spot an Antony in the street, if not quite a mile off, then several military paces away. Vile politicians are all in a day's work and headlines to journalists such as Jonathan Dimbleby and Fred Emery. Penelope Mortimer notices that some of Shakespeare's characters are alive but far from well in the pubs of Warwickshire, whereas John Mortimer finds them lurking with intent in Soho. It is important to doorstop the past to find out about Shakespeare's England, but that does not rule out the probability of finding some of it on your own doorstep. The programmes showed that the plays were not necessarily set in a far-away country or concerned with the lives of a people about whom we know nothing. Our guides to this country suggested that, although its attitudes and customs were often alien and remote, we know more about its inhabitants than we might think. Shakespeare's comedies do not just mock Tudor.

There have been many interesting theatrical attempts to convey Shakespeare's importance for today's audiences through modern dress productions. Judi Dench tells us about a gangster-style *Measure for Measure*. *Much Ado About Nothing* was recently taken on a successful passage to Kipling's India. Sebastian Shaw refers to perhaps the most sensational of all such re-interpretations, Peter Brook's discovery of the dark side of the moon in *A Midsummer Night's Dream*. Some of the other presenters suggest points of departure for modern productions by relating the plays to cinema and television. Anna Raeburn identifies Cleopatra's enigmatic appeal with that of the Goddesses of the silent cinema. Penelope Mortimer notices similarities between the verbal duels in *The Taming of the Shrew* and the wisecracks in early Frank Capra films. The critics might refer to these duels as examples of Elizabethan wordplay, but to see them as wisecracking sessions, or stand up turns, makes them a little bit more accessible. Critical terms and labels are somewhere between a hindrance and a help. *The Shrew*, which is usually tagged as an early comedy, is in fact a mixture of panto-mime and knockabout farce. Shakespeare's problem plays is hardly the catchiest of titles. A series called *Problem Plays of Yesteryear* would limp and limp, even though both *Measure for Measure* and *All's Well That Ends Well* have an appeal for a modern audience.

It would be quite possible to spend a lot of time teasing out the Elizabethan and Jacobean meanings of terms such as masque. The argument would become so weighed down with the techniques of patterned movement and symmetrical staging that we might forget that a masque and a Hollywood revue, or spectacular, are not poles apart. Shakespeare and Busby Berkeley were both, after all, in the entertainment business. It has become fashionable to talk about the emblematic structure of the plays. Once again, it would be possible to get so immersed in the depictions of Fortune's wheel in the Tudor emblem books as to forget that modern cartoons, comic strips and caricatures are all emblematic in a broadly similar way. *Timon of Athens* is, in the current jargon, a series of emblematic, morality tableaux. It is also a cartoon strip on the 'spend, spend, spend' approach to life. Falstaff may well be a personification of Vice or Misrule, but he might be more accessible if visualised in terms of a Gerald Scarfe caricature on conspicuous consumption.

Revenge could be defined exclusively in accordance with Elizabethan theatrical codes and conventions. Such an approach makes Shakespeare seem rather mysterious, whereas anybody who has seen films like *The Godfather*, with its code of 'my family right or right', or indeed been fed on spaghetti westerns, knows what a revenge drama is all about. Perhaps it helps to visualise the impetuous young men of Verona in *Romeo and Juliet* as high noon gunfighters as well as New York street gangs. It is certainly worth noticing that some of the scenes are macabre 'tales from the crypt'. Similarly, parts of *Hamlet*, particularly the Ghost's speeches, could put the ham back into Hammer horror films. The play within the play makes more sense if it is related to police procedure films in which the crime is reconstructed before the chief suspect. This is part of the cold, looking glass war which Hamlet and Claudius wage against each other. John Le Carré's George Smiley would understand Denmark rules. *Hamlet* is a difficult play, but it becomes even more mysterious if the themes of melodrama, detection and espionage are treated too reverently.

The Belmont scenes in *The Merchant of Venice* have been set in the divinely decadent world of Oscar Wilde, although they could just as appropriately be located in the damnably beautiful world of Scott Fitzgerald's *The Great Gatsby*. Timothy West also points out that the courtroom scene between Portia and Shylock needs to be seen as the forerunner of some of the classic confrontations in twentieth century dramas. Perhaps the prison scenes in *Measure for Measure*, particularly those in the condemned cell itself, should be seen as forerunners of those equally classic scenes in which Jimmy Cagney and others do not prepare to meet their maker. Portia is dressed as a man when she defends Antonio and Jessica disguises herself as a boy when she escapes from Shylock's house on the night of the carnival procession. Shakespeare's use of disguise both here, and in *As You Like It* and *Twelfth Night*, can be related to Renaissance concepts of metamorphosis, although Brigid Brophy is quite right to remind us that we are usually watching an outrageous drag show. *As You Like It* has been performed quite recently with an all male cast. The critical label – Shakespeare's festive comedies – seems a bit lame and tame.

The English and Roman history plays tend to evoke visual images from a whole range of 'room at the top', 'power game' and 'main chance' films and television series. The feuds between the Yorkists and the Lancastrians, or indeed between the Capulets and the Montagues, are not that different from the essentially dynastic struggles in soap-operas like *Dallas*. Jonathan Dimbleby suggests that we can see what Shakespeare described as 'the craft of smiles' being practised by politicians every day of the week on our television screens. The history plays are about 'the survival of the slickest', to appropriate A. P. Rossiter's immortal phrase. Fred Emery suggests that, if we are aware of at least some of the dirty tricks that were played behind those closed Washington doors during the Watergate scandal, then we should have no real difficulty in understanding *2 Henry IV*. Visual images from the cinema and television can often bridge the credibility gap caused by critical terms and labels.

The BBC TV Shakespeare is not offering modern dress productions, but there is still a dominant emphasis on the need to visualise rather than merely intellectualise the plays. The works of Rembrandt, Vermeer, Botticelli, Veronese, Breughel, Caravaggio and many other artists have suggested certain controlling visual images. The directors, set designers and costume experts have refused to treat either Shakespeare or these great artists as museum pieces, which can be looked at but not touched. They have used their own visual imaginations to initiate a creative interplay, or perspective, between plays and paintings. This would have pleased Shakespeare, who often reminded audiences at the Globe, bare boards bare to the sky, of the need to give their imaginations full rein, or play, to fill out some of those empty spaces. Just as the presenters of the *Perspective* programmes used locations to suggest a mood or atmosphere, so the productions themselves reflected a concern for the visual landscapes of the plays, whether this was achieved in the studio or on location. There is no play, and therefore no Shakespeare, unless actors, production teams and audiences respond to the challenge to bring their own perspectives to bear on it. The productions themselves represent a series of suggestive rather than definitive statements by actors and productions teams, which can now be supplemented by the radio talks in this volume. The television talks offer a series of personal reactions to past productions of the plays by members of the audience. The BBC TV Shakespeare has created a new audience for the plays, at the same time as allowing enthusiasts of longer standing, in theatre queues and elsewhere, to catch up with the more offbeat plays and to try to take an overview of the canon. The project as a whole, including the programmes that are collected together in this volume, has posed important general questions about the nature of the perspectives of actor, director and audience and the relationships between them. There may be more questions than answers, although the fundamental point to emerge is that each of these perspectives needs to be an active, creative and essentially personal one.

Some of the presenters suggest that Shakespearean form and structure needs to be related to music. *The Winter's Tale, The Tempest* and the other romances probably do have more in common with operas and ballets than with naturalistic theatre. Perhaps this is why there are no hard and fast distinctions nowadays between the Shakespearean and the operatic director. I suspect that the hardest single point for a modern audience to appreciate about Shakespeare is that his artistic vision could encompass both grand opera and soap opera and all stations in between. His plays are often a blend of what we have been conditioned to label the sophisticated and the popular: mythology and folk traditions, courtly literature and melodrama, high Renaissance art and strip cartoons, ballet and jigs. Television is probably the ideal medium through which to try to reawaken and recreate this kind of all-embracing cultural perspective. The plays themselves, and the radio and television programmes which introduce them, all suggest that the best context for an appreciation of Shakespeare's work is provided by the creative, performing and visual arts in all their diversity.

The message of the radio talks to students, teachers and the general reader is to leave the critical tracts in the classroom or study and to make tracks for the theatre, cinema or television screen. The suggestion is that you are not approaching Shakespeare properly if you read the plays as novels. The hope is that an awareness of performance and production might be imported back into the classroom or study. The message of the television talks is that everybody ought to write their own *Perspective* programme. This means making imaginative, creative voyages of discovery to country houses, art galleries and museums, but it also means trying to relate a particular play to personal experiences, environments and forms of entertainment. The message from both media is that these voyages of discovery should be ones of self-discovery as well. The contributors to this volume offer their travellers' tales to excite your curiosity and fire your enthusiasm for your own very different voyage.

My editorial policy, which has been carried out in consultation with the contributors, may be summarised under six headings. First of all, I have made some changes to the original scripts to try to achieve a uniform house style. The radio scripts took their quotations from a wide variety of editions, whereas I have standardised things by using the BBC TV editions throughout. Secondly, I decided to put all the scripts into essay form, in other words to publish them without production details or shot lists. This seems the most appropriate form for the radio scripts, although it obviously represents more of a compromise as far as the television ones are concerned. I and the contributors themselves have made a number of essentially stylistic changes to the scripts to make them more accessible on the printed page, but they have not been altered fundamentally. Thirdly, I decided not to include illustrations as I felt that the book could not possibly hope to emulate the television programmes. It would have been difficult, and somewhat invidious, to decide what to illustrate and what to leave to the reader's imagination. We might have ended up with a copiously illustrated volume as it usually turns out to be a case of all or nothing. There are enough good picture books on Shakespeare's life and times. The producers of both the radio and television programmes had a very different kind of volume in mind. They felt that a reasonably priced, simply laid out edition of talks by a distinguished repertory company of household names could make a very positive contribution to the way in which Shakespeare is approached in schools and further education colleges, without losing its appeal for the general reader. Illustrations seemed to point in the direction of the coffee table, whereas the producers felt that the hard school bench would be a more worthwhile destination. As somebody who has taught Shakespeare from 'O' level to university level, I agreed with them that we had a yawning gap to fill.

Fourthly, I asked all the contributors to accept some reasonably kind cuts to their original scripts. I usually suggested the omission of a quotation or two, or at least the shortening of some of them. The radio talks often contained some very long quotations, which I felt were more effective over the air than they were on the printed page. The quotations in the television programmes tended to be shorter, but there were occasions when they seemed either too action-packed or too character-packed to be anything but confusing when reproduced as part of an essay. I also suggested the omission of some of the larger signposts to the visual side of the programme. Fifthly, the decision to publish the talks in transmission order was almost inevitable given the fact that this volume just covers the first three years of the BBC TV Shakespeare. If it covered the whole of the six years, then it would have been perfectly possible to have arranged the talks according to the categories used by the editors of the First Folio, with the usual variants built into them. Transmission order seemed to be the safest way of proceeding, given the somewhat uneven distribution of categories in the first three years. I placed the *Perspectives* before the *Prefaces* as they tended to offer more of an overview of the plays. Finally, there were bound to be overlaps between some of the radio and television scripts, particularly as far as the history plays were concerned. I have to confess that I did not adopt a consistent policy on this issue. I sometimes suggested that the overall length of a script might be reduced without too much damage if overlaps and repetitions were taken out. I did point out that, whilst an individual programme on one of the histories might need to make quite detailed references to the cycle as a whole, this was not as necessary in a volume which would contain a number of essays on the history plays. I was very conscious, however, of the fact that all the contributors had been specifically asked for a personal view on Shakespeare by the BBC. If the text of the argument itself was altered too much then this vital ingredient might have disappeared. The volume may therefore be a little fatter than I originally anticipated, but it is certainly not scant of breath or life.

ROMEO AND JULIET

Germaine Greer

Germaine Greer researched and taught Renaissance literature before becoming a full-time writer. Author of The Female Eunuch *and* The Obstacle Race, *she is writing a book on* Shakespeare *for the Oxford Past Masters series. She made this programme on location in Italy.*

Nowadays few Italian fathers would think of giving away their teenage daughters to their friends. Italian girls date like girls anywhere else in the western world, worry about contraceptives, have voted in favour of divorce and abortion and yet, I'm not sure that Shakespeare would have been entirely in favour of this modernisation. One of the reasons why we cannot understand the tragic meaning of *Romeo and Juliet* is that we've allowed marriage to become anti-social in a way that Shakespeare would have deplored. Lovers need account to nobody but themselves when deciding to set up house and have children. Like the sixteenth century reformers, Shakespeare had a high ideal of marriage. He thought of it as superior to adultery and fornication because it was not simply regulated by lust. He knew too much about the changeability of human passions to give the cradle of children and cornerstone of the state no other bulwark. As a result of romantic criticism of Shakespeare we have come to believe that *Romeo and Juliet* is about the sovereignty of juvenile passion. It's not about that at all. It is about marriage as an honourable and public estate.

Romeo and Juliet seems so familiar to us because it has been the basis of so many other treatments since Shakespeare's. Probably the most familiar in our time is Leonard Bernstein's *West Side Story.* The story of *Romeo and Juliet* is not as important to Bernstein as the function of the love affair in showing the stupid destructiveness of inter-racial feuding. The two groups are sharply differentiated – the Puerto Ricans on the one hand, dark-skinned, Catholics with a culture of their own and the gang of Caucasian youths who call themselves the Jets. Now this, in fact, is not what is going on in Shakespeare's play. The

Montagues and the Capulets do not speak different languages, they haven't got different skins, they aren't even in different social classes. They are as alike as two peas in a pod. They are probably two of three most important families in Verona, the other being the family of Escalus, the Prince. Their quarrel has no explanation in a genuine conflict of interests or a struggle for room. In fact, Shakespeare deliberately avoids any explanation at all. Escalus says that the whole quarrel has been bred of an airy word and that gives us a clue to the sort of thing the play is about. Romeo goes on about the feud at great length and his sole purpose seems to be to show us that it doesn't make any sense at all, that it is chaos created out of nothing. So it seems then that if we are going to find out what *Romeo and Juliet* is about, we have to take the feud, not as an explanation, but as one of the conditions of the basic plot, as a starting point:

> Two households, both alike in dignity,
> In fair Verona, where we lay our scene,
> From ancient grudge break to new mutiny,
> Where civil blood makes civil hands unclean.
> From forth the fatal loins of these two foes
> A pair of star-cross'd lovers take their life; . . .

Prologue 1–6

While it is improbable that any couple called Romeo and Juliet ever lived and died, or carried on their strange six-day drama in the town of Verona, it is nevertheless very important that Shakespeare chooses to set his drama in Italy. The society of Verona is old and unchristian, evil and tortuous like the winding ways of a medieval town. In this town, men like Capulet who haven't danced for thirty years may have wives as young as Lady Capulet, who is not yet thirty. Young men like Tybalt have no useful thing to do but hang about flexing their muscles and causing trouble, for Tybalt is a totally Italian character. He is a virtuoso in the art of killing, in much the same way that Romeo wants to be a virtuoso in the art of loving.

We do not know, and will probably never know, whether Shakespeare was ever in Italy. Some people think he came to Italy as a soldier and travelled through the north. The odd thing is he never makes a mistake about Italy. For the Elizabethan audience, Italy was a land of popery first of all (about which they felt very passionate) and the land of poison. In fact they believed that Machiavelli taught 'the Prince' the use of poison in order to maintain the safety of his commonwealth. The brewing of poisons was thought of as a specifically Italian art. There was no truth in the English view. It was, like many other views held today, a prejudice. But the word Italian meant newfangled, difficult, indirect, subtle, artful, deceitful, the master of lies. It is important that *Romeo and Juliet* is set in Italy. It is not, however, to be thought that, in some way, the story of *Romeo and Juliet* is meant to be a gloss on Italian history. It is a thoroughly English view of events.

Romeo and Juliet presents a problem for actors because so many of the characters speak in a kind of clinking, clanking couplet form, which is very difficult to make any sense out of. Either you have to let the couplets sound and stall the action every time they occur, or you have to chop the lines up and pretend the couplets aren't there at all. A typical example of this kind of thing is Lady Capulet's speech to Juliet, describing Paris as a book:

> This night you shall behold him at our feast;
> Read o'er the volume of young Paris' face,
> And find delight writ there with beauty's pen;
> Examine every married lineament,
> And see how one another lends content;
> And what obscur'd in this fair volume lies
> Find written in the margent of his eyes.

1.3.81–7

There is another group of characters who don't speak in this way at all. In fact, you might say that this couplet form is limited to the Montagues and Capulets of a certain rank. The low life characters speak prose, as is usual with Shakespeare, except of course for the Nurse, who speaks a special form of lolloping verse which is all hers. Then there comes Mercutio, the champion of plain speaking, the man who calls a spade a spade. And the other person who refuses to speak in couplets unless she is speaking to her parents, or telling lies, is Juliet. Juliet speaks with the genuine accent of the greatest of Shakespeare's dramatic blank verse. One of the most extraordinary facets of the balcony scene is the way in which her direct language contrasts with Romeo's habit of falling forever into set speeches. So much so, that she virtually silences him when he falls into one of his postures:

> ROMEO: Lady, by yonder blessed moon I vow,
>   That tips with silver all these fruit-tree tops –

JULIET: O, swear not by the moon, th' inconstant moon,
    That monthly changes in her circled orb,
    Lest that thy love prove likewise variable.
ROMEO: What shall I swear by?
JULIET: Do not swear at all;
    Or, if thou wilt, swear by thy gracious self,
    Which is the god of my idolatry,
    And I'll believe thee.
ROMEO: If my heart's dear love –
JULIET: Well, do not swear. Although I joy in thee,
    I have no joy of this contract to-night:
    It is too rash, too unadvis'd, too sudden;
    Too like the lightning, which doth cease to be
    Ere one can say 'It lightens'. Sweet, good night!
    This bud of love, by summer's ripening breath,
    May prove a beauteous flow'r when next we meet.

                                      2.2.107–122

Possibly one of the most important aspects of Juliet is her youth. It is her youth which, in one way, saves her from being an ordinary Veronese. She hasn't yet been incorporated into the social whirl. She doesn't yet know the rules. When she meets Romeo at her parents' party and responds to him so fully, so utterly, she decides like a child might that 'this is it', that there will be no other lover for her, that she is wedded now for life with the kind of singlemindedness that only adolescents are capable of. That Romeo finds out about this child's decision is, of course, an unhappy circumstance. You might say that the tragedy of Juliet and her Romeo begins when Romeo, hiding in the orchard, hears what Juliet would never have told him to his face in the light of day, that she has devoted herself to him utterly.

Who is this Romeo with whom the child Juliet falls so utterly and disastrously in love? He is first described to us by his father and by Benvolio as suffering as suffering a disease which would have been known to Shakespeare's audience as 'melancholy' or 'love madness'. He is much like the figure in the famous miniature by Nicholas Hilliard, of 'An Unknown Youth Leaning Against a Tree Among Roses'. Everything he does is derived from one of the great sources, one of the great Petrarchan poets. The Elizabethan hinds in the audience might not have known who these Petrarchan poets were, they almost certainly had never read Petrarch, but everybody knew the kind of debased imitation of Petrarch which exalted adulterous love. What Romeo wants to be is a virtuoso in sexual passion.

The Palazzo Schifanoia in Ferrara, the name means 'begone dull care', was built in the late fourteenth and early fifteenth century by the d'Este family as a *palazzo di delizie* for balls, masquerades, banquets and receptions. The Duke Borso d'Este ordered its decoration by a remarkable series of secular frescoes, in which each scene could be interpreted in conflicting ways like a visual version of the riddling games that the boys of Verona so loved to play. The very top layer of the scene is of a kind called 'Trionfi'. In the first one, the triumph of Apollo, we see the first God of Romeo's idolatry – the God of poetry and of imagination. Apollo rides upon a car drawn by horses who are controlled by Poetry kneeling before him. On his left stand the figures of humanists and poets, the kinds of heroes a sixteenth century Veronese boy might have had instead of Emerson Fittipaldi or the Bionic Man. Behind him stand the nine Muses and on his right a very interesting group of tiny Amorini – little loves generated like Romeo's love, infinitely, by the power of the eye. Just as Romeo moves from imaginary passion to real passion, we move to the triumph of Venus. Before her kneels a knight, chained to her footstool. On the one hand an idealised version of the power of war conquered by the power of love, and on the other a very dubious image of valour subdued by lust. In the very next Triumph – the triumph of Minerva, the Goddess of discretion, judgement, magnanimity – we have the three Fates. Romeo and Juliet were unable to have their love sanctioned by law; here we see Minerva controlling lust in the form of the unicorns, who may only be dominated by a virgin and who, in this version, have the hindquarters of billy goats, a reference which needs no explanation. The Fates have their say in *Romeo and Juliet* too – love ungoverned by law brings the kind of destruction that Minerva existed to prevent. This is, if you like, the equivalent of a fourteenth, fifteenth century comic strip, and when Shakespeare writes about the bad, old Italian order, in his version of *Romeo and Juliet*, this is the kind of inauthentic, riddling world in which he wants us to see his characters as living.

No play of Shakespeare's contains more bawdry than *Romeo and Juliet*, notwithstanding the fact that it is a play about romantic love. It is as if Shakespeare wanted to keep us in mind of the real basis of all this high-falutin' brainstorm about sexual desire. In the very first scene, when they haven't been on the stage a full minute, Sampson and Gregory make for us the connection between the feud and sexual passion. Sampson claims he's going to push Montague's men from the wall and thrust his maids to it:

SAMPSON: . . . I will show myself a tyrant. When I have fought with the men, I will be civil with the maids – I will cut off their heads.

GREGORY: The heads of the maids?

SAMPSON: Ay, the heads of the maids, or their maidenheads; take it in what sense thou wilt.

GREGORY: They must take it in sense that feel it.

SAMPSON: Me they shall feel while I am able to stand; and 'tis known I am a pretty piece of flesh.

I.I.21–9

It's very unlikely, in my view, that if the Lord Chamberlain had had the same role in Elizabethan times as he used to have in England until a very short time ago, that *Romeo and Juliet* as a play would ever have seen the light.

The religion that kept the earthy passions of Verona in check is represented only by Friar Lawrence. Nobody in Shakespeare's audience was old enough to remember the dissolution of the monasteries, but ever since then the English had been inundated by floods of scurrilous propaganda about the viciousness of the monastic life, about convent fishponds that were dredged and found to be full of foetal skeletons, or young boys lured from healthy pursuits to become the catamites of the monks. The surprising thing is that Shakespeare's Friar Lawrence is so sympathetic. I wonder if he isn't too sympathetic. I wonder if we aren't lulled into a false sense of security. What he eventually decides to do is extremely dangerous and the catastrophe is entirely of his devising. We do not know how much Shakespeare knew about monasticism. Certainly all the elements of the character of Friar Lawrence are present in his source. If he had any extra knowledge he probably gleaned it on his travels through Catholic Europe when he would have seen friars who weren't subject to conventual discipline, who simply roamed about, begging on their own accord and making mischief, much as the hedge priests and travelling preachers of his own England. Among the kinds of mischief that these men made was the irresponsible marrying of people who were not fit to marry – marriages which afterwards could be neither proved nor disproved. Many an Elizabethan story turns upon the kinds of misery that this meddling induced. In Catholic theology, the sacrament of marriage consists in the words of consent, spoken in the present tense by the ministers of the sacrament who are the husband and wife. Thus a marriage exists which is known only to God, unless it is witnessed by others on earth who may live to tell the tale. For a long time canon lawyers made much of this apparent anomaly, but at last in the sixteenth century the Council of Trent decreed that the abuses resulting from secret marriage were such that in future, unless a marriage was witnessed by at least two people, the Church would deem that it had never occurred. Ironically, in Shakespeare's England the edicts of the Council of Trent did not apply and in England the abuse of clandestine marriage continued right up until the marriages in the Fleet Prison in the eighteenth century, when at last such marriages were declared, once and for all, invalid. The Church, thus, agreed to co-operate with the secular authorities. In the United States you must have a blood test and a licence. In England you need a licence to marry and so forth. In accepting Romeo and Juliet as bride and groom, without any recourse to the civil authorities, Friar Lawrence is taking a grave risk. He himself is not immortal. Romeo may disappear. Juliet may be condemned to a life of widowhood or to a bigamous marriage without having any security or any support from the social structures about her. In fact, in marrying herself in this way, the child Juliet embarks upon an extremely dangerous course in which her only guide is herself. Even the Nurse, her go-between, a bawd if ever there was one, is of the opinion that there's not much point in continuing to respect a few words spoken in the hugger-mugger of Friar Lawrence's cell.

The distinctions between tragedy and comedy were not as clear cut for Shakespeare's audience as they are for us. Right up until the time that Juliet is laid in the vault the tide could turn and the lovers could win the day. One of the things we demand of a tragedy is inevitability. But if Shakespeare cannot supply us with inevitability in terms of plot, he does supply us with inevitability in terms of character. What happy ending could there be for a thirteen or fourteen year old child of great seriousness and heroic intent who has fallen blindly in love with Romeo against her parents' wishes and in a situation where no happy outcome is possible? In what way is the Romeo and Juliet story the basis for a happy marriage? In fact, in moral terms, the catastrophe begins with Juliet's wedding and it can never be worked out. The extraordinary thing is that in a play which is, in itself, not a tragedy, in terms of its own structure not tragic, a character of true tragic dimensions emerges – young Juliet – and she herself makes of her coprotagonist also a hero, which by himself he would never have become. I believe that *Romeo and Juliet* is a play written by a master poet, who had very little to learn about the medium of poetry, but who had not yet become a master dramatist. It is not a real tragedy but it contains true tragic characters.

ROMEO AND JULIET
Dame Peggy Ashcroft

Dame Peggy Ashcroft is a director of the Royal Shakespeare Company. She has played all Shakespeare's leading ladies, apart from Lady Macbeth.

The BBC has taken on the rather risky venture of asking actors who have appeared in past productions to talk about the plays before they are televised. I say risky because actors are not scholars. We have a dangerously subjective attitude to any play. We have had to see it from the inside and it has become personal experience. I really believe actors should act in plays rather than talk about them, so perhaps these preliminary talks ought to be partially concerned with some of the problems actors have in approaching Shakespeare.

Every Shakespearean actor is frequently asked to name a favourite play or part. There isn't really an answer, although I would unhesitatingly put both the title part and the play, *Romeo and Juliet*, in my top . . . four. There has been a recent fashion in the theatre to define a certain kind of play as a 'black comedy'. I would define *Romeo and Juliet* as a 'golden tragedy'. George Meredith wrote:

> . . . In tragic life, God wot,
> No villain need be! Passions spin the plot:
> We are betrayed by what is false within.

Tragic heroes such as Macbeth and Hamlet do have something 'false within'. It is after all the definition of a tragic character that his fate lies in himself and in his own weakness. Romeo and Juliet are thus not strictly speaking tragic characters, since they are betrayed by what is false without. They are the epitome of youth awakening to life, joy, love and fidelity. Theirs is the tragedy of circumstance, which perhaps makes it all the more poignant. Is it youth betrayed by age or love destroyed by hate? I think that both these are simplifications. It is true that they are the victims of a family feud, but as the play unfolds one sees everything that happens as a series of fatal accidents. We are

never told the cause of the 'ancient grudge' between the
Capulets and the Montagues, which the Chorus refers to at the
very beginning of the play. It is accepted as a fact that the
servants of the two houses, as well as the young bloods, should
be ready to be at each others' throats. But we don't feel that this
'ancient grudge' is past remedy. After the opening brawl has
been put down by Escalus, the Prince of Verona, Old Montague,
who is Romeo's father, asks 'who set this ancient quarrel new
abroach'. Lady Montague is concerned for Romeo's safety:

O, where is Romeo? Saw you him to-day?
Right glad I am he was not at this fray.

I.I.II4–5

Capulet, who is Juliet's father, also appears to be concerned
with keeping the peace. He refuses to let Tybalt attack the
masked gate-crasher at the feast. But what we now call the
collision course is already set in motion. The background of
explosive anger and danger is an essential part of it, as is the heat
of Verona and the high spirits of its youth, whether picking
quarrels or falling in love.

And so the scene is set for the two lovers. Romeo is in love
with love and so has no difficulty convincing himself that he loves
fair Rosaline. Juliet is a child, not yet fourteen. When asked by her
mother what she feels about marriage, she replies 'it is an honour
that I dream not of'. Yet by the end of Act One she and Romeo
have met at her father's feast and fallen in love at first sight. This
is dramatised in the form of an exquisite sonnet:

ROMEO: If I profane with my unworthiest hand
This holy shrine, the gentle fine is this:
My lips, two blushing pilgrims, ready stand
To smooth that rough touch with a tender kiss.
JULIET: Good pilgrim, you do wrong your hand too much,
Which mannerly devotion shows in this;
For saints have hands that pilgrims' hands do touch,
And palm to palm is holy palmers' kiss.
ROMEO: Have not saints lips, and holy palmers too?
JULIET: Ay, pilgrim, lips that must use in pray'r.
ROMEO: O, then, dear saint, let lips do what hands do!
Then pray; grant though, lest faith turn to despair.
JULIET: Saints do not move, though grant for prayers' sake.
ROMEO: Then move not while my prayer's effect I take.

I.5.9I–I04

It is only at the end of the feast that they discover that they have each fallen in love with their fated enemy.

I was fortunate enough to attempt Juliet three times in the theatre and a fourth on radio. The first time was when I was twenty-three in John Gielgud's first ever-production. This was for OUDS, the Oxford University Dramatic Society, with George Devine as Mercutio, Christopher Hassell as Romeo, William Devlin as Tybalt, Hugh Hunt as Friar Lawrence and Terence Rattigan as the First Musician. The First Musician only has a few lines, one of them after Juliet's apparent death: 'Faith, we may put up our pipes and be gone'. Terry told me many years later that he thought I looked extremely critical of his interpretation as I lay on my bed. In fact, I was steeling myself not to cry, knowing that Edith Evans as the Nurse was about to say:

> Honest good fellows, ah, put up, put up;
> For well you know this is a pitiful case.

4.5.97–9

Philip Hope Wallace wrote 'This is the Nurse as Shakespeare might have dreamt of seeing it played. Each syllable has a perfect identification with the character'. He was obviously thinking of Edith's interpretation of the Nurse's great speeches:

> Even or odd, of all the days in the year,
> Come Lammas Eve at night shall she be fourteen.
> Susan and she – God rest all Christian souls! –
> Were of an age. Well, Susan is with God;
> She was too good for me. But, as I said,
> On Lammas Eve at night shall she be fourteen;
> That shall she, marry; I remember it well.
> 'Tis since the earthquake now eleven years;
> And she was wean'd – I never shall forget it –
> Of all the days of the year, upon that day;
> For I had then laid wormwood to my dug,
> Sitting in the sun under the dove-house wall;
> My lord and you were then at Mantua.
> Nay, I do bear a brain.

1.3.17–30

Perhaps for those who don't know this piece of ancient history I should explain that the OUDS always presented their winter production with a professional director and professional actresses. Whether that was a good idea or not is debatable. But I think it was a wonderful 'try-out' for John's original conception of the play. He saw it as above all a play about youth, to be acted by young men. It was a fast-moving, indeed a headlong and exhilarating production, on an open stage. There were no pauses between the scenes which was unusual in those days. This kept the tension and the ironic twists of fate always before the audience.

Romeo and Juliet meet, they love and they marry. Tybalt kills Romeo's friend Mercutio. Romeo kills Tybalt and is banished. The lovers consummate their marriage. Juliet is then betrothed by her father to Paris. She goes to Friar Lawrence, who had married her to Romeo. He gives her a potion which will simulate death and she is taken to the family vault. Romeo, hearing of her death, returns and finds her on her bier. Juliet wakes to find that he has killed himself. She then kills herself with his dagger. In the finale the parents are reconciled over the bodies of their children after they have heard Friar Lawrence's account of the events. That is the play in synopsis, but because of its extraordinary vivid reality and the depth of all the characters in it, it is, as well as a lyrical tragedy, an intensely human domestic drama. The lovers are framed by marvellously rich characters: Capulet, Friar Lawrence, Peter, Paris, Tybalt and, above all, two of Shakespeare's greatest characters, the Nurse, a rival to Falstaff in her earthy humanity, and Mercutio, the wit and eternal joker who is always remembered for the Queen Mab speech and his death scene. This scene is a central climax in the play and it is from that moment on that all the disasters occur.

My first attempt at Juliet was inevitably agonising as I was plagued by the idea of it being 'a great tragic role'. I learnt after that production, in a subsequent one at the Old Vic a year later, that it is essential for Juliet to be a child of fourteen. If that is credible, then her awakening, her passion, her refusal to compromise and, finally, her tragedy take care of themselves. So I think my third venture, in John's second production of the play when Laurence Olivier and he shared the roles of Romeo and Mercutio, came near to fully achieving John's original conception of the youthful nature of the play. Olivier's Romeo, a rash boy of sixteen, was a definitive one and Edith was once again our cornerstone as the Nurse. I know that we were all very proud to hear that Harley Granville-Barker thought it was 'by far the best bit of Shakespeare' he had seen for years.

I know it has been said that Juliet is an impossible part to play because, by the time an actress is experienced enough to play her, she's too old to look the part. I really think that is nonsense. An actress up to twenty years older than Juliet, if she is really capable of playing the part, is not too old to be convincing. Of course a very young girl, especially on the screen, will be at a great advantage, but she has to encounter a number of technical difficulties. These difficulties are, I would say, two-fold. Firstly, she has to be able to sustain a very long and demanding part on the stage. Secondly, she has to deal at times with extremely complicated verbal fireworks. The part is all simplicity, whereas the language is often complex in the extreme. Shakespeare was still experimenting with language. He uses verse and prose alternatively, as in all the plays, but at the height of a dramatic scene in *Romeo and Juliet* he sometimes uses conceits and puns which it is difficult to contain within the emotion. For instance, in the scene when the Nurse brings the news of the deaths of Tybalt and Mercutio, Juliet at first thinks that Romeo has been killed as well:

> What devil art thou that dost torment me thus?
> This torture should be roar'd in dismal hell.
> Hath Romeo slain himself? Say thou but 'I'
> And that bare vowel I shall poison more
> Than the death-darting eye of cockatrice.
> I am not I if there be such an 'I';
> Or those eyes shut that makes thee answer 'I'.
> If he be slain, say 'I'; or if not, 'No';
> Brief sounds determine of my weal or woe.

> 3.2.43 51

Compare the punning difficulties of such a speech with the directness of a later one, after the Nurse has tried to persuade her to marry Paris:

> Ancient damnation! O most wicked fiend!
> Is it more sin to wish me thus forsworn,
> Or to dispraise my lord with that same tongue
> Which she hath prais'd him with above compare
> So many thousand times? Go, counsellor;
> Thou and my bosom henceforth shall be twain.
> I'll to the friar to know his remedy;
> If all else fail, myself have power to die.

> 3.5.236–43

Of the productions I have seen, by far the most memorable was Franco Zeffirelli's at the Old Vic. He achieved that heat, danger and Italianate inflammability that we had striven for. I only quarrelled with some of his 'cuts'. As I have already said, this background of explosive anger and danger is an essential part of the play, as is the heat of Verona and the high spirits of its youth in picking quarrels or falling in love.

Richard II
Paul Johnson

Paul Johnson was editor of the New Statesman until 1970. He has published widely in the fields of history and current affairs, including a biography of Elizabeth I. Part of the programme was filmed on location at Leeds Castle.

On Saturday, 7 February 1601, one of the leading companies of actors in London, the Lord Chamberlain's Men, gave a special performance of Shakespeare's play, *Richard II*, at the Globe Theatre in Southwark. The play had been first written and presented six years before, in 1595, and the circumstances of this single revival were unusual. Giving evidence to the Privy Council afterwards, the spokesman for the players, Augustine Phillips, said they were asked to put on the play by a group of noblemen and knights, Sir Charles Percy, Lord Monteagle and others. The fee for this request performance was forty shillings above the ordinary cost of the tickets. At first, Phillips told the Council,

> We were determined to have played some other play, as we held that play of King Richard to be so old and so long out of use as that we should have small or no company at it. But at their request we were content to play it the Saturday and had out forty shillings more than our ordinary for it.

By the time Phillips appeared before the Council, he realised he was in a nasty political pickle. As he must have known, *Richard II* was no ordinary play in the minds of the Elizabethan public. It concerned the deposition of a king, that is essentially what the play is about, and although the event it described had taken place in 1399, two centuries before, the very phrase 'Richard II' was a fighting one to the Elizabethans.

There had already been a hint of trouble about this play, because when it was first published in 1597, the scene in which the King is actually deposed had been omitted. Moreover, the men who paid for this special benefit performance were by no means ordinary theatre-fans. On the contrary, they were

PAUL JOHNSON

notorious followers of the Earl of Essex, the most controversial man in British public life. Once the great favourite of Queen Elizabeth, now in deep disgrace and said to be plotting revenge against his enemies at court. The special performance was, in fact, intended by them as a symbolic celebration on the eve of their rebellion. The very next morning, Essex and his followers fortified Essex House, just across the river, kidnapped and imprisoned the Lord Chancellor and other crown officials, and then took part in an armed march on the City, to raise a mob as a prelude to storming the Palace at Whitehall. The ill-planned and ill-conducted rising, by a gang of hotheads, unemployed officers and bankrupts, was a complete fiasco. By nightfall on the Sunday, all the chief conspirators were under lock and key in the Tower. They included the Earl himself, his chief associate, the Earl of Southampton, one of Shakespeare's patrons, and most of the swashbucklers who'd attended the special performances of *Richard II*.

Thereafter the ponderous wheels of Tudor justice began to grind, and on 19 February, Essex and Southampton were tried for treason in Westminster Hall. Both were found guilty, and Essex was executed six days later. But there is no evidence that the authorities ever bothered Shakespeare. Less fortunate was Dr John Hayward, a writer and man about town. Dr Hayward was involved on the fringe of politics and in 1599 he published a book giving a historical account of the fall of Richard II and Henry IV's seizure of the throne. And more foolishly still, he dedicated the book to the Earl of Essex. Well, it caused trouble right from the start. The Council ordered the dedication to be removed and a second edition of the book to be destroyed. And then, when Essex returned in disgrace from his disastrous campaign in Ireland, Dr Hayward was hauled up before the Council, interrogated about the political implications of the book and put in the Tower. The book actually deals with events which took place 200 years before, in the last years of Richard II's reign, but the Council believed that they contained a hidden criticism of the Queen's regime. Hayward's plea to be treated as a serious historian was rejected. The Council continued to believe that he was a dangerous and subversive propagandist, and he remained in the Tower until the end of the Queen's reign.

Now you may ask: if Hayward was suspected of treason by association merely for writing history, why was it that Shakespeare, whose play had actually been used as a dangerous political instrument, was never, so far as we know, involved in the Council's enquiries? Throughout the Queen's reign, she and her ministers were hypersensitive to the very mention of Richard II. It was a synonym for autocratic government, government by courtiers, even by crypto-Catholics. Towards the end of her reign, in August 1601, shortly after the Essex rebellion, she gave an audience at Greenwich Palace to William Lambarde, who was her Keeper of Records at the Tower. Lambarde relates that when he presented her with a selection of records, her eye fell upon the reign of Richard II and immediately she said 'I am Richard the Second, know ye not that?' There must have been something very sad or bitter in her tone because immediately he made a disparaging reference to the Earl of Essex. Here is what William Lambarde said:

> Such a wicked imagination was determined and attempted by a most unkind gentleman, the most adorned creature that ever Your Majesty made.

Whereupon the Queen replied:

> He that will forget God will also forget his benefactors. This tragedy was played forty times in open streets and houses.

Forty times? Was the Queen exaggerating? The point she was making, surely, was that her name and rule had been associated with the fall of Richard II, even among the rabble of the city, and it was this she most resented, for in her day, history was not a dead but a living thing: a continuous series of messages and lessons from Providence.

Shakespeare found in the tragic circumstances of Richard II's life a very clear illustration of the general principle that the rule of law was the only barrier against anarchy. His bias was towards the claims of established authority and hierarchy. Every man in society, in his proper place and degree, had rights and duties and by the mutual respect for such rights, and the observance of such duties, the common safety and happiness of all was ensured. Hierarchy was ordained by divine justice and human law. This is why *Richard II* is one of the most formal and didactic of his plays, almost a miracle play in fact, full of elaborate *tableaux* and spoken mime.

Richard inherited as a boy, and never had the opportunity, as his father and grandfather had had, of fighting alongside the nobility in battle. As a boy, he had survived the crisis of the Peasants' Revolt and the infighting of his guardians, and had come to distrust those set in authority over him. As an adult

King, he determined to be his own master and to rule through men attached to his person, whom he had made. This was a not-uncommon monarchical tactic in the Middle Ages, but a risky one. A king who did not rule *through* his nobility had to rule *against* them. It was possible provided the king could ensure himself a large income and a standing army of mercenaries. In a feudal society that meant manipulating the law, and any king who brought the law into disrespect was asking for trouble. Therein lay the tragedy that Richard II wove for himself.

He took a higher view of the rights and dignities of a king than any of his predecessors. A contemporary records that, towards the end of his reign, Richard took to sitting after dinner, on a high throne, surrounded by silent courtiers. Any man upon whom his gaze fell had to kneel. And he took other steps to make his court more formal and hierarchical and to emphasise the divinity of his kingship. By Shakespeare's day, this behaviour of the King's had given him a quite unjustified reputation for profligacy and luxurious carnality. In point of fact, Richard was not a depraved man at all. He was an ideologue, a fanatic, an early supporter of the theory that kings ruled by divine right. But while insisting on his own titles and privileges, he made the great nobles feel insecure in theirs. He made illegal exactions and confiscations, and he exploited parliament to commit judicial murder against the nobles and despoil their estates. Now if he had been a born leader or a natural general, a man of great fortitude of mind and singleness of purpose, he might have got away with it. But as Shakespeare perceived, he always confused the realities of power with its mere externals:

> For God's sake let us sit upon the ground
> And tell sad stories of the death of kings:
> How some have been depos'd, some slain in war,
> Some haunted by the ghosts they have depos'd,
> Some poison'd by their wives, some sleeping kill'd,
> All murder'd – for within the hollow crown
> That rounds the mortal temples of a king
> Keeps Death his court; . . .

3.2.155–62

Richard II is a play about a crime and a curse. It's also a play about a prophecy. In Shakespeare's England, the most widely read book among all classes was the Old Testament. Indeed, many were brought up to believe that Protestant Englishmen, purged of the vices of Roman-Catholicism by the Reformation, had replaced the Jews as God's chosen people. Hence the story of the kingdom of Israel was studied with great care. That story has a recurrent theme. The rulers of Israel disobey God's explicit commandments. They are warned against doing so by a succession of inspired prophets – Isaiah, Elijah, Samuel and so forth. They choose to disregard this warning and therefore draw down upon themselves terrible calamities.

According to the orthodox Tudor view of history the deposition of the rightful and anointed King, Richard II, was a crime against God, which thereafter had to be expiated by the nation in a series of bloody struggles we call the Wars of the Roses. It was a popular justification of the strong Tudor monarchy that the first Tudor, Henry VII, had restored the crown to legality and by ending a century of conflict and inaugurating a long era of domestic peace, had completed the process of self-purging.

Shakespeare had the marvellous idea of combining the Biblical theme of prophecy fulfilled, with the Tudor theory of history, national crime and its expiation. And underpinning both was the notion he shared with Queen Elizabeth herself, that respect for the person and property of others, is the best guarantee of one's own. These ideas give the play an exceptionally strong moral and ideological framework. Even before it opens, the first crime has been committed – the murder, with the connivance of Richard, of his uncle Gloucester. This murder of royalty is itself a sacrilege, from which calamity must inevitably follow. The image of farming taxes, that is giving courtiers the power to levy taxes for their own uses, inspires Gaunt to the first great prophecy:

> This land of such dear souls, this dear dear land,
> Dear for her reputation through the world,
> Is now leas'd out – I die pronouncing it –
> Like to a tenement or pelting farm.
> England, bound in with the triumphant sea,
> Whose rocky shore beats back the envious siege
> Of wat'ry Neptune, is now bound in with shame,
> With inky blots and rotten parchment bonds;
> That England, that was wont to conquer others,
> Hath made a shameful conquest of itself.

2.1.57–66

But it is a recurrent theme of Biblical prophecy, and necessary to the mechanism of Shakespeare's play, that such warnings are ignored by the foredoomed Monarch.

Richard now proceeds to his next crime, the fatal one. Not

only does he ignore Gaunt's dying plea, but as soon as he is dead, he confiscates his property. The crime is fatal, because it means that Gaunt's heir, Bolingbroke, who has already been exiled, is deprived of his rightful inheritance. This turns him into Richard's implacable enemy and worse, it undermines Richard's own position, because if a duke of the blood royal cannot be secure in his own titles and property, what guarantee is there that even a king can be safe? In effect Richard bows his head to treason. In doing so, he repeats old Gaunt's warning that there is no way in which an anointed king can be dethroned. Whatever the specious justification, to do so is treason and an affront to God, and in consequence, he prophesies that England will become the victim of war:

> For well we know no hand of blood and bone
> Can gripe the sacred handle of our sceptre,
> Unless he do profane, steal, or usurp.
> And though you think that all, as you have done,
> Have torn their souls by turning them from us,
> And we are barren and bereft of friends,
> Yet know – my master, God omnipotent,
> Is mustering in his clouds on our behalf
> Armies of pestilence; and they shall strike
> Your children yet unborn and unbegot,
> That lift your vassal hands against my head
> And threat the glory of my precious crown.

3.3.79–90

Again the prophecy is ignored. Bolingbroke proceeds with his seizure of the crown and in Westminster Hall Richard is dethroned. Stressing, as he always does, the sacerdotal nature of kingship, he chooses to turn the ceremony into a religious occasion, a sort of coronation-in-reverse:

> I give this heavy weight from off my head,
> And this unwieldy sceptre from my hand,
> The pride of kingly sway from out my heart;
> With mine own tears I wash away my balm,
> With mine own hands I give away my crown,
> With mine own tongue deny my sacred state,
> With mine own breath release all duteous oaths;
> All pomp and majesty I do forswear;
> My manors, rents, revenues, I forgo;
> My acts, decrees, and statutes, I deny.

4.1.204–13

And in this magnificent panoramic scene which sums up the whole style of the play, we get the third and last prophetic warning, uttered this time by the orthodox Bishop of Carlisle, who opens up for his hearers, and for Shakespeare's audience, the entire calamitous perspective of the civil wars which were to engulf England for the best part of a century:

> My Lord of Hereford here, whom you call king,
> Is a foul traitor to proud Hereford's king;
> And if you crown him, let me prophesy –
> The blood of English shall manure the ground,
> And future ages groan for this foul act;
> Peace shall go sleep with Turks and infidels,
> And in this seat of peace tumultuous wars
> Shall kin with kin and kind with kind confound;
> Disorder, horror, fear and mutiny,
> Shall here inhabit, and this land be call'd,
> The field of Golgotha and dead men's skulls.

4.1.134–44

The rest of the play shows the curse and the prophecy begin to take effect, as treason and rebellion swirl around the freshly-crowned Monarch. It ends on a note of unrelieved gloom, as Henry IV receives the news of Richard's murder, an act he has willed but not wished. Struck with horror and premonition of disaster, he vows to go on pilgrimage to purge his guilt. But Shakespeare's audience knew, and we know, that such a resolve, even if carried out, will be ineffectual. The fatal sacrilege has been committed, and nothing can now prevent the inexorable divine revenge on the nation that has committed it. Of course, the Elizabethan crowd could enjoy this vicarious shiver of fear, safe in the knowledge that earlier generations had paid the penalty and purged the guilt, and that their country was now protected by Tudor legitimacy.

Richard II
Ian Richardson

*Ian Richardson is a member of the Royal Shake-
speare Company. His parts have included Cassius,
Angelo and Prospero. Television appearances include
Bill Hayden in* Tinker, Tailor, Soldier, Spy. *He
has already published a preface to* Cymbeline.

Imagine to yourselves a land full of castles. In each one a lord
keeping his power jealously over the surrounding countryside,
with power of life and death over the illiterate peasantry and the
turbulent fighting men who are his subjects. There are few
roads. Journeys are made on horseback and news travels slowly.
Many days journey away, in the fairest castle in the land, there is
a sacred king, the figurehead and unifying factor, that makes the
island a nation rather than a tract of earth. His power is absolute,
and in his name laws are passed, wars are made, men live and
die. He is eternal. The king is dead, long live the king! The
lords in their lonely castles are mostly united to him by blood,
and so the threads spread out from the centre to hold the country
together. It has been thus for hundreds of years. Now, if the
sacred king proves unsatisfactory, how can he be replaced
without invoking the wrath of Heaven, both for the sacrilege of
his removal, and the equal sin of abandoning the ties of kinship?

This is the basic situation contained within the play of *Richard
II.* It is a psychological drama. We must not just ask the question
of whether right will triumph over wrong, but also consider from
what point of view we look at right and wrong and how we define
triumph. Taking the long and unwieldy chronicles of the reign,
Shakespeare weaves his story by a marvellous use of the
character of King Richard. As is usual with Shakespeare when
dealing with history, he telescopes time and adapts facts to suit
his dramatic intention, and the character of the King is Shakespeare's and not history's, but it contrives to make sense of the
bare narrative in a totally convincing way.

The events of the play are baldly as follows. Two noblemen
quarrel and are banished. One of them is the King's cousin,
Henry Bolingbroke. Bolingbroke's father, John of Gaunt, dies and
the King seizes his lands and goods, setting off immediately

afterwards for war in Ireland. Bolingbroke returns from exile, demanding the restitution of his titles and his estates, and is supported by various powerful nobles. The King, on returning from Ireland, finds that he has too few supporters to fight his cousin and surrenders to him both his person and his crown. Several of the nobles shilly-shally in their allegiance. The King says goodbye to his Queen, goes to prison where he is murdered.

For the first third of the play, we're presented with a King who is capricious, callous and irresponsible – a child playing with power for his own amusement. In the matter of the nobleman's quarrel, for instance, it's made clear to us that both parties are, in a sense, in the right. Bolingbroke accuses Mowbray, the other nobleman, of complicity in the death of the King's uncle, the Earl of Gloucester. Richard had ordered it and so Mowbray from sheer loyalty keeps his mouth shut, beyond affirming that he is a true and loyal subject. The lords arrange for a formal duel, which Richard permits. He allows it to get as far as lowered lances for the onslaught, but then intervenes and banishes both the faithful Mowbray and Bolingbroke. It's a dirty trick in all directions.

Further, we are told that he consistently overspends and listens to flatterers, such as the ubiquitous Bushy, Bagot and Green, 'the caterpillars of the Commonwealth'. Richard also commits the no doubt heinous sin of laying out lavish amounts to maintain himself in Italian fashions. The well-intentioned uncles, of whom there are still some left, warn him constantly that he is on the road to ruin, both his own and the country's, but he is deaf to advice until it is far too late. Richard is presented at his worst when he receives the news of John of Gaunt's death:

> The ripest fruit first falls, and so doth he;
> His time is spent, our pilgrimage must be.
> So much for that. Now for our Irish wars.

2.1.153–5

This flippant, doggerel epitaph has all the marks of something remembered from a Christmas cracker, which makes it all the more offensive. And our playboy King follows it up by cheerfully availing himself of all his uncle's property to finance the Irish war.

Why is he allowed to get away with it? The answer lies in the concept of kingship as held by the medieval world, the Elizabethan world and indeed the world of England up to and including the reign of the ill-fated Charles I. A king was believed to have a divine right to his position, which he held in trust directly from God Himself. He was God-appointed and, however perverse or unsatisfactory he might seem, he was the worker of God's will on earth. It was therefore heretical presumption to question or defy the king because it was tantamount to defying the Supreme Being Himself. As Richard so confidently puts it:

> Not all the water in the rough rude sea
> Can wash the balm off from an anointed king;
> The breath of worldly men cannot despose
> The deputy elected by the Lord.

3.2.54-7

The king's sanctity, inherent in himself by right of succession and fortified by the holy oil with which he was anointed at his coronation, was a necessary adjunct for self-preservation in a society only half civilised. The great earls and barons who effectively ruled most of the country by right of the feudal system had more real power, in terms of lands and troops, than the king. Their belief in his divinity was what placed their resources at his command. Loyalty had become religion and a point of honour. This attitude was also important to Elizabethan politicians and the sensible playwright took good care to uphold it. The censorship of the theatre at the time was entirely political and religious not moral, and the status quo, only recently achieved after the unrest and rebellion of the previous reigns, was to be supported in the arts as elsewhere.

On one level of interpretation almost the most important thing about Richard is that he is King. When I played the part I wanted to stress this, which meant examining what were the external and noticeable characteristics of royalty. I watched films of the coronation in 1953 and a newsreel of an investiture. And what struck me most was the expert stage-management of those about the Sovereign. She never needed to ask for anything. She extended an arm and the sword was placed in her hand. She sat and knew that the chair would be there. She moved to the exit knowing without looking that the way would be cleared and the door open. I tried to do the same. I never looked to see if my commands were obeyed because I knew they would be. I handed objects with which I had finished to hands I knew would be there to relieve me of them. Remember that Richard had been King since he was eleven and that these habits were thus deeply ingrained. His own concept of kingship, at this point expressed when he finds it challenged, reflected the contemporary view;

> We are amaz'd; and thus long have we sood
> To watch the fearful bending of thy knee,
> Because we thought ourself the lawful king;
> And if we be, how dare thy joints forget
> To pay their awful duty to our presence?
> If we be not, show us the hand of God
> That hath dismiss'd us from our stewardship; . . .

3.3.72–8

Yes, that was the whimsical, effete King, who reveals himself in the teeth of adversity to be a superb actor, who has at last found a part worth playing. As King, he has had little scope for his talents, beyond a parade of magnificence and the demonstration of power. He is given cue after cue to perform as the play progresses and the events of his own life become increasingly dramatic. He seizes these cues hungrily. He is never without an audience and it's interesting to note that, unlike most Shakespearean 'heroes', he has no soliloquy until the penultimate scene of the play. For the rest of the time there are always spectators. It would be over-cynical to say that Richard acts consciously. No, what makes him such a good actor is that he can make himself believe everything he is saying and create realistically for himself the situations in which his poetic gifts and histrionic powers can give themselves full rein. He simply cannot help dramatising every event. For instance, Bolingbroke returns from exile and requests, quite politely, the return of his lands and titles which have been illegally confiscated. On his way to meet Richard he is joined by many adherents to his cause, so that his men outnumber the King's. Now, if Richard were any other King, he would have accepted the impossibility of fighting his cousin and granted his request which was in all conscience modest enough. But he doesn't. Like a child who finds a bit of paint has come off a new toy, he doesn't want to play with it anymore. The gloss of his royalty is spoilt. So he proceeds with an amazing scene of outraged dignity and injured innocence. He says, in effect, 'You want my crown? Take it! Take it!'

The opposition continues to be restrained and civil, but Richard plucks defeat from the jaws of victory and wilfully destroys himself:

What must the King do now? Must he submit?
The King shall do it. Must he be depos'd?
The King shall be contented. Must he lose
The name of king? A God's name, let it go.
I'll give my jewels for a set of beads,
My gorgeous palace for a hermitage,
My gay apparel for an almsman's gown,
My figur'd goblets for a dish of wood,
My sceptre for a palmer's walking staff,
My subjects for a pair of carved saints,
And my large kingdom for a little grave,
A little little grave, an obscure grave –
Or I'll be buried in the king's high way,
Some way of common trade, where subjects' feet
May hourly trample on their sovereign's head;
For on my heart they tread now whilst I live,
And buried once, why not upon my head?

3.3.143–59

But none of these things have been asked of him, although there is one present who would have forced his hand if he had not so conveniently given up. This is the Earl of Northumberland, a powerful war-lord from the wild north, who is ambitious, ruthless and totally cynical about the King's divinity. He knows that soldiers mean more than holy oil any day and sees Bolingbroke as his means of indirect rule of the kingdom. The royal blood, which Henry Bolingbroke possesses, is still an essential for the role of king, but for an eminence grise like Northumberland the identity of the puppet who sits on the throne is unimportant so long as the strings are in his hands.

Bolingbroke, whether genuinely or not, still maintains that he has come but for his own. But there is no stopping Richard. He has made a superb gesture, placed his cousin in the wrong and himself in the role of a holy martyr and he is not going back on it now. The irony of his closing remarks, bearing in mind what has gone before, is considerable:

What you will have, I'll give, and willing too;
For do we must what force will have us do.

3.3.206–7

The man who is now, apparently against his will, about to ascend the throne, is very different from Richard, although it could be said that he began the play not unlike him. The royalty of their blood is identical, since they are both grandsons of Edward III, and their upbringing has been similar. When we first meet Bolingbroke, his language is as full of ornament and eloquence as the King's. At his banishment he cries out against the folly of being comforted by thoughts of home:

O, who can hold a fire in his hand
By thinking on the frosty Caucasus?
Or cloy the hungry edge of appetite
By bare imagination of a feast?
Or wallow naked in December snow
By thinking on fantastic summer's heat?
O, no! the apprehension of the good
Gives but the greater feeling to the worse.
Fell sorrow's tooth doth never rankle more
Than when he bites, but lanceth not the sore.

1.3.294–303

But this great gift of hardship and misfortune is the most supreme blessing that Bolingbroke could have had, for he returns matured and improved. He is now a man of few words and those are to the point. Rhetoric he leaves to his cousin, the King. The paucity of words means that he is to some extent an enigmatic figure. One is never quite sure how much he joins in the plots to make himself King and how much he just lets them happen. His greatest asset is his common touch, as reported early in the play by Richard, who is shrewd enough even then to see that his cousin may in the future be a threat. But things are never so simple in Shakespeare. Certain unalterable dogmas are always present. One being that kingship is sacred, even if the king is bad, and that those who defy the established order, even if they are the instruments of God's will in the overthrow of that order, must be at the last condemned and suffer for their sins. It's important for Henry Bolingbroke to have had no hand in Richard's overthrow, at least as direct instigator, if he is to maintain the audience's sympathy within Shakespeare's moral framework.

When Richard is brought to Westminster Hall for the formal renunciation of his crown, his performance is faultless and one feels the pity of it – that this man should have had the misfortune to be merely the King of England and at that particular time. What a Prince of the Renaissance he would have made, with his love of music and poetry, his grasp of philosophy and his almost excessively developed aesthetic sense. For now we do feel sorry

43

for him. The situation in which he finds himself may have been of his own making, but it is none the less real and pitiful. He realises his own humanity in rare moments of simplicity:

> For you have but mistook me all this while.
> I live with bread like you, feel want,
> Taste grief, need friends: . . .

3.2.171–6

Nothing can lie before him but imprisonment and death and the present is full of bitter humiliation. It is perhaps unkind to imagine Richard preparing for his last great public scene, again as an actor, but it's irresistible. I am sure he dressed with care to present just the right image of humility and distress. He certainly pulls out all the stops when he renounces for ever his sovereignty before his cousin and the assembled lords. This is his swan-song and he is going to make sure that none of his audience forgets it. He is magnificent, and no doubt deeply embarrassing to Henry, who hardly speaks throughout the scene.

Richard accuses the assembled company of betraying him, as Christ was betrayed. It becomes plain that this is the seed he wants to sow. However and whenever he dies, after this, it will be as a sacrificial victim, and Henry will be – at best – Pontius Pilate. The moral problem posed to those among his listeners who are well-meaning, honest men is also a very real one. They had, indeed, sworn loyalty to King Richard, but was it loyalty to Richard or to the King? And is not Henry King? The transference of loyalty is not so simple as it may first appear, and consciences are stirred. Henry's reign is not going to be easy. If there is anything so simplistic in a Shakespeare play as a message, then in *Richard II* it seems to be this. Men are discontented but every change is not necessarily for the better. Men must work out their destiny and Richard's destiny, indeed his only option, is to die. Anything less would be for him an anti-climax. He has become, through the course of the play, a better person, although his misfortunes have come too late to make him into a good King. His reflections in prison contain a kind of serenity totally alien to his earlier character. The play is in no way depressing or pessimistic, even though Richard's great discovery is that death is the only recipe for happiness:

> But whate'er I be,
> Nor I, nor any man that but man is,
> With nothing shall be pleas'd till he be eas'd
> With being nothing.

5.5.38–41

AS YOU LIKE IT
Brigid Brophy

Brigid Brophy is an active campaigner for authors' rights. Her own publications include The King of a Rainy Country *and* Flesh. *Part of the programme was made on location at West Wycombe Park.*

As You Like It is a play I've loved virtually all my life, but it was only recently that I realised that it isn't what the Copyright Act would call an 'original work'. This is not a great feat of literary detection on my part. Almost all Shakespeare's plays have sources of some kind and any school text will tell you that the source of *As You Like It* is a novel called *Rosalynde* by Shakespeare's contemporary, Thomas Lodge. However, very few people bother actually to read Lodge's novel, and that's a pity, because it is a highly interesting novel in its own right – rather eccentric, deeply charming, very shrewd about psychology, very lively, very well written – and the moment you do read it you realise that it is very much more than just a source for *As You Like It. As You Like It* is, in fact, an absolutely straightforward dramatised version of Lodge's *Rosalynde.*

The novel was first published in 1590 and it evidently had a considerable success. It ran to three editions within the next decade. That, presumably, made it worthwhile for someone to cash in on it. It's notable that Shakespeare didn't change the name of the heroine, which the novel had made famous by its title. He kept the name Rosalind, though not for his title. It was eight or nine years after the novel was published, in 1598 or 1599 (no one knows for sure which), that the dramatised version appeared on the stage, under the title *As You Like It.*

Shakespeare did change the names of several of the other characters, but he didn't change the characters themselves or – which is more important – the relationships between them. He cut down the time spanned by the novel, because a novel has more room to stretch than a play has. But on the whole he made fewer changes than a modern writer might if he were adapting a modern novel for the theatre or for television.

Having stayed with Lodge in all the big things, relationships, characters, plot and sequence, Shakespeare often chose to stay with him right down to smallish detail. For example, here are some details as they occur in Lodge:

> After his repast he fell in a dead sleep. As thus he lay, a hungry lion came hunting down the edge of the grove for prey, and espying Saladyne, began to seize upon him. But seeing he lay still without any motion, he left to touch him, for that lions hate to prey on dead carcasses, and yet desirous to have some food, the lion lay down and watched to see if he would stir. While, thus, Saladyne slept secure, fortune . . . brought it so to pass that Rosader . . . came . . . pacing down by the grove with a boarspeare in his hand in great haste. He spied where a man lay asleep and a lion fast by him. Amazed at this sight, as he stood gazing, his nose on the sudden bled, which made him conjecture it was some friend of his. Whereupon drawing more nigh, he might easily discern his visage, and perceived by his physionomy that it was his brother Saladyne.

When Shakespeare came to dramatise this minor episode, he got rid of the nose bleed and inserted a snake. Otherwise he changed very little. He kept even the detail that lions won't eat dead carcasses:

> A wretched ragged man, o'ergrown with hair,
> Lay sleeping on his back. About his neck
> A green and gilded snake had wreath'd itself,
> Who with her head nimble in threats approach'd
> The opening of his mouth; but suddenly,
> Seeing Orlando, it unlink'd itself,
> And with indented glides did slip away
> Into a bush; under which bush's shade
> A lioness, with udders all drawn dry
> Lay couching, head on ground, with catlike watch,
> When that the sleeping man should stir; for 'tis
> The royal disposition of that beast
> To prey on nothing that doth seem as dead.
> This seen, Orlando did approach the man,
> And found it was his brother, his elder brother.

4.3.105–20

Lodge's novel and Shakespeare's play are set in France. One thread concerns a king of France who is driven out of his court by his usurping brother. Shakespeare demotes this pair of brothers from kings of France to dukes of an unnamed part of France. The exiled king or duke is eventually followed into exile by his daughter Rosalind, but not before she has fallen in love with another ill-used brother, who has been driven out of his inheritance by his elder brother and who also goes into voluntary exile.

The place where all these exiles take refuge and where the threads of the story are woven is what Lodge and Shakespeare called the Forest of Arden and what we should call, now that it's no longer fashionable to anglicise French names, the Ardennes. The ups and downs of fortune, which have turned these people into exiles, give them all the opportunity to reflect on blind fortune – or random chance, as we would probably call it – and this gives the play its fashionable philosophical tone; and the fact that they have all taken refuge in the forest puts the play slap in the middle of another high fashion of the Renaissance, which remained in high fashion deep into the eighteenth century, the fashion for the pastoral.

Although a pastor is, literally, a shepherd who puts his sheep out to pasture, I can assure anyone who feels, as I do, that the countryside is highly overrated that the pastoral fashion has remarkably little to do with real countryside or with real sheep-rearing. When they arrive in the forest Rosalind and Celia do buy a sheep farm, but even in Lodge, who has more room, they are only moderately serious about working it. In Shakespeare, it is obviously left to run itself. The object of the pastoral was not really to draw any morals from nature. It was to re-create the literature of the ancient world – in particular, the pastoral poems, the dialogues mainly between shepherds, which Theocritus wrote in Greek in the third century BC and Virgil imitated in Latin a couple of centuries later.

If you bought a pastoral novel or went to see a pastoral play, you knew pretty much what you were going to get, just as nowadays you know pretty much what you're going to get if you buy a thriller. You were going to get shepherds, with Greek or Latinised names like Sylvius, Corin, Lycidas, Damon, and shepherdesses called things like Phoebe and Corinna. The point of the whole piece was going to be that people were going to fall desperately in love, and you knew also that you'd get large quantities of lyric verse. The idea that shepherds were poets may have begun, I think, from the thought that shepherds piped to their flocks and perhaps, having piped a tune, they then set words to the tune.

However it arose, one of the rules of the pastoral convention is that shepherds are poets. In Shakespeare's dramatised version, only one of the characters, Orlando, had the actual verse-writing mania. No doubt he picks it up from the pastoral setting like an infection when he arrives in the forest. Orlando's verses, incidentally, are all bad. However, the entire play is punctuated by songs, which seem to leave their echo in the forest, creating patches of mood, like mist, in the play.

The shepherds in Theocritus and Virgil often fall passionately in love with shepherdesses and they also quite often fall passionately in love with shepherds. The same is probably true of the cowboys in the modern Western, which is a diluted descendant of the pastoral.

This tradition of the pastoral made it a particularly apt mode for Lodge and for Shakespeare in Lodge's tracks to set their story in. When the girl cousins and best friends, Rosalind and Celia, run away to the Forest of Arden, Rosalind – and it is Rosalind rather than Celia because, as she explains, she is the taller of the two – dresses up as a boy. As you'd expect, given that the novel is knee-deep in classical allusions and the play is at least ankle-deep, some having been cut out to make it more easily assimilable in the theatre, the name which Rosalind chooses for herself while she's disguised as a boy is Ganymede, the name of the page whom Zeus, King of the Gods, fell in love with.

Lodge plays with grammar. He calls Rosalynde 'Ganymede', 'he' and 'she' within a single sentence. Shakespeare, of course, had an extra decorative dimension to play with, because women didn't appear as actors on the English stage for another generation, and therefore all the parts in *As You Like It* were taken by men. Rosalind was that old favourite of the English theatre, a drag act, from the word go, and when she disguises herself as a boy she goes into double drag; and at the same time a very delicate and charming air of sexual ambiguity comes over the story. Phoebe falls in love with Ganymede, but of course Ganymede doesn't really exist. Is she in fact in love with Rosalind? Orlando constitutes an even greater dilemma. He believes that, if he pretends (as he thinks it is) that Ganymede is his Rosalind and he woos him, he will be cured of his love for her; and so he does woo the boy and in the process falls deeper and deeper in love with the woman. Or *is* it with the woman? Is it in fact with the boy?

ROSALIND: But come, now I will be your Rosalind in a more coming-on disposition; and ask me what you will, I will grant it.

ORLANDO: Then love me, Rosalind.

ROSALIND: Yes, faith, will I, Fridays and Saturdays, and all.

ORLANDO: And wilt thou have me?

ROSALIND: Ay, and twenty such.

ORLANDO: What sayest thou?

ROSALIND: Are you not good?

ORLANDO: I hope so.

ROSALIND: Why then, can one desire too much of a good thing? Come, sister, you shall be the priest, and marry us. Give me your hand, Orlando. What do you say, sister?

ORLANDO: Pray thee, marry us.

CELIA: I cannot say the words.

ROSALIND: You must begin 'Will you, Orlando –'

CELIA: Go to. Will you, Orlando, have to wife this Rosalind?

ORLANDO: I will.

ROSALIND: Ay, but when?

ORLANDO: Why, now; as fast as she can marry us.

ROSALIND: Then you must say 'I take thee, Rosalind, for wife'.

ORLANDO: I take thee, Rosalind, for wife.

4.1.98–121

If I ask myself what makes *As You Like It* so moving, I locate the answer in two elements that Shakespeare dramatised quite brilliantly from Lodge's novel: the erotic love between Rosalind and Orlando and, slightly less obviously, the non-erotic love between Rosalind and Celia. The dialogue that expresses these relationships may not be positively witty in the sense that you could go through it taking out bits for an anthology of aphorisms, but it is witty in tone, witty in rhythm – and its tone is, of course, the tone of flirtation. Rosalind and Celia are limbering up their flirtatiousness on one another.

If I go on to ask myself how Shakespeare achieved this technically, the answer is one that I think is rather surprising or would be surprising if you knew only his other comedies. He does it in prose:

CELIA: Trow you who hath done this?

ROSALIND: Is it a man?

CELIA: And a chain, that you once wore, about his neck. Change you colour?

ROSALIND: I prithee, who?

CELIA: O Lord, Lord! it is a hard matter for friends to meet; but mountains may be remov'd with earthquakes, and so encounter.

ROSALIND: Nay, but who is it?

CELIA: Is it possible?

ROSALIND: Nay, I prithee now, with most petitionary vehemence, tell me who it is.

CELIA: O wonderful, wonderful, and most wonderful wonderful, and yet again wonderful, and after that, out of all whooping!

ROSALIND: Good my complexion! Dost thou think, though I am comparison'd like a man, I have a doublet and hose in my disposition? One inch of delay more is a South Sea of discovery. I prithee tell me who is it quickly, and speak apace . . . I prithee take the cork out of thy mouth, that I may drink thy tidings.

CELIA: So you may put a man in your belly.

3.2.164–190

Even if you discount the superstitions about the innocence and simplicity of life in the country, there is a way in which shepherds can truly be said to be innocent. This doesn't apply to cowboys, incidentally. Shepherds are innocent of bloodguilt. Human beings don't always choose to do so but it is possible to live on reasonably fair terms with a flock of sheep. You can deprive the sheep of their wool, which they are quite glad to be rid of, and not deprive them of their lives. One of the changes that Shakespeare did make in dramatising Lodge's novel was to shift the economy from sheep-minding to hunting. His exiled courtiers in the forest kill the deer. And in this way he darkens the sunny landscape that he found in Lodge.

All the same, through that imperfect windy instrument, Jaques, Shakespeare does allow the point of view of the deer to be stated. It's Jaques who has pointed out to his fellow courtiers in exile that wounded deer weep, which is a matter of fact, incidentally, not a matter of folklore as is usually thought. Jaques makes his entrance, asking the telling question 'Which is he that killed the deer?', a question in which he, as well as looking for someone to congratulate on his victory, is also the detective hunting out a killer; and the song that follows – although it does congratulate the killer on his victory – also makes a mockery of him:

JAQUES: Which is he that killed the deer?

LORD: Sir, it was I.

JAQUES: Let's present him to the Duke, like a Roman conqueror; and it would do well to set the deer's horns upon his head for a branch of victory. Have you no song, forester, for this purpose?

(ANOTHER) LORD: Yes, sir.

JAQUES: Sing it. 'Tis no matter how it be in tune, so it makes
 noise enough.

song; What shall he have that kill'd the deer?
 His leather skin and horns to wear.
 Then sing him home.

4.2.1–12

The English-speaking theatre's other grand master of dramatic
prose, Bernard Shaw, considered *As You Like It* a 'melodrama',
on the grounds that the hero and heroine have no disagreeable
qualities. Presumably he missed (or didn't consider disagreeable) the distinct touch of sadism which I discern in Rosalind's
personality. He considered that *As You Like It* gives unmixed
delight, but he thought this was simply a bid for popularity. He
said Shakespeare flung Rosalind at the public with a shout of 'As
you like it'.

 And, of course, it *was* a bid for popularity. It was a bid for the
popularity which Lodge's novel had already established with
readers. My guess is that, when Shakespeare had finished
making his adaptation, he riffled through the pages of Lodge's
novel, casting about for a title, and finally he turned back to the
beginning and came upon Lodge's preface, which is addressed
to 'the gentlemen readers'. 'To be brief, gentlemen', Lodge says,
after relating how he wrote the book on a sea voyage when he
was taking part in a military expedition, 'room for a soldier and a
sailor, that gives you the fruits of his labours that he wrote in the
ocean, when every line was wet with a surge, and every
humorous passion counterchecked with a storm. If you like it so
. . .' By the time Shakespeare made his adaptation, the gentlemen readers had already proved that they did indeed like
Lodge's novel. It was no longer a question of '*if* you like it', but
'*as* you like it'.

AS YOU LIKE IT
Janet Suzman

Janet Suzman is a member of the Royal Shakespeare Company. Her parts have included Portia, Ophelia and Cleopatra. She has also appeared in several television productions of Shakespeare.

There is a wild wood, an old religious man, an abandoned cave, a hungry lioness, a weeping deer, a green and gilded snake, a grove of olives, a palm tree with a poem on it and an old oak tree. Where are we? In fairyland? Will Merlin pop out with his owl on his head? Will St George slay the fiery dragon any minute now? Or perhaps we are looking over the shoulder of the painter Cranach the Elder as he touches in the last brush stroke of a great court painting. No, for all those unlikely things belong to the imaginary world of the Forest of Arden, where *As You Like It* is set.

You would be wrong to think of it as a real geographical place that you could find on a map. Some mysterious substance called 'traditional Shakespeare' has been poured like porridge into our collective skulls, so we tend to assume that supposedly historically accurate settings and costume will give us Shakespeare as Shakespeare intended. The characters in the plays may belong to a particular world, but that world can be an imaginary one. It does not have to be historically accurate. We may be infected with 'authenticity-fever', but Shakespeare wasn't. He flung a toga over a doublet and hose to create Rome. His words tell you where you are rather than the costumes or props. No-one has trouble with the fantastic world of the Muppets. What's so different about Shakespeare? Everyone has an imagination, which some use to earn their livings whilst others use it to enjoy their leisure. Why on earth should theatre audiences expect to be pictorially spoon-fed, instead of imaginatively filling in the spaces by actually listening to the word-picture drawn by the actor?

Jaques's speech on the ages of man is the most famous one in the whole play. You'll have probably heard it or read it a great many times, but let's pretend that this is the first time:

All the world's a stage,
And all the men and women merely players;
They have their exits and their entrances;
And one man in his time plays many parts,
His acts being seven ages. At first the infant,
Mewling and puking in the nurse's arms;
Then the whining school-boy, with his satchel
And shining morning face, creeping like snail
Unwillingly to school. And then the lover,
Sighing like furnace, with a woeful ballad
Made to his mistress' eyebrow. Then a soldier,
Full of strange oaths, and bearded like the pard,
Jealous in honour, sudden and quick in quarrel,
Seeking the bubble reputation
Even in the cannon's mouth. And then the justice,
In fair round belly with good capon lin'd,
With eyes severe and beard of formal cut,
Full of wise saws and modern instances,
And so he plays his part. The sixth age shifts
Into the lean and slipper'd pantaloon,
With spectacles on nose and pouch on side,
His youthful hose, well sav'd, a world too wide
For his shrunk shrank; and his big manly voice,
Turning again toward childish treble, pipes
And whistles in his sound. Last scene of all,
That ends this strange eventful history,
Is second childishness and mere oblivion;
Sans teeth, sans eyes, sans taste, sans every thing.

2.7.139–66

Twenty-eight lines and the world has passed by us in review. I defy any set designer to create this panoramic picture. What I am really saying, as a fanatical lover of Shakespeare, is that when you see *As You Like It* don't get too easily seduced by pretty or authentic pictures and wonder why on earth they are being spoilt by all that talk. Try it the other way round. Give yourself to all that pretty talk and only start to wonder if the pictures seem to be getting in the way.

If I were to say to you 'once upon a time there was a wicked duke', you would have no difficulty at all in sitting bolt upright, eyes wide awake with interest, waiting for me to carry on. This duke has a daughter called Celia and this is the first line she speaks in the play: 'I pray thee, Rosalind, sweet my coz, be merry'. What a host of things we learn from this one line! Celia's cousin Rosalind is sad. Celia loves her very much and so begs her to put off her sadness. It sounds as if Rosalind has been sad for quite a time, maybe hours, maybe days. The tone is familiar, friendly and filled with concern. Shakespeare has introduced us to his two heroines in a mere nine words. There's a poet and storyteller for you! We immediately want to know more about them and the next four speeches make it clearer why Rosalind is sad: a father banished, a guilty uncle and an injustice done.

As You Like It – with what smiling expansiveness the title invites you to view the play. It is very difficult to say it with a frown. It does not come out right because the vowels are open. The beckoning finger asks you to make no comment but rather simply to listen and watch in a quiet, friendly fashion. It asks you to make no harsh, modern judgements. Goodness and wickedness spring unbidden into the hearts of people. It is impossible to have one without the other, since opposites hold the balance of the world. We swing with natural ease from friendliness to viciousness, from court to country, from warmth to cold, from riches to poverty, from repletion to hunger, from youth to age and from the single state to the married. The wheel of fortune whirls us around and we are victims of its whims. Even the form of the writing reflects this kind of pendulum-swing, as it moves from verse to prose and back again. Poetry, to put it crudely, means you are in love, whereas prose usually means that you are still thinking about it!

What is the play about? It appears to be about getting married. Indeed, the God Hymen turns up at the very end to bless that happy institution and to shower goodwill on the four prospective couples. Yet it is more particularly concerned with the suitability of these couples. The state of marriage is joked about, laughed at and lauded as the proper end for mutual attraction. Marriage is presented as the expression of order rather than chaos. This may seem to be nothing new, but what is in fact acted out before our eyes is how men and women find the actual basis on which to build their lives together. The conclusion is that common backgrounds are the most important ingredient. Shakespeare, I suppose, was the first person to make ordinary, bourgeois, middle class ideals actually irresistible. I am very tempted, once again, to recount the story in fairy-tale rather than operatic terms. If I say 'once upon a time there was this wicked duke', you will accept his wickedness without question. If I say 'Duke Frederick has usurped his elder brother from his rightful station and banished him', you will either start yawning or wanting to know why he did such a wicked thing. It would be a dreadful waste of time to find out why. He did and that allows the story to take place. Once upon a time in a rich palace, a girl fell in love with a young man. She is the daughter of a banished duke. The young man, whose name is Orlando, is the son of an honourable but dead father. They are both forced to flee to the forest, where they meet again. Rosalind is dressed as a boy to protect herself from the world, so Orlando does not recognise her. She decides to use her disguise to test his love and so pretends to be his real love. At last neither of them can bear to pretend any longer. They stop the game. Orlando is very happy to find his real Rosalind and they become engaged. She finds her lost father, who gives them both a title, and they live happily ever after.

Or do they? A seedling of doubt is sown during the course of the play about the cure-all properties of matrimony. Rosalind and Orlando might live happily ever after, but they are surrounded by a crowd of untried and untested couples, whose chances of happiness may not be quite so secure even though their search for love and companionship is no less assiduous. Who are these others? There's our Celia, who falls head over heels in love with Orlando's beastly brother, Oliver. Then there's Touchstone the fool. Fools were one of Shakespeare's obsessions because they could tell the truth while appearing not to. Touchstone lusts after a country bumpkin called Audrey, who, like all women, is dazzled by the smooth tongue of a nifty talker. Then there's sweet, constant, gentle Silvius, who loves a termagent shepherdess called Phoebe. She can't stand being fawned on and needs a man who does not plead. Perhaps she too is like all women. *As You Like It*, more than any other comedy I can think of, suggests that everyone, even that crusty old vegetarian Jaques and his dying deer, is able to love. They are able to love others even with their faults and to sacrifice safety and comfort for friendship. The play praises patience, kindness and faithfulness. It deals with adultery, foolishness and lust and, without dismissing their existence, opts for marriage. Yet marriage is not a way of playing it safe. It is a gamble.

I am in danger of having so simplified the subject matter of the play that you will, when you see or read it, be surprised at how busy it is. It is a very sociable play indeed. No-one is ever alone for very long in this forest. People are continually plumping down like dropped acorns to have a good old chat about some subject or other. It seems that out there in the forest, rather like those stories of life during the Blitz, the best is brought out in everyone. People are very ready to help each other. The enclosed society of the court, by contrast, seems to breed jealousy, fear and selfishness. Despite this contrast, the play is not in any way seriously disturbing. For it is a play about falling – and I mean falling, plonk! – in love, or falling in and out of wickedness. It's about taking a fall in a wrestling match, falling over in a faint, falling in and out of captivity, falling over your words to get your thoughts out, talking before thinking and loving without considering. It is the most impetuous of plays. It is, to repeat, such a romantic, impetuous play that you have to work very hard to find the sour note. Cynicism, blaséness, fibrous intellectualism and black moods are swatted aside as if they were flies by everyone in the forest. Jaques, for example, tries in vain to find acceptance amongst the many self-absorbed natures of the forest folk, busy sorting out their own pleasing problems. We listen to him. We even wish him no harm, but we can't somehow be bothered with him. But we ought to, for his dark mutterings heighten the heady glow round lovers.

I have played both Rosalind and Celia. I discovered in playing Celia what a card she is. As she is uninfected by love right until the end of the play, she casts a nicely unsentimental eye on the cavorting of her mad cousin. Her spiky observations are only silenced when she too falls in love and finds herself made speechless by the experience. She should under no circumstances be played as a second fiddle. She's just a late starter. Celia, Touchstone and the audience are the only ones who know the secret of Rosalind's disguise. The two central scenes of the play would be contrived and unacceptable, without Celia there to share the joke. It's Celia as an audience, as well as the audience as an audience, that enhances the delight. The audience knows that Celia knows about Rosalind's disguise. They also know that Rosalind knows that Celia knows, so the danger of Celia giving the game away heightens the comedy. The other characters are all innocents and there is something finally tiresome about deceiving innocent people, although it makes for wonderful comedy!

Rosalind falls in love first. We are completely hooked, since she feels it so deeply, has so much to say and is so desperately silly and adorable about it. You can't cast a glow like she does and expect people to remain impervious. She infects the air with love. It becomes catching and suddenly everyone is up to it. She has no time for bores and cynics. Jaques bores her because he's out of love with life. It's a bit like being caught by a horticulturist discussing the potato blight when you've just dined off caviar at Maxim's! The girl is ripe and ready for love – and bingo! When it strikes it strikes deep:

> ROSALIND: O coz, coz, coz, my pretty little coz, that thou didst know how many fathom deep I am in love! But it cannot be sounded; my affection hath an unknown bottom, like the Bay of Portugal.
>
> CELIA: Or rather, bottomless; that as fast as you pour affection in, it runs out.

4.1.184–9

If you don't bother to feel to bursting when you play Rosalind, she will become dangerously near to being just a nice girl who unaccountably talks too much. If you play upon her anti-romantic side, she will appear to be callously teasing Orlando out of love and into marriage just for the hell of it. If you play upon her garrulity, she'll become long-winded and tedious. If you play upon her expertise at being a forest lad, she'll become only a callous temptress. And here we come to one of the most central themes of so many of Shakespeare's plays – disguise. Innocence is cruelly tested, but through deception comes clarity. Disguise allows you both to play the archetypal spy and time to think. It also makes you unhappy because, although you can say what you really feel, you're not taken seriously because it's not really you saying it. Disguise makes you feel a cheat, so you long to be recognised in order to stop having to be so careful about giving yourself away. These days when both girls and boys wear jeans and nobody seems to have too much trouble differentiating between the sexes, you might think that the point of being in disguise is somehow lessened. The point is 'look but don't touch'. If Orlando were to scrap with Rosalind, or play football with her, or give her a bear-hug, he'd soon know who she was. The success of disguise depends upon being able to tease at a distance. Innocence has to be the keynote and mannish rough and tumble has to be delicately avoided. So now I leave you to this improbable forest, where a lot of crazy people are having an engagement party. You get the point, I know. It's not real or authentic in the sense that it obeys the rules of the camera, but it is believable in its own terms.

JULIUS CAESAR
Jonathan Dimbleby

Jonathan Dimbleby has worked on current affairs programmes such as This Week, as well as making his own documentaries on the Middle East and South America. He made this programme at the BBC TV Centre and used a number of extracts from contemporary news and current affairs programmes.

I first saw *Julius Caesar* at school and I didn't like it very much. There was a conspiracy I didn't really understand, a murder which made me giggle and a very long speech which didn't move me as it had been suggested it should. I was, you will correctly conclude, a callow youth. Coming back to it I've discovered at least some of what I missed. The play may have been written by Shakespeare 400 years ago about events which took place 2,000 years ago, but it's only glancingly about the past. It speaks to us about the present, and not only to a modern age but particularly to those of us who live in a good, old-fashioned, democratic country like Britain. The play is a chillingly precise metaphor about power and politicians.

Of course we can play safe. We can choose to see the play as a statement about the struggle between freedom and tyranny. And then we can summon images from elsewhere in the world, where martial music wearily proclaims that one tyrant has been over-thrown by another who believes greatly in freedom but carries a gun in his hand. And then we in the West say, with some complacency, and forgetting yesterday's dictators, that we've given up such barbarity long ago and how wonderfully Mr Shakespeare portrays the frailties of others. But we can't really get away with that. Shakespeare requires us to reach rather further for the meaning. People in power survive by secrecy and salesmanship and *Julius Caesar* is about individuals who inhabit the citadel of power and conspire against each other in its corridors. But it's a paradox of power, even absolute power, that it requires a measure of consent. Public opinion does matter. Contact with the populace may be distressing, as it evidently is for the Roman élite, but it is necessary. There's no power without the people.

The Roman mob is ignorant and therefore it's easily swayed. It's volatile, and therefore it is dangerous, so for me the play is about the political process. It's this, not the murder that matters; it's the decision, not the way it's made.

Cassius is a politician for any age. He's clever, manoeuvres well, has his scruples well under control and counts heads like the best party whip. Brutus is needed if the plot is to succeed. Cassius recognises this instinctively and knows how to get him. For Brutus, much honoured by the masses as a man of integrity, has a flaw. He is mighty susceptible to flattery. Nor is he without ambition, so he's ripe for Cassius to pluck:

> 'Brutus' and 'Caesar'. What should be in that 'Caesar'?
> Why should that name be sounded more than yours?
> Write them together; yours is as fair a name.
> Sound them: it doth become the mouth as well.
> Weigh them: it is as heavy. Conjure with 'em:
> 'Brutus' will start a spirit as soon as 'Caesar'.
> Now, in the names of all the gods at once,
> Upon what meat doth this our Caesar feed,
> That he is grown so great? Age, thou art sham'd!
> Rome, thou hast lost the breed of noble bloods!

I.2.142–51

Now Brutus has a moment of real turmoil, but significantly it's only a moment. He does have doubts, but they're despatched with singular speed by the convenient device of persuading himself that what he *ought* to do coincides with what he *wants* to do. He alights upon a proposition, much favoured by those in search of power and in need of justification. Let's think of Caesar, he says, as a serpent's egg 'which, hatch'd, would as his kind grow mischievous,/And kill him in the shell'. It must be by his death. You would expect even the most robust conscience to be troubled by such reasoning. But Brutus is now a prisoner; obedient to a political logic which won't permit him to dally with moral niceties. The hunger for power imposes its own irresistible and unsavoury rules. When Shakespeare takes us into these secret chambers where power lurks we meet a cast of familiar figures – politicians plotting. Do we need Cicero? Can we get him? And what about Mark Antony? What are we going to do about him? And then there's public opinion. Our course must seem necessary, not envious. Hungry politicians: some who'll stop at nothing, some who calculate, the squeamish, the indecisive, the ones who can't sleep at night for anxiety and the eternal placeman who retains his position by assenting in quick succession to quite contradictory propositions according to the prevailing wind.

Perhaps it is different today. After all, our politicians don't behave like conspirators. They don't go about with their hats plucked 'about their ears/And half their faces buried in their cloaks'. And yet they manage to conceal their purpose with remarkable effect. Indeed Brutus would be delighted by their ability to 'hide it in smiles and affability'. And they do understand secrecy because they rule behind closed doors. In Britain, as in Caesar's Rome, the substance of power lies in the shadows. In *Julius Caesar* the struggle for power engulfs the state, but the protagonists challenge nothing except each other. They trade limp slogans about peace, liberty and freedom, but they don't ask 'whose freedom?'. The people matter only insofar as they give or withhold their consent. Today it's almost different and nearly the same. We try to avoid murder, preferring that more civilised institution, the general election. Here again, there's much talk of freedom, but we're inclined to suspect that, like their predecessors, our politicians have themselves in mind as much as the people. Those who jostle and turn on each other in the hope of advancement compete to be at the heart of that secret network, that centre of great influence, which forms the British establishment. To that end, factions wage permanent war against each other, though their conflicts break out into the open only on the rarest of occasions, usually when the victim has fallen, the knives have been sheathed and the new leaders are delivering the old speeches. It may be as good a way of running things as any other, but for most of the time we, like the Roman mob, are left in ignorance about it – in the national interest, of course. We become spectators in the public gallery, where the rhetoric of our representatives offers us an opaque echo of the secret chambers, an exclamation mark put in to assure us that democracy is alive and well and living in Westminister.

Whether it be murder or election, the politician must perform upon a public stage. The contest between Brutus and Mark Antony over the murdered body of Julius Caesar is between two salesmen. Brutus may be sincere. He may be convinced by now that his was an honourable deed, 'Not that I lov'd Caesar less, but that I lov'd Rome more', as he explains it. Politically that's irrelevant. What matters is whether the speech works, who wins. That issue is not for long in doubt, for while Brutus is painfully pedestrian, Mark Antony delivers a speech of genius, surely the best ever written for a politician. It's so good that we can hardly resist joining the mob ourselves. We remain detached only if we detect its purpose:

> He hath brought many captives home to Rome,
> Whose ransoms did the general coffers fill;
> Did this in Caesar seem ambitious?
> When that the poor have cried, Caesar hath wept;
> Ambition should be made of sterner stuff.
> Yet Brutus says he was ambitious;
> And Brutus is an honourable man.
> You all did see that on the Lupercal
> I thrice presented him a kingly crown,
> Which he did thrice refuse. Was this ambition?
> Yet Brutus says he was ambitious;
> And sure he is an honourable man.

3.2.88–99

Mark Antony has the mob in his hands and we are reminded of a basic law of politics: the more devious your purpose, the more open you must appear to be. To which, I suspect, there is a corollary: the more open a politician seems to be, the more surely should you question his purpose. I wonder how Mark Antony would have fared trying to do the same thing in the age of television. Imagine him giving a party political broadcast:

> Good evening. First of all, I should say that on this sad occasion I am not here to make party political points. That would be quite wrong. I am here, simply and plainly, to remind you of the facts as we all know them. It's not my job to try to persuade you, the British people, of anything that you don't know already.

The purpose remains the same, but television has made oratory redundant, which doesn't mean that a politician can't make good speeches, or that he's always insincere, but that the most passionate speech, however sincere, simply doesn't rattle the teacups in the living room, let alone change the public mind. Television intrudes between the performer and his audience, detaching the one from the other. Their contact is by remote control and this forces the diligent salesman to adapt. Rather than whipping up the masses on the hustings, they now try to massage them in the home, and because they've discovered that we respond to appearance and impression, they've concluded that we ignore the argument, and so rather than peddling rhetoric they now package images.

So while our leaders deliberate in private, in public they and their PR men devise an endless series of mindless non-events in the hope that a susceptible news editor in search of some pictures, will help them sell the product simply by reporting its presence and then the image need do nothing but plead silently that it too could bestride the narrow world like a colossus. It's an old device, as old as Julius Caesar himself, and it treats us with just about the same respect as he offered the Roman mob when he took to the streets in search of its good opinion. Even today, unfortunately, the image is not called to account. When our leaders descend into the public arena, apparently in search of democratic discussion, they do so with their image very much in their mind. It's a dumb politician indeed who destroys his image in the television studio. Politicians in public are their one-dimensional image and in *Julius Caesar* it's likewise. In public, the protagonists are posturers, whose ambition we despise, and whose bad faith we condemn, and yet we care about them and are moved by their destiny. This is the heart of the play for me. We can actually be touched by plotters and salesmen. This happens because Shakespeare takes us into their inner world from which the populace is inevitably barred and then we see that what would otherwise be a penetrating and exciting political drama is in fact one of the great tragedies.

There's a moment in the play when you would expect to feel the most profound contempt for Brutus and Cassius. Their poor, honest, ignorant foot-soldiers are about to be hacked to pieces in a struggle which they didn't start and don't understand and these two men choose this moment to start a bitter but irrelevant row:

CASSIUS: You wrong me every way; you wrong me, Brutus;
   I said an elder soldier, not a better.
   Did I say 'better'?
BRUTUS: If you did, I care not.
CASSIUS: When Caesar liv'd, he durst not thus have mov'd me.
BRUTUS: Peace, peace! You durst not so have tempted him.
CASSIUS: I durst not?
BRUTUS: No.
CASSIUS: What, durst not tempt him?
BRUTUS: For your life you durst not.
CASSIUS: Do not presume too much upon my love;
   I may do that I shall be sorry for.

BRUTUS: You have done that you should be sorry for.
   There is no terror, Cassius, in your threats;
   For I am arm'd so strong in honesty
   That they pass by me as the idle wind.
   Which I respect not. . . .

4.3.55–69

It's a revelation. The Brutus lurking behind the image emerges as a sneering prig, the possessor of a vicious tongue. And Cassius, the dedicated schemer, is suddenly out of control, beside himself with rage and pain. We feel for him and we're shocked by Brutus and yet neither man is diminished. Indeed, the humanity of both is enhanced. When they die, it *is* a tragedy, not because their strategies collapsed, not because some great ideal perished with them, but because they were rather ordinary, vulnerable human beings, almost pathetically trapped in power, who over-reached themselves.

This sense of private tragedy haunting public men is pervasive, but it's not only personal. Take perhaps the most poignant moment of all, which comes early in the play before the deed's done. Brutus is desperately ill-at-ease. Portia, his wife, detects this and begs the man she loves to confide in her, but he, fearing that she might dissuade him, doesn't dare unburden himself.

PORTIA: . . .   Dwell I but in the suburbs
   Of your good pleasure? If it be no more,
   Portia is Brutus' harlot, not his wife.
BRUTUS: You are my true and honourable wife,
   As dear to me as are the ruddy drops
   That visit my sad heart.
PORTIA: If this were true, then should I know this secret.
   I grant I am a woman; but withal
   A woman that Lord Brutus took to wife.
   I grant I am a woman; but withal
   A woman well reputed, Cato's daughter.
   Think you I am no stronger than my sex,
   Being so father'd and so husbanded?
   Tell me your counsels, I will not disclose 'em.
   I have made strong proof of my constancy,
   Giving myself a voluntary wound
   Here, in the thigh. Can I bear that with patience.
   And not my husband's secrets?
BRUTUS: O ye gods,
   Render me worthy of this noble wife!

2.1.285–303

Of course that intimate moment is a private tragedy. Brutus the man lacks the moral courage to listen to his heart. He obeys the rules of power. But it is also a public tragedy. History is hung in the balance, until Brutus the Senator chooses the course which leads to chaos and bloodshed. But more than that, the tragedy is universal. Brutus the eternal politician is driven by laws which are unchanging and which he is compelled to obey, or to give up the search for power. And even if somewhere, there were some ideals which prompted that search, the process turns the politician into a victim. To feel for the victim you have to see through the image. The Roman mob couldn't and nor can we. Modern politicians obeying ancient laws keep us in the dark and treat us with contempt by pretending to treat us with respect. And because we can never reach into their inner world, perhaps it's *their* tragedy that we can't extend to *them* what we offer to Brutus, Cassius and even Caesar – not cynicism, but compassion.

JULIUS CAESAR
Ronald Pickup

Ronald Pickup played Rosalind in the all-male As You Like It. *Besides Cassius, his other Shakespearean parts have included Richard II.*

Julius Caesar is an enormously popular play. It contains, certainly, all the most colourful aspects of a good blood and thunder epic film. After all, Hollywood has twice realised its commercial qualities. political assassination, the grandeur of ancient Rome and doses of some of Shakespeare's most soaring, massive rhetoric. It must also appeal to the moguls of education, since it's a play that appears on the GCE syllabus with faithful regularity. The play is called *Julius Caesar,* yet the title role is one of the smaller parts in Shakespeare. Unlike Macbeth, Othello, Lear, Hamlet, Henry V, Coriolanus, Caesar himself has relatively little to say. He's also dead about half-way through. And yet his presence broods over the whole structure. As Brutus says long after Caesar's death:

> O Julius Caesar, thou art mighty yet!
> Thy spirit walks abroad and turns our swords
> In our own proper entrails.

5.3.94–6

In fact, beneath the apparently noble march of the play lies the probing examination of the meaning of power: the use and abuse of it and whether or not violent means produce anything better or more than violent ends.

Julius Caesar himself need not be dragged by the scruff of his neck into the twentieth century as being a Hitler figure with his flunkeys dressed in jackboots. He's not presented in such a clear-cut, black and white way. In Shakespeare's world, the king is the natural head of society. Shakespeare believed in a natural law and order. I emphasise the fact that it sprang from nature because it wasn't a Nixonian concept of law and order. And whether or not we now believe otherwise, the good health of the Elizabethan world depended on the strength of its God-given natural leader, the king. Tangles of bureaucracy and the Civil

Service hadn't yet exerted the sophisticated tyranny over our lives that they do nowadays. Put simplistically perhaps, all good and all evil emanated from the king, the natural head of society. Hence the importance in the early part of the play that is placed on the question of whether or not Caesar should be allowed to become king, which, according to all the reports we are given he is certainly likely to be.

In the very name Julius Caesar Shakespeare chooses perhaps the most famous name in history, resonant with power and energy. A man destined to be a great leader, but a good leader, a good king? That's the vital question. And Shakespeare deliberately presents us with a brief wonderfully *ambivalent* sketch of someone teetering on the edge of being a demagogue. He's vain, superstitious, over-wheening and arrogant and yet, at the same time, with that mischievous ability to play with his audience's emotions, Shakespeare gives him, just at the moment before he is murdered, a glorious blaze of rhetoric:

> I could be well mov'd, if I were as you;
> If I could pray to move, prayers would move me;
> But I am constant as the northern star,
> Of whose true-fix'd and resting quality
> There is no fellow in the firmament.
> The skies are painted with unumb'red sparks,
> They are all fire, and every one doth shine;
> But there's but one in all doth hold his place.
> So in the world: 'tis furnish'd well with men,
> And men are flesh and blood, and apprehensive;
> Yet in the number I do know but one
> That unassailable holds on his rank,
> Unshak'd of motion; and that I am he,
> Let me a little show it, even in this –
> That I was constant Cimber should be banish'd,
> And constant do remain to keep him so.

3.1.58–73

Now rhetoric it may be. It's almost ridiculous in its grandiloquence. Fascistic yes, but it also has irresistible force, magnificence, glitter – 'I am what I am'. However ambivalently Caesar may have been presented, when this man crashes to the floor of the Capitol, we should feel that something momentous and catastrophic has happened. The presence of an actor like Ralph Richardson in the part can only help to enhance this. I have also been lucky enough to have been in a production with

John Gielgud playing Caesar. At this, one of the great climaxes of dramatic literature, a violent operation is performed not only on the body of Caesar, but on the whole body of society and the rest of the play traces the convulsions the body has to suffer as a result.

Early in the play, after the great opening procession briefly introducing Caesar at his most powerful and public, we first meet two of the main protagonists, Brutus and Cassius. In the production with Gielgud, I played Cassius. It's rather like an assault course: indeed any major Shakespearean part is. However, I certainly realised early on in rehearsals that this manic, febrile, fanatic creature is the motor, the generator of the energy at this point in the play. Cassius has boiled quietly for many years, but once he starts to speak, he doesn't draw breath. It's an exhausting, exhilarating part. You have to draw very, very deep breaths and be prepared to sweat a lot. Years of pent-up frustrated ambition, hatred of tyranny in general and of Caesar in particular, make Cassius the explosive force that gives the play its dramatic lift-off. The actor has to blast the plot of the play and the plot against Caesar off the ground:

> I was born free as Caesar; so were you.
> We both have fed as well, and we can both
> Endure the winter's cold as well as he.
> For once, upon a raw and gusty day,
> The troubled Tiber chafing with her shores,
> Caesar said to me 'Dar'st thou, Cassius, now
> Leap in with me into this angry flood,
> And swim to yonder point?' Upon the word,
> Accoutred as I was, I plunged in
> And bade him follow. So indeed he did.
> The torrent roar'd, and we did buffet it
> With lusty sinews, throwing it aside
> And stemming it with hearts of controversy;
> But ere we could arrive the point propos'd,
> Caesar cried 'Help me, Cassius, or I sink!'
> I, as Aeneas, our great ancestor,
> Did from the flames of Troy upon his shoulder
> The old Anchises bear, so from the waves of Tiber
> Did I the tired Caesar. And this man
> Is now become a god; and Cassius is
> A wretched creature, and must bend his body
> If Caesar carelessly but nod on him.

1.2.97–118

67

What an amazing mixture of motives emerge. A genuine sense of honour mixed with petty, human jealousy of Caesar. 'Why shouldn't I be as great as Caesar, since I was able to swim better and save him from drowning?' Now this doesn't belittle Cassius, it humanises him. In other words, revolutionaries do not necessarily become revolutionaries only from honourable motives but for petty ones too. Cassius is an almost anarchic figure of misrule at this point. Brutus, reluctant, slightly constipated, needs this injection of massive, gutsy energy to get him moving.

The energy of Cassius spills over into the next scene. A scene of storm at night during which Cassius exults in the tempestuous omens which he sees as the natural forces at work to rid the world of Caesar. It's a wild and irrational scene. Cassius is himself a figure of storm and tempest, who gives neither his companions on the stage, nor the audience any time in which to debate his reasons, to rationalise, but urges us to follow him, breathless from his own excess of energy. Then, as in a film, the most abrupt cut to the silent orchard of Brutus. The storm has miraculously and conveniently dropped a bit and we first get to know something of the man who is Shakespeare's moral centre – the man who has to agonise over the rights and wrongs of killing a leader, a king, or indeed anyone:

> It must be by his death; and for my part,
> I know no personal cause to spurn at him,
> But for the general: he would be crown'd.
> How that might change his nature, there's the question.
> It is the bright day that brings forth the adder,
> And that craves wary walking. Crown him – that!
> And then, I grant, we put a sting in him
> That at his will he may do danger with.

2.1.10–17

Calvinistic in his austerity, Brutus tortuously decides on death as the only solution and when the other conspirators arrive, he then proceeds to claim the centre of the stage. Shakespeare, almost mischievously I suspect, then shows us what a disastrous choice Brutus is as a man of action. Cassius shrewdly suggests that Mark Antony, Caesar's favourite, should be eliminated as well and the whole group agree. But from Brutus, we are treated to a sermon on the morality of murder.

When I said Shakespeare is mischievous I meant that he has a satirical, oblique view of a man for whom he also has great compassion and admiration. Brutus may be thought by many to be an older version of Hamlet. He does indeed think too precisely on the event. He knows the whys and wherefores, but cannot commit himself with every vein in his body. Hence the importance of Cassius, who is a man of blood, instinct and intuition. Brutus can go through with the murder only in a religious frame of mind. 'Let's carve him as a dish fit for the gods', he says. And indeed when Caesar lies dead at his feet, he follows this through with his actions:

> Stoop, Romans, stoop.
> And let us bathe our hands in Caesar's blood
> Up to the elbows, and besmear our swords.
> Then walk we forth, even to the market-place,
> And waving our red weapons o'er our heads,
> Let's all cry 'Peace, freedom, and liberty!'

3.1.106–11

Antony enters and plays it very cool with the conspirators, showing he means no criticism, but allowing himself a genuine display of emotion at the sight of Caesar. Within an amazingly short space of time, he wins from Brutus a promise to speak in Caesar's funeral and is then left alone over the body and murmurs what we have not yet been allowed to feel:

> O, pardon me, thou bleeding piece of earth,
> That I am meek and gentle with these butchers!
> Thou art the ruins of the noblest man
> That ever lived in the tide of times.
> Woe to the hand that shed this costly blood!
> Over thy wounds now do I prophesy –

3.1.255–60

And the prophecy is one of the most apocalyptic descriptions of civil war in all of literature. A description that should perhaps mean more to us today than even in Shakespeare's time.

After this scene, Brutus has made an eloquent speech, in *prose,* and has won the approval of the crowd. All is going well. But, as Cassius knew he would, on comes Antony to speak in *verse* and win his place in the hearts of all the Romans and all schoolchildren ever since. When Marlon Brando played the part he caught something which is very difficult to analyse – the stealth. It emanates partly from this actor's own incredible animal stealth. The whole speech is a blueprint for anyone either wishing to win the school debating prize, or wishing to take over a nation. Antony is exemplary in bowing to the courtesy with which he has been allowed by the 'honourable' men to make this speech. He's not going to contradict anything they've said, merely to say a few words of praise for an old friend, now dead. And never, directly, does he contradict anything Brutus has said. He simply emphasises the sentimentally acceptable side of Caesar. The fact that he cried sometimes, well, who doesn't? He gave a bit of his money away to charity, well, what rich man doesn't? It's good public relations stuff. Also, his most telling point, Caesar refused to accept the crown, the ultimate symbol of absolute power. What Antony does not say is, that given another chance, Caesar probably would have accepted it. He describes for the people Caesar's death, which he didn't see at all, with all its imagined pity and terror. Perhaps his most brilliant stroke is the use of Caesar's robe. It may not even have been his robe, but by choosing a specific garment, some object that is intimate to the person dead, he heightens the emotional sympathy of the crowd. He moves them as a skillful barrister would move a jury by showing something like the handbag of the murdered victim. It moves them as we are moved when we are shown on television a scene of some air-crash and there's a quick shot of a child's toy in close-up. He brings the emotional impact of death into sharp focus for the crowd and indeed for us. And having used sharp focus, he can then afford to generalise and wallow in melodramatics which the crowd are now thirsty for:

> And in his mantle muffling up his face,
> Even at the base of Pompey's statue,
> Which all the while ran blood, great Caesar fell.

2.2.187–9

What a wonderful Hammer-horror film image that is!

It would take too long to analyse all the techniques in this amazing speech. It's remarkable for its combination of genuine passion and political cunning, which were themes very close to Shakespeare's heart in this play. And if it has worked we, along with the crowd, should want to stream out into the streets in a state of blood-lust. And after the crowd has left what does Antony say to himself?

> Now let it work. Mischief, thou art afoot,
> Take thou what course thou wilt.

2.2.261–2

I think that they are two of the most chilling, prophetic lines in the play. Antony may or may not be a mere opportunist. I think he's more than just that. But it is true of his actions here that the awful consequences of violence erupt. With their leader gone, the people go mad in a blood-lust or pogrom, and Shakespeare, as ever specific and not general, gives us a brief, horrific scene in which a gentle poet named Cinna is murdered by the mob, simply because his name is the same as that of one of the conspirators.

Laurence Olivier once said with characteristic accuracy that the climax of the play is reached with the assassination. Certainly in terms of high theatricality much capital has been spent by the time Antony has finished work for the day. But Shakespeare, approaching the height of his powers, deliberately ends the play on a disjointed, moody, despairing note. The passions of the characters are increasingly personal and private, particularly in the famous and moving quarrel scene between Brutus and Cassius. The specific reason for quarrelling is not in itself important. Out of exhaustion and disillusionment people, be they generals or lovers, will always quarrel, to vent their frustration and bitterness at having failed. This part of the play is about failure and the scene has an almost embarrassingly petty note as well. The two men catch each other out and yet yearn for the moment when they can let all their defences down and simply say 'I'm sorry'. The sheer mess of it all lies at the heart of this final movement of the play. Not only do the two friends bicker, but the opposing generals line up face-to-face and simply hurl impotent insults at one another in front of their respective armies. The battle scenes themselves have an almost farcical lack of order even to the extent that the audience finds it difficult to follow quite what is happening. It seems to me a deliberately chaotic montage of the effects of violence. Caesar, the dead Leviathan, still lashes his tail, not dead in spirit but brooding over all, appearing to Brutus in a nightmare as his evil spirit and driving the protagonists more and more in upon themselves. Cassius, for instance, in an awkward, embarrassing moment of stillness has to take one of his generals aside and, in a rush of naked, vulnerable despair, confesses his terror at the black omens he has seen:

> . . . ravens, crows, and kites,
> Fly o'er our heads and downward look on us
> As we were sickly prey.

5.1.84–6

'Sickly prey' is for me the most vivid image in these dying moments of the play. The noble acts of unselfish generosity in battle, the noble farewells, the noble deaths of Brutus and

Cassius, the noble speech of Antony over the dead body of Brutus are all undercut by giving the enigmatic, tight-lipped, cold Octavius the final word:

> So call the field to rest, and let's away
> To part the glories of this happy day.

5.5.80–1

The rhyming couplet is just too glib to be true. It seems that the assassination has achieved nothing. There is still a vacuum to be filled. The world is still 'sickly prey' to the opportunists.

MEASURE FOR MEASURE

John Mortimer

John Mortimer has taken part in a number of celebrated trials of moral conduct. He is also a playwright and author whose publications include A Voyage Round My Father *and* Will Shakespeare: An Entertainment. *He made this programme on location at the Inns of Court.*

I work as a lawyer at the Inns of Court. In this warren of passages and courtyards and lawyers' chambers, in this nest of dining halls, which has been the home of lawyers since the Middle Ages. It's a city of lawyers inside the City of London. And here the Elizabethan students learned to argue obscure points of law and flatter judges and made love and got drunk and fought, just as students do now. And here Elizabethan judges dozed over their port and dreamt of old sentences and perfect judgements, just as lawyers do now. In Shakespeare's day the students acted for the lawyers after dinner in the Middle Temple Hall, which has survived everything, even the German bombers. They did a perfect comedy here, *Twelfth Night,* on a stage at the end of the room.

We can't be sure if they did Shakespeare's great tragi-comedy *Measure for Measure* here. But it would have been a perfect play for lawyers. Because it's a play that sets the judges in the dock, makes the prisoner the prosecutor and raises huge questions of law and morality. It's a play guaranteed to wake every judge from his complacent snooze and set him worrying about the fallible nature of human judgement. And it's a play which poses to all lawyers that great fundamental question: 'must the law be obeyed because it's there, simply because it's the law, or is there a higher, deeper, more profound sort of justice which is something apart from the laws of our society, and may even contradict them?' You hear it often when mothers are quarrelling with their children. 'Why should I?', says the child. 'Because I tell you to', says the mother, adopting the same strict view of law relied on by Angelo in *Measure for Measure.* 'But it isn't fair', says the child, appealing to the great principle of natural justice, call it God, or the Benign Spirit of the Universe, or even the vanished Duke in Shakespeare's play, who is finally there to see that virtue and fairness triumph in spite of the law and not because of it. Man's justice and natural justice, and the eternal conflict between them, is what Shakespeare's *Measure for Measure* is all about.

The play is set in a city. It could be Vienna, which Shakespeare says it was, or in London in 1604, which is when he wrote it, or any city today, in which men and women are no more or less lustful and hypocritical, saintly or weak than they were in Shakespeare's day. We look out on the same river that separated our Inns of Court and his playhouse over on the South Bank. We live in a town bursting with life. In Shakespeare's day you could pay a penny to see the bear baiting or apes torn to pieces by dogs, or the wonderful mermaid of Gravesend. Most days there was that great free entertainment, a public hanging. Old soldiers begged in the gutter and the Puritans announced the Day of Judgement from street corners. And there was the seedy side of the town. Not much different from today. In Shakespeare's time there were the noted whores like Lucy de Negro, Abbess de Clerkenwell, a great favourite of the young lawyers, who was praised in the Christmas revels at Gray's Inn. In the red light district the ponce and the brothel keeper, like Pompey and Mistress Overdone in *Measure for Measure*, exercised their trade. And there Lucio, the cynical man about town, mused wisely on the law's impossible demands on human frailty.

And in the back of everyone's frightened mind, in our day as in Shakespeare's, the cold, relentless power of the law, that huge blunt instrument there to preserve society. The seemingly blind justice, ready to strike out blindly at whoever defied her. But let me tell you a secret about the figure of Justice on the dome of the Old Bailey. She's not blindfold at all. And in *Measure for Measure* justice had the blindfold ripped from its eyes and was made to stare at its own guilt. Princes couldn't do much about the law in those days. It was the time of the Ecclesiastical Courts when bishops sat as judge and kings feared the popes and there was absolutely no distinction between law and morality. Most sins were crimes in those days and certainly all crimes were sins.

Westminster Hall was then the seat of the English Parliament; a body which was growing in power and influence during Queen Elizabeth's reign. It was jealous of the legal power of the Church and anxious to protect the independence of the English Common Law. And in that they had one great ally. Sir Edward Coke wasn't a particularly attractive character. He was a courtroom bully and a ferocious prosecutor of Sir Walter Raleigh and the Earl of Essex. He forced his fourteen year old daughter to marry Sir John Villiers, the elder brother of the King's favourite, in order to improve his position at court. But he was a brilliant lawyer, the first man to be called Chief Justice of England, and a strong defender of the Common Law against the power of the new King, James I. By the time Shakespeare wrote *Measure for Measure* the golden age of the great Queen Elizabeth was over. The small, intelligent, stupid, drooling, messy King James came down from Scotland, speaking in an incomprehensible accent, and on his way to London he hanged a pickpocket at Newark without charging him and without a trial. King James had a new idea of the law, not the Church's law, founded on the laws of God, not the English Common Law founded on the practical experience of judges and handed down from the rights of Magna Carta, but the King's law, the law which was the law because the King said so: 'The Right Divine of Kings to govern wrong'. This led King James into immediate conflict with Coke. The peppery Lord Chief Justice denied James's right to try his own cases and started to frame his Bill of Liberties. This would lead to the great English revolution and finally to the trial of King Charles I, James's son, and the triumph of the Common Law of England over kings and bishops. When King Charles was led out to his execution Parliament asserted the principle that although a king may be the fountain of justice, he's still subject to the law.

But for Shakespeare, working as an actor and a playwright in the theatre, such struggles were in the distant future. Shakespeare knew two faces of the law. On the one hand he followed Aristotle, who believed in the law as the embodiment of reason and good sense in society. Shakespeare was a great man for order which he thought led to peace and stable government:

DUKE: We have strict statutes and most biting laws,
    The needful bits and curbs to headstrong steeds,
    Which for this fourteen years we have let slip;
    Even like an o'ergrown lion in a cave,
    That goes not out to prey. Now, as fond fathers,
    Having bound up the threat'ning twigs of birch,
    Only to stick it in their children's sight
    For terror, not to use, in time the rod
    Becomes more mock'd than fear'd; so our decrees,
    Dead to infliction, to themselves are dead;

> And liberty plucks justice by the nose;
> The baby beats the nurse, and quite athwart
> Goes all decorum.

1.3.19–31

But as a humanist alive in 1604 Shakespeare was as conscious as anyone of the law's appalling cruelty. In those days you could be hanged for stealing anything worth over twelve pence. Out of a population of only five million people, 800 men and women in England were executed in only one year. After one Exeter Assize there were seventeen hangings. This appalling carnage even won the sympathy of the Lord Chief Justice Coke, who was no sentimentalist:

> What a lamentable case it is to see so many Christian men and women strangled on that cursed tree of the gallows: insomuch as if in a large field a man might see together all the Christians that, but in one year, throughout England, came to that untimely and ignominious death, if there were any grace or charity in him, it would make his heart bleed for pity and compassion.

I can't think of many occasions when Shakespeare would have agreed with a judge, but I'm sure he would have agreed with that. The need for justice and the need for compassion are the two great conflicting claims in the mind of anybody who has to think seriously about the law. Those are the two themes of *Measure for Measure.*

Who is the Duke? Perhaps he's the King. I think that maybe he's God, a somewhat eccentric God who, although he is the source of all law, is content to leave its operation in the hands of fallible human beings. The Duke pretends to disappear, and he leaves the laws of Venice in the hands of Angelo, a cold-blooded judge who regards the law as a kind of perfect computer to be operated without human feelings. Lawyers all know judges like Angelo, whom you can't imagine ever having had a mother. Now there is for the purposes of this play a law making sex outside marriage punishable by death. We know to our horror that in some countries there still is. It's a law which fails to pass the test of natural justice because it quite fails to take into account the reality of human nature. But for the cold-blooded Judge Angelo, it's the law and that's enough. The law has to be enforced because it's the law. It's a theory which didn't provide a defence to the Nazi war criminals in the Nuremberg trials. But many lawyers hold it, as does the mother who says to the child 'you do what I tell you because it's what I tell you to do'. If you criticise or question the law, so the theory goes, then the whole concept of law and order is endangered and may crumple like a pack of cards.

Angelo believes that

> We must not make a scarecrow of the law,
> Setting it up to fear the birds of prey,
> And let it keep one shape till custom make it
> Their perch, and not their terror.

2.1.1–4

So he condemns Claudio, a very normal young man, to death for getting his girlfriend pregnant before they are married. Claudio's sister, Isabella, comes to plead with Angelo for mercy and for her brother's life. Isabella is very religious and devout and about to enter a convent, and she brings the first conflict into the play, which is between society's need for a strong law based on fear and Christ's call for compassion. Pleading for her brother's life she reminds stern Judge Angelo of the religion based on the cruci-fixion as the forgiveness and remission of sin:

> ANGELO: Your brother is a forfeit of the law,
>   And you but waste your words.
> ISABELLA: Alas! Alas!
>   Why, all the souls that were were forfeit once;
>   And He that might the vantage best have took
>   Found out the remedy. How would you be
>   If He, which is the top of judgement, should
>   But judge you as you are? O think on that;
>   And mercy then will breathe within your lips,
>   Like man new made.
> ANGELO: Be you content, fair maid,
>   It is the law, not I condemn your brother.
>   Were he my kinsman, brother, or my son,
>   It should be thus with him. He must died to-morrow.

2.2.71–82

So up to then the dialogue between Isabella and Angelo follows the lines of any barrister today mitigating before a judge in the Old Bailey after his client had pleaded guilty. 'The law must be strictly upheld', says the judge, 'otherwise those who might be tempted won't be deterred'. 'But my client is a special case, my Lord', says the barrister,' and in any event, justice must always be tempered with mercy'.

That's the argument at the start of the play. But then Shakespeare gives it the twist which makes this great drama. Isabella makes Angelo look at his own guilt. Her innocence makes him desire her with an avid, burning, irresistible longing which makes Claudio's lust look like a passing summer fancy. Shakespeare has hit on the great paradox which lies behind all human law giving. We are all born with the same imperfections, call it human frailty if you are an Atheist or original sin if you happen to be a Christian. Judges are wise men, perhaps, but as prey to lust and envy and prejudice as those they have to try. So *Measure for Measure* quickly shifts from the question of the criminal's guilt to that far more interesting matter, the guilt of the judge. Even judges today are not computers. You don't put the question in at one end and get out the perfect, correct judicial answer. They are men and women with their own set of temptations and sexual hang-ups and midnight terrors. So are jurors: twelve averagely sinful men and women taken off the street to decide the question of guilt and innocence, which is supposed to be the sole province of God.

Of course lawyers recognise this. 'Judges are only human', they say, 'they have their prejudices, it's a risk you're bound to take.' But the law is above all that, and it's the law that has to be preserved, even by imperfect judges. This is Angelo at the start of the play:

> 'Tis one thing to be tempted, Escalus,
> Another thing to fall. I not deny
> The jury, passing on the prisoner's life,
> May in the sworn twelve have a thief or two
> Guiltier than him they try. What's open made to justice,
> That justice seizes. What knows the laws
> That thieves do pass on thieves? 'Tis very pregnant,
> The jewel that we find, we stoop and take't,
> Because we see it; but what we do not see
> We tread upon, and never think of it.
> You may not so extenuate his offence
> For I have had such faults; but rather tell me,
> When I, that censure him, do so offend,
> Let mine own judgment pattern out my death,
> And nothing come in partial. Sir, he must die.

2.1.17–31

But Isabella won't accept the theory of a huge, soulless machine of justice being operated by one set of half criminals against another. She argues

> Go to your bosom,
> Knock there, and ask your heart what it doth know
> That's like my brother's fault. If it confess
> A natural guiltiness such as is his,
> Let it not sound a thought upon your tongue
> Against my brother's life.

2.2.136–41

In other words, the Christian message in all its simplicity and power:

> Judge not, and yet shall not be judged; condemn not and ye
> shall not be condemned; forgive and ye shall be forgiven.

So Shakespeare, with that complete intellectual honesty which is often given to poets, and less often to lawyers, asks the final fundamental question, which is as subversive, in a way, as Christianity itself. Is any man or woman fit to sit in judgement on a fellow human being?

Of course we all want to judge each other, it's so easy to denounce other people's crimes, condemn their mistakes, crow in righteous rage when other people are caught out doing the very things we long to do ourselves. But is judgement on our fellow human beings at best any more than hypocrisy? When King Lear, in another of Shakespeare's great Jacobean tragedies, was thrown out into the storm, he lived with the poor, the foolish and the half mad and he knew then, in his madness, his first true sanity. He came to understand that the rulers and the ruled, the criminals and the judged, are all brothers and sisters under the skin. Uniform is the only thing that can show us the difference between the justice and the thief. In voicing such dangerous sentiments Shakespeare the upholder of law and order, the respectable burgher and householder of Stratford-upon-Avon is forgotten, and he becomes the passionate questioner of all the assumptions of a structured society. And Isabella in her pleading to Judge Angelo goes far beyond her brief and denounces in unforgettable language the very impertinence of human judgement:

> ISABELLA: So you must be the first that gives this sentence,
>   And he that suffers. O, it is excellent
>   To have a giant's strength! But it is tyrannous
>   To use it like a giant.
> LUCIO: That's well said.
> ISABELLA: Could great men thunder
>   As Jove himself does, Jove would never be quiet,

For every pelting petty officer
Would use his heaven for thunder,
Nothing but thunder. Merciful Heaven,
Thou rather, with thy sharp and sulpurous bolt,
Splits the unwedgeable and gnarled oak
Than the soft myrtle. But man, proud man,
Dress'd in a little brief authority,
Most ignorant of what he's most assur'd,
His glassy essence, like an angry ape,
Plays such fantastic tricks before high heaven
As makes the angels weep; who, with our spleens,
Would all themselves laugh mortal.

2.2.106–23

Of course we make 'the angels weep'. But we imperfect human lawyers, scurrying from court to chambers, from murder to arson, from rape to petty theft, must do our imperfect best, and imperfect human judges, let's hope with perpetual compassion and due humility, must pass sentence – I suppose. A great play doesn't answer questions, it asks them. *Measure for Measure* asks enormous questions about law and judgement. We don't know the answers. But we should all be better, wiser, perhaps, for seeing or reading a play which subjects human justice to a devastating cross-examination.

Measure for Measure
Judi Dench

Judi Dench is a member of the Royal Shakespeare Company. Her parts have included Hermione, Perdita and Viola. She is also an award-winning television actress.

*M*easure *for Measure* is a marvellous morality play. Like a medieval morality play, it contrasts human corruption with virtue, but much more subtly. The play may seem to be black and white but Shakespeare was much more interested in showing that there are also shades of grey. Everybody in the play is corrupt in one way or another, though this is not apparent at first. People who appear to be one thing are not necessarily that thing at all:

> O, what may man within him hide,
> Though angel on the outward side!

3.2.253–4

In fact, nearly everybody in the play does a kind of volte face. The Duke is physically disguised for most of the play in order to observe without being observed. The blame for the state of Vienna should probably be laid at his door initially. If he had governed more firmly, then the city wouldn't be in a state of social and moral disorder. Angelo, his deputy, appears to be a man of incredible iron and puritanical iciness, just the man to stand in for him while he's supposedly away on a journey. In actual fact he's a man who is seething inside with terrifying emotions which he eventually discovers he can't control, and when they suddenly break out this is his downfall. Lucio, called a 'fantastic' by Shakespeare, is the most obviously two-faced character. He's a man who never conforms and is neither true to himself nor to anyone else. He's everybody's confidante and nobody's friend. Mariana, Angelo's ex-girlfriend, dons a disguise so that Angelo thinks that she is Isabella. Isabella herself professes she's a nun and in the end marries the Duke. It's an extraordinary play of what seems and what doesn't seem. But in the end, it's a play that balances. Everyone in it gets their just

desserts as it were and 'Measure still for Measure' is handed out
by the Duke:

> Haste still pays haste, and leisure answers leisure;
> Like doth quit like, and Measure still for Measure.

5.1.408–9

It's a very moral play but there's a very good story line to follow.
It's still a hard play to perform because it's difficult to make this
plot convincing to a modern audience. At the beginning of the
play the Duke announces that he's going to leave the country and
put his deputy, Angelo, in charge while he's away. He disguises
himself as a friar and remains in the city to observe its corruption. Angelo governs with a rod of iron, sticking absolutely to the
letter of the law. He starts by sentencing Claudio to death for
making his girlfriend, Juliet, pregnant. Claudio's sister, Isabella,
who is a novice in a nunnery, assures her brother that she will
plead with Angelo for his release. Although Angelo refuses to
grant Isabella's plea, he finds himself deeply disturbed by her
presence. So he asks her to visit him the next day. And by this
time, sexually aroused by the thought of her, he agrees to pardon
Claudio if she will give herself to him. Isabella now turns to a
holy father, who we alone know is the Duke. He persuades
Isabella to agree to Angelo's request, having planned to substi-
tute Mariana for Isabella. The play ends on a note of forgiveness,
with Angelo marrying Mariana, Claudio marrying Juliet, who's
about to have his baby, and the Duke marrying Isabella.

I have never felt that this fairy-story conclusion was really
satisfying because Isabella has to undergo a remarkable change
of character in order to accept the Duke. It seems an extraordinary way to behave for both of them. After all, Isabella has
refused to give up her virginity for her brother's life. There
seems to be no explanation for the way she suddenly renounces
her vocation to become a nun, but I think that she has learnt
about weakness. It's as if she was, at the beginning of the play, a
very young girl, who sees everything as either positive or negative, good or bad, white or black. Her character is flawed because
of this but during the play she learns about human weakness, not
only from the Duke, but also from Angelo. The change that
Shakespeare intends her to undergo is that she should see that
everything is not so simple and straightforward and that there are
shades of grey. She learns to be compassionate and to make
allowances for other people.

It's a particularly difficult play to do nowadays because our

82

conventions and attitudes have changed. After all, if one were put in the same situation today and, in order to save your brother's life or even a very good friend's, the same proposition was made, I don't think that you would think twice about it – or would you? You must remember when watching or reading the play that it's about Elizabethan and Jacobean England. Isabella's behaviour would have been understandable then because it would have been a venial sin to have to go to bed with Angelo. Isabella's a novice in a nunnery and in order to be a nun she has to be pure. Now, whether or not your sympathies lie with Isabella, or you have any kind of compassion for her, it's a very difficult job to make the audience somehow believe in her decision not to save her brother's life. 'More than our brother is our chastity' she cries out at one point. She's alone on the stage at this moment, as Angelo has left the room after making it plain what he wants from her. I've played Isabella twice and, each time I've come to that agonised line, I've tried to convey the dilemma she's facing:

> To whom should I complain? Did I tell this,
> Who would believe me? O perilous mouths
> That bear in them one and the self-same tongue
> Either of condemnation or approof,
> Bidding the law make curtsy to their will;
> Hooking both right and wrong to th'appetite,
> To follow as it draws! I'll to my brother.
> Though he hath fall'n by prompture of the blood,
> Yet hath he in him such a mind of honour
> That, had he twenty heads to tender down
> On twenty bloody blocks, he'd yield them up
> Before his sister should her body stoop
> To such abhorr'd pollution.
> Then, Isabel, live chaste, and, brother, die:
> More than our brother is our chastity.

2.4.171–85

Now in the theatre that line would have to be magnified. It's a thought on its own, bounded by two full-stops. I'm sure that that one line, 'More than our brother is our chastity', is a kind of wrench from the heart. She has to cry it out as some kind of excuse because she's at terrible odds with herself.

She believes she understands her brother well enough to know just how he will react but she underestimates the strength of his emotions. Just before the scene between Isabella and

Claudio in the prison, the Duke, disguised as a friar, has been to visit Claudio in his cell to prepare him for his execution. The Duke puts forward a marvellous case for dying by pointing out that life is hardly worth holding on to. I used to stand spellbound in the wings listening to this speech at Stratford in 1962 when Tom Fleming played the Duke:

> Be absolute for death; either death or life
> Shall thereby be the sweeter. Reason thus with life.
> If I do lose thee, I do lose a thing
> That none but fools would keep. A breath thou art,
> Servile to all the skyey influences,
> That does this habitation where thou keep'st
> Hourly afflict. Merely, thou art Death's fool;
> For him thou labour'st by thy flight to shun
> And yet run'st toward him still. Thou art not noble;
> For all th' accommodations that thou bear'st
> Are nurs'd by baseness. Thou'rt by no means valiant;
> For thou dost fear the soft and tender fork
> Of a poor worm. Thy best of rest is sleep,
> And that thou oft provok'st; yet grossly fear'st
> Thy death, which is no more. Thou art not thyself;
> For thou exists on many a thousand grains
> That issue out of dust. Happy thou art not;
> For what thou hast not, still thou striv'st to get,
> And what thou hast, forget'st.

3.1.5–23

Claudio seems reassured but, confronted immediately afterwards by Isabella, his courage fails him and life becomes infinitely more desirable. Our sympathies can only be with Claudio:

> Ay, but to die, and go we know not where;
> To lie in cold obstruction, and to rot;
> This sensible warm motion to become
> A kneaded clod; and the delighted spirit
> To bathe in fiery floods or to reside
> In thrilling region of thick-ribbed ice;
> To be imprison'd in the viewless winds,
> And blown with restless violence round about
> The pendent world; or to be worse than worst
> Of those that lawless and incertain thought
> Imagine howling – 'tis too horrible.

The weariest and most loathed worldly life
That age, ache, penury and imprisonment,
Can lay on nature is a paradise
To what we fear of death.

3.1.119–33

Every night on hearing that speech in the production with Ian Holm and later with John Shrapnel, I was struck by the terrifying ordeal the condemned man faces. It's at this point in the play that the Duke, having overheard the scene, takes a hand in Isabella's plight. By the end of the play, Isabella, like Angelo, has been made to face reality and has even questioned her decision to become a nun. So the acceptance of the Duke doesn't come as such a surprise and is perhaps a marriage of minds anyway.

Angelo is also an incredibly difficult part to play. I don't think that he should be a villain at all. It's too easy to label characters mentally as heroes and villains. When the Duke hands over the government to Angelo he is probably unaware of his deputy's weaknesses. He does it in good faith, believing that Angelo is the best man for the job. He's a very promising young member of the Cabinet, maybe a bit too perfect in the Duke's eyes:

Lord Angelo is precise;
Stands at a guard with envy; scarce confesses
That his blood flows, or that his appetite
Is more to bread than stone. Hence shall we see,
If power change purpose, what our seemers be.

1.3.50–4

Angelo in fact does appear to be a man who lives an incredibly disciplined and abstemious life. We find out later that he didn't marry Mariana because she had no dowry; not a very commendable way to behave, but not a sin. He leads a moral upright, puritanical life and there's nothing particularly wrong with that. And then suddenly he meets Isabella who comes to plead for her brother's life and she completely destroys his composure. It's a terrifying prospect for a man who's regarded in the way he is. Lucio says of him:

a man whose blood
Is very snow-broth, one who never feels
The wanton stings and motions of the sense, . . .

1.4.57–9

85

He's never before been moved by anything or anyone but I can understand his feelings at the end of the scene with Isabella. He just can't believe what's hit him when he says 'What's this, what's this?', as though he's been caught totally off-guard:

> What's this, what's this? Is this her fault or mine?
> The tempter or the tempted, who sins most?
> Ha!
> Not she; nor doth she tempt; but it is I
> That, lying by the violet in the sun,
> Do as the carrion does, not as the flow'r,
> Corrupt with virtuous season. Can it be
> That modesty may more betray our sense
> Than woman's lightness? Having waste ground enough,
> Shall we desire to raze the sanctuary,
> And pitch our evils there? O, fie, fie, fie!
> What dost thou, or what art thou, Angelo?

2.2.162–73

Angelo, bewildered, shocked and horrified by what's just happened to him has to try to reconcile his feelings with the man he has set himself up to be: 'What dost thou, or what art thou, Angelo?' Up till now he's always been in charge of the situation, now he suddenly finds himself overwhelmed by it. Angelo is usually played as a man who ought to be in a psychiatrist's chair, but there's a great deal to pity him for.

Of the productions I have been involved in probably the most interesting was a modern-dress one at the Nottingham Playhouse. The whole play was performed as though it were set in the Vienna of the thirties: a police state with black hombergs and astrakhan collars and everybody looking, on the face of it, frightfully respectable. It was a Chicago-style, gangster-type Vienna and it worked extremely well. Edward Woodward played Lucio as a too-smooth character in dark glasses and white tuxedo jacket with a carnation in his buttonhole. Pompey, played by Harold Innocent, wore a much too wide grey and white striped suit, a slouch hat and black and white co-respondent shoes. He was in charge of the seediest bunch of ladies, played by Mary Healey and Ursula Smith as Kate Keepdown and Mistress Overdone. The production had its worries. I remember that John Neville, who was directing, had made the moated grange a night club and there was Mariana smoking heavily and sitting with a drink at a table, obviously in the first stages of alcoholism. The waiters were brushing up the tables and the musical director,

Ewan Williams, was sitting at a piano with a green Chicago shade over his eyes, playing 'Take O Take Those Lips Away'. The atmosphere was terrific. But then, as Isabella, I had to come bursting in through the door after-hours at this night club in a white nun's costume. I asked John Neville how on earth I was to do this. He replied that I was to come on like any nun would come on after-hours in a night club. The challenge of the whole production was terrific and because it was in modern dress the audience was able to identify more quickly with the characters. I'm talking principally about a young audience who may never have seen the play before.

Whenever I've done the play and I've been in it three times, once as Juliet and twice as Isabella, I think about it only in terms of a modern audience, the specific audience I'm playing to on that night. I am using Shakespeare's words and trying to tell his story, but trying to tell it in terms that will relate to a modern audience. This particular play, depicting a corrupt state, is something we can all understand today. There are many things in it that a modern audience can recognise very easily about corruption in a city on every level throughout government, throughout society as a whole. Corruption is not just confined to pimps and prostitutes. That's why it is, as I said, a very difficult play to wind up in a satisfactory way because this kind of corruption is a cancer. It's something that will break out again and again. It's meant to be a really tidy end but, my goodness, who can tell what might happen after the curtain comes down on that particular city with its seemingly redeemed society?

HENRY VIII
Anthony Burgess

Anthony Burgess's numerous publications include a novel about Shakespeare, Nothing Like the Sun, as well as a biography of him. He made this programme at his home in Monaco and used a model of Shakespeare's stage to demonstrate some of the points about stagecraft.

*H*enry VIII is different from all the other plays of Shakespeare in one important respect. We know the date of its first public presentation, which was 29 June 1613. Try and find the date for the first public performance of *Hamlet* or *As You Like It* or *Twelfth Night* and you're in trouble. But this date we know because a terrible thing happened. The playhouse where this play was presented was burnt to the ground. Ben Jonson, who wasn't much given to hyperbole, said: 'See the world's ruins'. What he was referring to there, I think, was the name of the playhouse, which was the Globe, the home of the Lord Chamberlain's players, later the King's Men, and of Shakespeare's plays from 1599 on.

That first performance of *Henry VIII* came to an abrupt end at line 49 in Act 1, Scene 4:

> WOLSEY: Y' are welcome, my fair guests. That noble lady
> Or gentleman that is not freely merry
> Is not my friend. This, to confirm my welcome –
> And to you all, good health! (*drinks*)
> SANDYS: Your Grace is noble.
> Let me have such a bowl may hold my thanks
> And save me so much talking.
> WOLSEY   My Lord Sandys,
> I am beholding to you. Cheer your neighbours.
> Ladies, you are not merry. Gentleman,
> Whose fault is this?
> SANDYS: The red wine first must rise
> In their fair cheeks, my lord; then we shall have 'em
> Talk us to silence.
> ANNE: You are a merry gamester,

My Lord Sandys.

SANDYS: Yes, if I make my play.
   Here's to your ladyship; and pledge it, madam,
   For 'tis to such a thing –

ANNE: You cannot show me.

SANDYS: I told your Grace they would talk anon.

(Drum and trumpet. Chambers discharg'd.)

WOLSEY: What's that?

CHAMBERLAIN: Look out there, some of ye.

At this point, with everybody waiting for the arrival of King Henry and the revellers, the first signs of a fire were noticed.

Sir Henry Wotton, who was present at the play, wrote a letter three days after the event:

> Now, King Henry making a masque at the Cardinal Wolsey's house, and certain chambers being shot off at his entry, some of the paper, or other stuff, wherewith one of them was stopped, did light on the thatch, where being thought at first but an idle smoke, and their eyes more attentive to the show, it kindled inwardly, and ran round like a train, consuming within less than an hour the whole house to the very grounds.

Sir Henry is rather light-hearted about the tragedy:

> This was the fatal period of that virtuous fabric, wherein yet nothing did perish but wood and straw, and a few forsaken cloaks; only one man had his breeches set on fire, that would perhaps have boiled him, if he had not by the benefit of a provident wit put it out with bottle ale.

He can be frivolous about it, but we can't help romantically imagining that more than straw and old cloaks went up in the blaze. Probably in the poet's room or the players' library, manuscripts of William Shakespeare perished as well. We don't know, but we do know that with this conflagration a great period in dramatic history came to an end. That mass of wood with straw on the top, always highly combustible, had seen *Henry V*, *Julius Caesar*, *Hamlet* and *King Lear*.

From about 1610 on, Shakespeare had been living in semi-retirement in Stratford. As for the plays themselves, he didn't seem to care very much about them. Seven years after his death it was left to two of his friends and fellow players, John Heminge and Henry Condell, to bring out the First Folio. Why did Shakespeare re-enter the theatre from his retirement with *Henry*

VIII? Let's imagine that one day Shakespeare went to London from Stratford and met his old friends, his fellow actors, in the Mermaid Tavern, the great fish restaurant of the time, and after the meal, over the wine, they talked about plays and Shakespeare perhaps talked about the cycle of great historical life he had written, telling the whole English story from the assassination of Richard II to the accession of the first Tudor, Henry VII, after the death of Richard III on Bosworth Field, the end of a bad period of strife and the beginning of a new period of peace. Would it be possible to bring the story up to his own time? Henry VII was very dull and not a good subject for a drama. Elizabeth would be difficult and dangerous as she was a bit too close. But in the middle stood the great, bluff, popular tyrant, Henry VIII, whom the fathers of many of Shakespeare's own contemporaries must have seen and who was, after all, the father of the great dead Queen herself.

This is a possibility, but I don't think for one moment that it happened that way at all. I believe that the impulse came not from within, but was imposed from without. Shakespeare, remember, was one of the King's Men still. He held shares in the company and, as Groom of the Royal Bedchamber, he was one of the King's Officers. He had to obey orders and I'm pretty sure that an order came down from above that the King's Men must act, and Shakespeare must write some great, magnificent, spectacular play based on a subject like Henry VIII to be presented on the occasion of some great public event. Then, as now, people loved a show, and in 1613 the River Thames was the scene of riotous celebrations. The year before a marriage contract had been signed between the Princess Elizabeth of England, daughter of James I, and the German Prince Frederick. The wedding took place on 14 February, St Valentine's Day, 1613. Celebrations like this fulfilled an important function. It was a visual affirmation of the power and majesty of the State. It united the common people and renewed the bond between king and subject. Ceremony was an essential part of government, more pertinent than it is today. It was also very costly. £100,000 of their money was spent on lavish junketings, which was a large amount for a shaky economy.

I'm afraid we have no actual proof that *Henry VIII* was presented at court during the wedding celebrations, but we can be quite sure that King James I saw this play and liked it. And he'd like it, I think, for the following reason: that he saw in Henry VIII something of himself, or perhaps something of what he'd like to be. He saw in Henry a man, for instance, who had created his own Church, had been given the title of Defender of the Faith by the pope himself, which Henry had hypocritically then made to mean Defender of the Faith against the pope, and James, also as head of the Church, was trying to defend that Church not against the pope this time but against the Puritans, the Calvinists who were baying and howling all around him in England and had made his life such a misery in Scotland. Henry had been something of an amateur theologian. He'd written a Treatise on the Seven Sacraments which had been a bestseller in its day. James wrote a little theology, but he prided himself rather on being able to preside over such great ecclesiastical conferences as the one at Hampton Court in 1604 and more than anything at having brought into being perhaps the greatest achievement of his reign, the Authorised Version of the Bible, the King James Version of 1611. Henry had been trying to assert his authority over his ministers, both lay and ecclesiastical, and James was trying to the same thing. For example, James turned himself into his own Secretary of State. The sight of Henry disposing of the overweening Wolsey must have given James a great deal of pleasure:

KING: Read o'er this; (*Giving him papers.*
  And after, this; and then to breakfast with
  What appetite you have. (*Exit the King* . . .
WOLSEY: What should this mean?
  What sudden anger's this? How have I reap'd it?
  He parted frowning from me, as if ruin
  Leap'd from his eyes; so looks the chafed lion
  Upon the daring huntsman that has gall'd him—
  That makes him nothing. I must read this paper;
  I fear, the story of his anger. 'Tis so;
  This paper has undone me. 'Tis th' account
  Of all that world of wealth I have drawn together
  For mine own ends; indeed to gain the popedom,
  And fee my friends in Rome.

3.2.201–13

King James would have liked that. But how about the people? What did the people think about this play? We have to remember that this year, 1613, was a time of great uneasiness and great fear in England. There was a feeling that the Spaniards, those old enemies, were going to come back and try to re-impose Catholicism on the Protestant English. There was a lot of anti-Spanish and anti-Catholic sentiment about. To mirror this sentiment there's a poem by a very minor writer, George Wither, who just a year before had said this:

> But more *Romes locusts* do begin to swarme . . .
> Yea Hell to double this, our sorrowes weight,
> Is new contriving to old *Eighty-eight* . . .

It's a reference, of course, to the year 1588, when the Spanish Armada tried to invade England but had been beaten back, soundly trounced, chiefly because there was a great Monarch on the throne at that time, Elizabeth. Her successor, James, was a cowardly weakling; he had no great fire in his belly or burning words in his mouth. So perhaps the English people at this time of fear were drawn back instinctively to the Tudors and glad to be reminded of the huge, fearless King Henry VIII, who had defied the Spaniards and the pope and everybody. When Elizabeth appeared as an infant on the stage, I'm sure there must have been a great roar of nostalgic affection. Shakespeare was showing his old skill in arousing, or reflecting, popular sentiment, a skill he had shown twenty years previously with his very first plays, *1, 2 and 3 Henry VI*, written in the same sort of national circumstances. Here he is up to his old tricks again, giving the people what they want and giving the ruler of the people what might conceivably please him.

But now I must ask a very awkward question. Did Shakespeare really write this play? Whenever I re-read *Henry VIII*, I'm tormented by a rather illogical conviction that this is not the work of Shakespeare but the work of some other man, some great or certainly highly competent playwright who may have learnt something from Shakespeare but is not Shakespeare himself. Most critics and scholars say that Shakespeare didn't write it all, but he wrote some of it. He probably collaborated with John Fletcher, a very popular playwright who was mostly a collaborator with Francis Beaumont, and that the two worked together on this. But I'm not convinced. I still have this curious hunch that there's a great unknown, missing name, to whom we can attribute not only this play but various others and that some day we'll find him and then we'll discover there was a rival to William Shakespeare, or certainly a legitimate heir. Meanwhile, as I'm not a scholar myself, I have to bow to the real scholars. When I look at the First Folio, I am reminded, of course, that this was put together by a couple of men, who knew Shakespeare very well indeed and they should know who wrote the play. This is a

very firm argument indeed for believing that Shakespeare wrote
it all, especially when we remember the words of T.S.Eliot concerning John Fletcher who was supposed to have collaborated
with him. John Fletcher, said Eliot, was incapable of putting
reality into his plays. Everything is artificial. It's like a set of
artificial flowers stuck in artificial soil. There's no bloom, there's
no perfume, there's no colour. Well, with this play, whoever
wrote it, we get the impression of reality and truth. The subtitle
of the play was *All Is True*. The flowers are real, they have a
colour and an odour. This speech, for instance, of Cardinal
Wolsey must either have been written by Shakespeare, or somebody very like him:

> Cromwell, I did not think to shed a tear
> In all my miseries; but thou hast forc'd me,
> Out of thy honest truth, to play the woman.
> Let's dry our eyes; and thus far hear me, Cromwell,
> And when I am forgotten, as I shall be,
> And sleep in dull cold marble, where no mention
> Of me more must be heard of, say I taught thee –
> Say Wolsey, that once trod the ways of glory,
> And sounded all the depths and shoals of honour,
> Found thee a way, out of his wreck, to rise in –
> A sure and safe one, though thy master miss'd it.
> Mark but my fall and that that ruin'd me.

3.2.428–39

Most people look at the question of authorship this way. There
was a job for the King's Men to do and Shakespeare was called
in from retirement in Stratford to do it. He got as far as the
Third Act, probably grew bored with the job and handed over to
John Fletcher who, more than Shakespeare, was aware of the
royal wedding, the pomp and circumstance side of the work, and
thus completed it.

It was this gorgeous, magnificent aspect of the play that
appealed to a great showman like Sir Henry Irving. The whole
work does, in fact, suggest a long procession – from the King
and his Council to Wolsey's sumptuous party, to Katharine's
trial and to the christening of Elizabeth and the hope of a glorious
Tudor future with which the work ends. But with all its elaborate
Victorian resources, I doubt if Irving could have out done the
vision that Shakespeare had in his own mind, or the transference
of this vision to Shakespeare's own stage. Irving would have
had to bring his curtain down to effect the scene changes,

ANTHONY BURGESS

but the Elizabethan or Jacobean playhouse alternated its acting areas. A scene on the balcony, or tarrass, would be followed immediately by a scene on the main stage, with its huge, jutting apron. Then there could be a more intimate episode in the study at the back part of the stage, which could either be disclosed or covered by means of a curtain. For the great trial scene, we can imagine all the areas in use at once, with the side doors opening and closing to admit or dismiss fresh participants in the scene. Everything in use, except the cellar or trap where ghosts moaned or from which, in Christopher Marlowe's *Dr Faustus*, ugly Hell gaped. And all this was done by the light of day. The common folk or groundlings stood for a penny and the better sort of people occupied the balconies for a shilling. Shakespeare thrust his action forward, right into the middle of this audience. That's the big difference between his theatre and our theatre of illusion. We like lights and demand atmospheric effects of all kinds, but Shakespeare had no effects and lights. Everything depended on the actor's capacity to overpower the audience which he could so clearly see there before him. And the over-powering was effected through great, ebullient language. The audience was used to this kind of language, expected it, wanted it. After all, they went to church every Sunday, that was the law, and there they had fine, strong, eloquent, ebullient sermons hurled at them for ninety minutes. In the playhouse, they not only expected poetry, they wanted it, whether it was in verse or in prose. And again, whether this poetry was thundering or whether it was intimate, it was thrust out to them and they, in turn, were drawn into the rhetoric of the drama.

All Is True, that's the title, remember, under which the play was first presented:

> Think ye see
> The very persons of our noble story
> As they were living; think you see them great,
> And follow'd with the general throng and sweat
> Of thousand friends; then, in a moment, see
> How soon this mightiness meets misery.
> And if you can be merry then, I'll say
> A man may weep upon his wedding-day.

Prologue 25–32

It's worth remembering this wasn't remote, fantasticated, romanticised history. It was still pretty close to the collective memory of the English people. The monuments of that great but

94

bloody reign were all about. Indeed, they still are. Hampton Court, for example, with the ghost of Cardinal Wolsey walking in the garden. And Henry VIII, that most substantial of English monarchs, is as much a dramatic draw now as he was in 1613. He gets a certain affection from us which he doesn't really deserve, and we know it. But he still stands for a kind of bluff patriotism, a concern for England expressed in open defiance of popes and emperors, expressed in notions like 'We'll have our own church, and we'll keep our own customs, and we'll build a great navy to keep the foreigner out'. He stands for roast beef, ale and chauvinism. Perhaps it's right that the greatest of English dramatists should end with the most spectacular, if not the greatest, of English monarchs. But in my mind a doubt still remains. Did Shakespeare write this play? And if not, who did?

Henry VIII

Donald Sinden

Donald Sinden played the King of France in the BBC
TV *Shakespeare production of* All's Well That Ends
Well. *Besides* Henry VIII, *his other Shakespearean
parts have included Malvolio, King Lear and
Othello.*

'I come no more to make you laugh; . . .'. That is the rather
ominous first line of the Prologue of Shakespeare's *Henry VIII*
and it pretty well holds good for the rest of the play. There's
hardly a laugh in it, which of course distresses me as an actor
because I enjoy getting laughs. The scholars, who know about
these things, tell us that *Henry VIII* was not the unaided work of
Shakespeare but was written in collaboration with a young playwright named John Fletcher. Now, sometimes these scholars are
right and, having spent a year of my life playing the part of
Henry, I find myself agreeing with them wholeheartedly.

Let me tell you my own theory abou the authorship of the play.
At some time during the middle of his playwriting years, Shakespeare first conceived the idea of a play about the father of
Queen Elizabeth the First.. Possibly in 1597, which would have
been the fiftieth anniversary of Henry's death. Having mapped
out his original plan, he found himself in trouble. In all honesty,
and he was a playwright who could never be dishonest, he
would have to show Henry VIII as the ogre and tyrant that he
undoubtedly was. This would not have exactly been wise with his
daughter Elizabeth still on the throne and herself noted for
wielding a pretty bloody axe. But, having done considerable
research on the subject, Shakespeare was loathe to waste it.
What if he were to concentrate on the early years of Henry's
reign when Cardinal Wolsey was his Chancellor? What a
splendid, colourful character he would be! Henry could be
shown as the David who overthrew this Goliath. He could show
Wolsey's rather than Henry's fall from grace. Henry's first wife
Katharine could be the villain of the piece as well. The audience
would sympathise with Henry over the divorce. The young,
beautiful and innocent Anne Boleyn could be Shakespeare's
heroine because she finally gave birth to, guess who? – Eliza-

beth, Our Elizabeth, Good Queen Bess. There was, however, no getting away from the fact that Henry VIII was the villain. The audience could not be expected to forget that he had chopped off the head of Elizabeth's mum, and possibly the heads of their own parents as well. He had no alternative but to drop the idea. If he offended the Queen and the court, he and his colleagues would be out of work or, worse still, in the Tower. So Shakespeare put all the relevant papers, his research notes, his synopsis and a few odd speeches he had already drafted, into his desk and set about writing something easier.

The years rolled by and Shakespeare entered the mature years of his playwriting. *Twelfth Night* and *Hamlet* fell from his pen. Queen Elizabeth died in 1603 and James I became King. Merrie England was a thing of the past and Shakespeare set to work on the great tragedies of *Othello, Measure for Measure, King Lear, Macbeth* and *Antony and Cleopatra*. His last play, his swan song, *The Tempest*, was produced in 1611 and he could now enjoy his retirement in Stratford-upon-Avon. His place as resident playwright to the King's Men had been taken by a young fellow called John Fletcher who, while clearing out his predecessor's desk, came across a bundle of notes on the subject of Henry VIII. He wrote to the grand old man at Stratford and asked if he could please make use of the notes. 'Of course you can, my boy', replied Shakespeare, 'You'll find it a very difficult task. Take my advice and make all the speeches ambiguous and call the play *All is True*. If you need my help just let me know. I enclose two or three speeches you can use, one for Buckingham, several for Wolsey and Katharine. Good luck, and for heaven's sake don't put my name on the play-bills. Yours, W.S.'. Well that, as I said, is my own theory. However, the play, under its title of *Henry VIII* first appeared in print as being the work of William Shakespeare in the collected edition of his works edited by John Heminge and Henry Condell in 1623. Poor Fletcher doesn't get a mention.

The play is rarely produced today because of the enormous cost involved. The cast list is the longest list in any play by Shakespeare. There are scenes of great pageantry: a great ball given by Wolsey, and enormous courtroom scene, the splendid coronation procession for Anne Boleyn, the dancers who appear to Katharine in a vision and, finally, the impressive baptism ceremony for Elizabeth. Just think of the costumes! the court of Henry VIII did not stint themselves so when the play is presented today it must look sumptuous. Wolsey is the only character who can get away with only one costume. He is dressed in cardinal red throughout.

So why bother to do it? Well, it contains two smashing parts, Wolsey and Katharine, and over the centuries leading actors and actresses have wanted to play them. The part of Buckingham is pretty good too, but the part of Henry is a stinker! He is one of those few historical characters whose appearance is known to every man in the street. More than any other monarch, with the possible exception of Queen Victoria, everybody has a pre-conceived idea of what Henry looked like because of those end-less reproductions of Holbein's portrait. There he stands, this great bulk of a man, his feet astride, hands on hips, with vast, hunched shoulders. All the poor actor can do is to try to look like that portrait and therein lies the problem. You see, an actor is quite safe with Richard II, Henry IV, Henry V and Henry VI because nobody knows what they looked like. Yet, if you don't look like Holbein's Henry, the public think you have failed.

I found this to my cost when I played the part. I wore a padded wig (to make my head look larger) glued to my forehead. My own eyebrows were obliterated and false ones stuck in their place. I had a false nose glued on, then a moustache and beard were gummed into position. There was Henry's face but where was Sinden's? By measuring the inside of Henry's armour which stands in the Tower of London, we know that he was six foot three inches tall. Very few actors are that tall. Then comes the costume – calamity! If you make a study of the human anatomy, you will discover that the distance between the knee and the ground is one quarter of the overall height of a man. Holbein has cheated! In trying to make Henry's vast bulk look in proportion, he has made the distance a third of Henry's height! Now no actor will undergo a bone graft, especially not for a part as poor as Henry, so when he dons the skirt-like lower part of the costume his shin bone is too short and again it appears to be the fault of the actor. In the portrait, Henry's calves are at least six inches in diameter. Well, that is easy enough to overcome, so on went enormous padded calves. To underline Henry's virility, Holbein shows a massive codpiece protruding from a split in the skirt. The wardrobe made me one of equal size but at each move the skirt covers it up. Painter's licence I suppose. Then comes the problem of the hat. The one in the portrait is totally two-dimensional. The moment an attempt is made to reproduce it 'in the round' it looks quite wrong unless the actor faces front the whole time. So on go the great padded shoulders and the cloak with enormous sleeves which covers the dagger on the belt, unless the actor keeps his hand on it all the time. There you stand, gummed up, stuck up, glued up, padded up, encased in a costume weighing a ton, and you look stupid. In fact, with my face gummed up, I did not have the freedom to add much of myself to the character. So I can't say I enjoyed the part although I did enjoy certain scenes.

The play concerns the fall of Buckingham, the greatest man in the kingdom, the meeting between Henry and Anne Boleyn, his divorce from Katharine of Aragon to whom he had been married for twenty years, the fall of Cardinal Wolsey whose ambition has over-reached itself, the death of Katharine and, finally, the birth of a daughter, Elizabeth, to Anne. Now remember that *All is True* is the alternative title of the play. But, if you study history, you will find that practically everything shown or talked about in the play is only a veneer of the truth. The divorce scene is really the centre-piece, so one needs to understand the background to it. Katharine of Aragon had been married as a child to Henry's elder brother, Arthur, when he was also a child. She had always maintained that the marriage was never consummated and when Arthur died, still a child, she was allowed to marry his brother Henry, now heir to the throne. During their twenty years of marriage, Katharine produced many children, all of whom either died at birth, or shortly after, except for one daughter, Mary, who thus became heir to the throne. It grieved Henry that he had no son to carry on his line so, when he fell hat over codpiece for Anne Boleyn, he was determined to get rid of Katharine and marry Anne. But how to do it? The Roman Catholic church would never countenance divorce but what about an annulment on the grounds that his entire marriage to Katharine was illegal because he should never have been allowed to marry his brother's wife? It all hinged on two quotations from the Bible, one from *Leviticus* and the other from *Deuteronomy*. One maintains that a marriage is a marriage once you have 'taken a wife' whilst the other maintains that a marriage is only a marriage once it is consummated. Ecclesiastics from all over the world argued that one out. Henry of course chose the side that would suit him best and the pope chose the other one. It was a very difficult situation for Wolsey who, as a good Catholic who did not want to act against his king, was caught between king and pope. Luckily for Henry, all this occured at the time when the Reformation was gaining ground in Europe. Henry jumped on the bandwagon, made himself head of the Church of England and pushed through the divorce.

In the play the divorce scene takes place in what is called a

consistory court. This comprised a sort of fenced-in area in the
centre of a large room. The judges, the defendant and the
witnesses sat in this area and, during the scene, Katharine is told
several times to 'come into the court'. She refuses to enter the
small, box-like structure because there she would have been
under oath. This is how she answers Henry's accusations:

Sir, I desire you do me right and justice,
And to bestow your pity on me; for
I am a most poor woman and a stranger
Born out of your dominions, having here
No judge indifferent, nor no more assurance
Of equal friendship and proceeding. Alas, sir,
In what have I offended you? What cause
Hath my behaviour given to your displeasure
That thus you should proceed to put me off
And take your good grace from me? Heaven witness,
I have been to you a true and humble wife,
At all times to your will conformable,
Even in fear to kindle your dislike,
Yea, subject to your countenance – glad or sorry
As I saw it inclin'd. When was the hour
I ever contradicted your desire
Or made it not mine too? Or which of your friends
Have I not strove to love, although I knew
He were mine enemy? What friend of mine
That had to him deriv'd your anger did I
Continue in my liking? Nay, gave notice
He was from thence discharg'd? Sir, call to mind
That I have been your wife in this obedience
Upward of twenty years, and have been blest
With many children by you. If, in the course
And process of this time, you can report,
And prove it too against mine honour, aught,
My bond to wedlock or my love and duty,
Against your sacred person, in God's name,
Turn me away and let the foul'st contempt
Shut door upon me, and so give me up
To the sharp'st kind of justice.

2.4.13–44

Vintage Shakespeare, obviously written by the old man himself!
Katharine's speech is actually twice as long as this. Throughout
the scene Shakespeare, brilliant as ever, does not allow Henry to

speak one word to her. He has been married to her for twenty years but what could he say? Her argument is unanswerable. If he dared to join in his cause would be lost, so it is better to keep his mouth shut. If he were even to look at her and see her tears, compassion would get the better of him. It is far safer to turn his head away and try not to look or listen. But hasn't Henry fallen in love with Anne Boleyn? Well, she's a very, very attractive popsie and eminently bedable. She might produce a son and heir. The combination is irresistible to Henry but is he in love with her? That's a debatable point. When Katharine makes her exit, Henry speaks for the first time and shouts after her 'Go thy ways, Kate'.

That half-line raises an interesting point of how Shake-spearean verse should be spoken. We work on a principle at Stratford-upon-Avon that one should not pause during, but only at the end of, a line. Everybody knows that the major part of Shakespeare is written in iambic pentameters, that is, a beat of five feet to the line. One should keep that stress going through-out each line and the only time you should pause is at the end of a line. If a full-stop is in the middle of a line, you can break the line but not stop. Now Katharine's last full line is 'Upon this business my appearance make/In any of their courts'. Whereupon Henry completes the line by saying 'Go thy ways, Kate'. Now there must be no pause between her half-line and Henry's. After he's said 'Kate' he can wait an hour but before that he must keep the rhythm going. He's got to slap his half-line in immedi-ately after Katherine's. He then embarks upon a very long, very dreary speech, obviously pure, unadulterated Fletcher, in which he tries to excuse himself. He finishes up with the very clever ruse of saying words to the effect of 'If you can't see my argu-ment that the marriage was unlawful, the onus is on you to prove that it was lawful.'

Now for some time, Henry, unobservant and insensitive as he is, had been aware that Wolsey was getting above himself and was feathering his own nest. In a moment of extraordinary mental aberration Wolsey had put the wrong letter into an envelope that he had sent to Henry. He knows the game is up and in a very inept scene, obviously by Fletcher, he makes this melodramatic speech:

What should this mean?
What sudden anger's this? How have I reap'd it?
He parted frowning from me, as if ruin
Leap'd from his eyes; so looks the chafed lion

Upon the daring huntsman that has gall'd him –
Then makes him nothing. I must read this paper;
I fear, the story of his anger. 'Tis so;
This paper has undone me. 'Tis th'account
Of all that world of wealth I have drawn together
For mine own ends; indeed to gain the popedom,
And fee my friends in Rome. O negligence,
Fit for a fool to fall by! What cross devil
Made me put this main secret in the packet
I sent the King? Is there no way to cure this?
No new device to beat this from his brains?
I know 'twill still him strongly; yet I know
A way, if it take right, in spite of fortune,
Will bring me off again. What's this? 'To th' Pope'.
The letter, as I live, with all the business
I writ to's Holiness. Nay then, farewell!

3.2.203–22

Then suddenly, after that claptrap, we are given five glorious lines:

I have touched the highest point of all my greatness,
And from that full meridian of my glory
I haste now to my setting. I shall fall
Like a bright exhalation in the evening,
And no man see me more.

23–8

It's like ten bars of Beethoven after forty of Havergal Brian. Thank God we are now back to Shakespeare and we have the glorious scene of Wolsey's final downfall, with Shakespeare's great phrases soaring and swooping like an eagle. Brilliantly, we are now made to feel sorry for the man who has risen from being the son of an Ipswich butcher to become the greatest man in the kingdom. It's really rather an English attitude of not wanting to kick a man when he is down.

We next see Queen Katharine on her death bed in a tragic scene in which she sends her blessings to Henry, who has by now married Anne Boleyn. After this the play might just as well be over and everybody might just as well go home. The fireworks have all fizzled out. In what follows it is up to the actor playing Henry to try to keep the play alive for the next half-hour. Nothing happens that the audience are at all interested in until Cranmer introduces the infant Elizabeth and prophesies what a wonderful reign she will have. Well, it was if you were *in* but if you were *out* it was a very different story. All is True? Again we are left with the question mark. The play is finished with an Epilogue which begins ''Tis ten to one this play can never please/ All that are here'. Between them, Shakespeare and Fletcher had skated over some very thin ice.

I HENRY IV
George Melly

George Melly was the film and television critic for
The Observer *before returning to a full-time
career as a blues singer. He made some of this programme on location in Shrewsbury.*

All over the country, aiming at a greater or lesser degree of
authenticity, and at a price which would have kept a real Tudor
family for a month, Elizabethan banquets have become enormous tourist and indeed native attractions. The city traffic may
roar past outside, the trains rumble overhead, but for an hour
or two the real estate agent from Dallas or the motor-car salesman and his wife from Wolverhampton can imagine themselves
at the court of Good Queen Bess or her father, bluff King Hal,
wassailing and gorging and eyeing the serving wenches. A
musician wanders amongst them, picking out 'Greensleeves' on
an electronic lute. They dream of uninhibited drunkenness,
gluttony and lechery from a simple and more colourful age, the
lost land of Cockaigne.

The real Elizabethan feasts were pretty lavish by all accounts.
It was an age of the nouveau riche and there was that typical
love of ostentation and showing off, of proving they'd made it.
They were shrewd and unscrupulous but full of energy and lust
for living. Supper in Shakespeare's time was actually about 5.30
in the afternoon. Vast quantities of beef were consumed in
the ordinary course of events but, at feasts, food was provided
in enormous and quite unnecessary quantities. The dishes
tended to be rather elaborate, such as swan and peacock
smothered in sauces containing ambergris, musk and saffron,
which was probably rather disgusting. The booze was formid-
able: great hogsheads of beer and wine as well as sack, Falstaff's favourite, which was actually the Elizabethan name for all
wines that came from Spain. I believe that there at least our
modern Elizabethan feasts are probably rather authentic.

All this misrule, this riot, this wenching, this total lack of in-
hibition is summed up for us, perhaps best of all, in Shakespeare's marvellous creation, Sir John Falstaff:

FALSTAFF: Now, Hal, what time of day is it, lad?
PRINCE: Thou art so fat-witted with drinking of old sack, and
  unbuttoning thee after supper, and sleeping upon benches
  after noon, that thou has forgotten to demand that truly
  which thou wouldst truly know. What a devil has thou to do
  with the time of day? Unless hours were cups of sack, and
  minutes capons, and clocks and tongues of bawds, and dials
  the signs of leaping-houses, and the blessed sun himself a
  fair hot wench in flame-coloured taffeta, I see no reason
  why thou shouldst be so superfluous to demand the time of
  day.

I.2.I–II

Although Falstaff was, historically speaking, a medieval character, he seems to us the essence of an Elizabethan. This is
because Shakespeare didn't aim at historical accuracy. He wrote
as an Elizabethan for Elizabethans and all his characters,
whether they are ancient Romans or medieval kings and knights,
think like Elizabethans. They live in the Tudor world and are
heirs to its vices and virtues.

Falstaff spent, or rather mis-spent, much of his time in the
stews of Eastcheap, now levelled by bulldozers, but then a
warren of the kind of Elizabethan jerry-building which keeps the
tourists' cameras busy. I don't know if they'd be quite so happy if
they could go back in time. The Elizabethans had a rather casual
approach to sewage that wouldn't really have appealed to the
patrons of the Holiday Inns. The country was flooded with
sturdy beggars and crime was almost on a level with that around
Times Square in New York today. There were numerous con
men, highwaymen, cutpurses, pimps and whores, and many of
the less reputable inns doubled as brothels. Falstaff made use of
them in both capacities. He was as lecherous as he was greedy
and as greedy as he was thirsty. In the lechery department, however, there is some doubt, which is expressed by Poins, Prince
Hal's companion, when he finds Falstaff with a whore on his
knee. 'Is it not strange', he says, 'that desire should by so many
years outlive performance'.

The play is based on historical fact as is Shakespeare's usual
practice. He made use of chronicle histories such as Holin-
shed's. After a few years of uneasy peace, rebellion is threatening. The Welsh are rising and they're helped out by the Percies,
who have originally put Henry IV on the throne. They now feel
that they've been hard done by. Young Percy, Harry Hotspur, in

particular is thirsting for a fight. Prince Hal, by contrast, is content to spend his time in the stews and bagnios of London, an apt and willing disciple of that old reprobate, Sir John Falstaff. Falstaff represents misrule, anarchy, the riot of the senses and is thus a very unsuitable companion for the heir to a rather shaky throne. Henry IV certainly regrets his son's friendship with Falstaff but then he admires his enemy, Hotspur. Young Percy wants glory on the bloody fields of war so he would never waste his time in drunkenness and horseplay. As far as I am concerned Hotspur seems rather like the priggish headboy of a school, randy for glory, but Henry IV admires him as much as he despises his own son. He wishes there was some way to change one for the other:

> Yea, there thou mak'st me sad and mak'st me sin
> In envy that my Lord Northumberland
> Should be the father to so blest a son –
> A son who is the theme of honour's tongue;
> Amongst a grove, the very straightest plant;
> Who is sweet Fortune's minion and her pride;
> Whilst I, by looking on the praise of him,
> See riot and dishonour stain the brow
> Of my young Harry. O that it could be prov'd
> That some night-tripping fairy had exchang'd
> In cradle-clothes our children where they lay,
> And call'd mine Percy, his Plantagenet!
> Then would I have his Harry, and he mine.

1.1.78–90

Shakespeare was, politically speaking, a conservative, that is to say, a survivor. It was necessary to be a conservative in Elizabethan England. You had to use history as a way of propping up the status quo in order to keep the savage royal babies and their cold-eyed servants happy. And perhaps it's this that accounts for Shakespeare's obsession with the divine right of kings. The Tudors did not have all that firm a right to the throne and, for that reason, they believed in divine right all the more. As to whether Shakespeare believed in it, I always seem to detect a certain cynicism but I think he knew that regicide led to political disorder because, once you deposed a king, you could in your own turn be deposed. This is certainly the theme of both parts of *Henry IV*. They are plays of mirrors. Each part, while complete in itself, reflects the other. There isn't a character that doesn't have his alter ego. There isn't a historical event which isn't echoed in some absurd tavern jape or ridiculous drunken foolery. Falstaff and King Henry are both, for instance, father-figures to Prince Hal. Falstaff is disreputable, a lesson in humanity, however flawed, whereas King Henry is cold and demanding. Yet in the end Hal knows that he must seek to emulate his father. The absurd robbery at Gadshill, where Hal and Poins, in disguise, rob Falstaff of the purses he's just taken from the rich merchants, in order to prove him both a coward and a fool, has its parallel in the great Battle of Shrewsbury upon which King Henry's crown depends. It's point counterpoint throughout.

And yet how gracefully Falstaff can wriggle for all his bulk. Accused by Hal of lying when he claims that the purses have been taken from him by an ever-increasing number of armed men, he gets out of it by explaining that it was all down to his instinct:

> By the Lord, I knew ye as well as he that made ye. Why, hear you, my masters: was it for me to kill the heir apparent? Should I turn upon the true prince? Why, thou knowest I am as valiant as Hercules; but beware instinct – the lion will not touch the true prince. Instinct is a great matter: I was now a coward on instinct. I shall think the better of myself and thee during my life – I for a valiant lion, and thou for a true prince.

2.4.258–66

Falstaff is a liar but at the same time human and affectionate. I first fell in love with him when I was a sailor stationed at Chatham just after the end of the war. I was always going up to London and going to the New Theatre where the Old Vic had a season running with Laurence Olivier and Ralph Richardson. There were three plays, the two parts of *Henry IV* and *Oedipus*. I saw both parts of *Henry IV* and then I wanted to see *Oedipus*, so I kept coming back again and again to the matinees. I always found that one or another of the Henries was on, so I saw them each several times and got to know them really very well. The thing I find most attractive about Falstaff is his ability to cast an eccentric glow on all around him. Even Prince Hal, cold, calculating Hal, is humanised by his presence, and yet Hal knows very well that he's going to have to get rid of his dubious tutor. It should come as no surprise to us. There's a marvellous scene in the tavern where Falstaff play-fully imitates King Henry and Hal represents himself as being reprimanded for keeping such low companions, although, as

Falstaff is the King, he naturally excludes himself from these low companions. Then they change places: Hal represents his father and Falstaff represents Hal:

PRINCE: Now, Harry, whence come you?

FALSTAFF: My noble lord, from Eastcheap.

PRINCE: The complaints I hear of thee are grievous.

FALSTAFF: 'Sblood, my lord, they are false. Nay, I'll tickle ye for a young prince, i'faith.

PRINCE: Swearest thou, ungracious boy? Henceforth ne'er look on me. Thou art violently carried away from grace; there is a devil haunts thee in the likeness of an old fat man; a tun of man is thy companion.

2.4.425–33

The King, played by Hal, really lays into Falstaff and tears him to shreds. One detects a cold, cruel, cutting edge under all the fun and exuberance of this attack:

PRINCE: Why dost thou converse with that trunk of humours, that bolting-hutch of beastliness, that swoll'n parcel of dropsies, that huge bombard of sack, that stuff'd cloak-bag of guts, that roasted Manningtree ox with the pudding in his belly, that reverend vice, that grey iniquity, that father ruffian, that vanity in years? Wherein is he good, but to taste sack and drink it? Wherein neat and cleanly, but to carve a capon and eat it? wherein cunning, but in craft? wherein crafty, but in villainy? wherein villainous, but in all things? wherein worthy, but in nothing?

FALSTAFF: I would your Grace would take me with you; whom means your Grace?

PRINCE: That villainous abominable misleader of youth, Falstaff, that old white-bearded Satan.

2.4.433–47

Falstaff's rejection later on should therefore come as no surprise to us.

Shakespeare neatly solves all the equations he's set earlier in the play at the Battle of Shrewsbury, although much more neatly than in reality because medieval battles were uncertain and bloodthirsty affairs. The mounds of dead and dying symbolised the sacrifice that had to be paid for the medieval concept of honour, which Falstaff, in my view quite rightly, attacks so eloquently:

Can honour set to a leg? No. Or an arm? No. Or take away the
grief of a wound? No. Honour hath no skill in surgery, then? No.
What is honour? A word. What is in that word? Honour. What is
that honour? Air. A trim reckoning! Who hath it? He that died o'
Wednesday. Doth he feel it? No. Doth he hear it? No. 'Tis insensible, then? Yea, to the dead. But will it not live with the living?
No. Why? Detraction will not suffer it. Therefore I'll none of it.

5.2.130–8

Later on Falstaff lies down in self-preservation during the height of
the battle and feigns death next to the real corpse of young Hotspur.
He is discovered by Prince Hal who speaks, looking at the two
corpses, with admiration for the courage and honour of Hotspur, but
with true love for the corpse of the old, all too human reprobate,
Sir John Falstaff.

What, old acquaintance! Could not all this flesh
Keep in a little life? Poor Jack, farewell!
I could have better spar'd a better man.
O, I should have a heavy miss of thee,
If I were much in love with vanity!
Death hath not struck so fat a deer to-day,
Though many dearer, in this blood fray.
Embowell'd will I see thee by and by;
Till then in blood by noble Percy lie.

5.4.102–10

Falstaff couldn't be left dead on the field at Shrewsbury, he had to
get up and waddle off into *2 Henry IV*. His death is described at the
beginning of *Henry V*. Shakespeare knew he couldn't be left alive to
unbalance that noble piece of jingoistic ranting. His description of
the last moments of Falstaff on the lips of a bawdy-house keeper is
perhaps the most moving account of a deathbed in the whole of our
literature:

Nay, sure, he's not in hell: he's in Arthur's bosom, if ever man
went to Arthur's bosom. 'A made a finer end, and went away an it
had been any christom child; 'a parted ev'n just between twelve
and one, ev'n at the turning o' th' tide; for after I saw him fumble
with the sheets, and play with flowers, and smile upon his fingers'
end, I knew there was but one way; for his nose was as sharp as a
pen, and 'a babbl'd of green fields.

2.3.9–16

It's Arthur, you notice, not Abraham. Arthur was the traditional guardian of the English spirit and so is more appropriate, since Falstaff represents that spirit which lasts, lasts and preserves itself against the heel of kings and tyrants: 'Banish plump Jack, and banish all the world'.

I HENRY IV
Sir Michael Redgrave

*Sir Michael Redgrave has played Hamlet at Elsinore,
done one-man shows based on Shakespeare and
played so many Shakespearean parts that they are
too numerous to mention.*

So shaken as we are, so wan with care,
Find we a time for frighted peace to pant
And breathe short winded accents of new broils
To be commenc'd in strands afar remote.

I.I.I–4

With these words from the opening of the play, King Henry
IV hopes for an end to the troubles that have beset his reign.
Since coming to the throne in 1399, he has had to cope with
rebellions by the English nobles and attacks from Wales and
Scotland. *I Henry IV* tells the story of yet another rebellion. It is
led by the Earl of Northumberland and his son, Henry Percy,
better known as Harry Hotspur. They join forces with a number
of other powerful nobles who, like themselves, had first helped
King Henry and then turned against him. The rebellion fails and
the rebel armies are defeated at the Battle of Shrewsbury by the
army of King Henry and his son, Prince Hal. Hotspur is killed in
the battle by Hal. That, in a nutshell, is the story of *I Henry IV,*
or, at least, that part of the story which shows us 'man in shining
armour'. The figure of Sir John Falstaff, one of the truly great
comic figures of world drama, and his cronies, the riff-raff of the
tavern and the town, bustle at the heels of these great men.

The leading characters form a strong quartet in which the
grave and troubled King Henry is a counterweight to Falstaff, in
much the same way as Prince Hal balances Harry Hotspur. The
contrasting characters of Hal and Hotspur are pitted against
each other throughout the play until Hotspur's death at the end.
The two young men represent two versions of the concept of
chivalry. The contrast in their characters is brought out very
early on in the play by King Henry himself, when he hears that

the brave and valiant Hotspur has defeated a Scottish army and taken many prisoners:

A son who is the theme of honour's tongue;
Amongst a grove, the very straightest plant;
Who is sweet Fortune's minion and her pride;
Whilst I, by looking on the praise of him
See riot and dishonour stain the brow
Of my young Harry.

1.1.81–6

Hotspur is certainly brave and warlike, but he is also young, tempestuous and quick-tempered. When I played him at Stratford during the Festival of Britain celebrations in 1951, I felt that the clue to his character lay in the fact that he was a rough, down-to-earth countryman, who was ignorant in the ways of the court and proud of it. Hotspur, whom his wife refers to as 'thick of speech', also makes references to himself which show that he is ill at ease with words:

Arm, arm with speed! and, fellows, soldiers, friends,
Better consider what you have to do
Than I, that have not well the gift of tongue,
Can lift your blood up with persuasion.

5.2.76–9

A little later on, he thanks a messenger for interrupting him because he professes 'not talking'. He dies in mid-sentence when he is killed by Hal and the majority of actors have used that to give him a stammer. Yet Anthony Quayle, the Director at Stratford that year, suggested to me that Hotspur ought to speak in the Northumbrian dialect, which has a kind of French or Scottish 'r' sound or burr. So I went up to Northumberland for a week or more and acquired something that passed as a countryman's accent with the local people. To show how small the world is, one Northumbrian who came to see the play thought that my accent was just right, whereas another felt that it was 'more Wooller than Alnwick'. Wooller and Alnwick are less than twenty miles apart and yet there is still a difference in the dialect.

Hotspur's brother-in-law, the Earl of Mortimer, had been captured by the Welsh under Owen Glendower. In the normal course of events King Henry would have been expected to pay the ransom for Mortimer, although Mortimer had in fact gone over the other side, as we'd say today, and married into the Glendower family. Hotspur is, nevertheless, still annoyed with

Henry's action, particularly as it is coupled with a demand that he has to hand over some of the prisoners he has captured in Scotland. He later explained that he could not control his rage when he saw King Henry's messenger:

> My liege, I did not deny no prisoners.
> But I remember when the fight was done,
> When I was dry with rage and extreme toil,
> Breathless and faint, leaning upon my sword,
> Came there a certain lord, neat, and trimly dress'd,
> Fresh as a bridegroom, and his chin new reap'd
> Show'd like a stubble-land at harvest-home.
> He was perfumed like a milliner,
> And 'twixt his finger and his thumb he held
> A pouncet-box, which ever and anon
> He gave his nose and took't away again;
> Who therewith angry, when it next came there,
> Took it in snuff – and still he smil'd and talk'd–
> And as the soldiers bore dead bodies by,
> He call'd them untaught knaves, unmannerly,
> To bring a slovenly unhandsome corse
> Betwixt the wind and his nobility.
> With many holiday and lady terms
> He questioned me: amongst the rest, demanded
> My prisoners in your Majesty's behalf.

1.3.29–48

King Henry refuses to listen to these arguments, but merely reminds Hotspur and his father rather curtly of their duty:

> Send me your prisoners with the speediest means,
> Or you shall hear in such a kind from me
> As will displease you. My Lord Northumberland,
> We license your departure with your son.
> Send us your prisoners, or you will hear of it.

1.3.120–4

The stubborn Hotspur will not, of course, do this and so a conspiracy is hatched.

It might sound odd for me to say that, in spite of his rashness, petulance and immaturity, I find Hotspur a lovable and humorous character to play. This comes across in the scene in which he gets together with Owen Glendower to hatch the plot against Henry. Glendower starts boasting of his magical powers and the

supernatural circumstances of his birth, but is soon deflated by
Hotspur:

> GLENDOWER: . . . at my nativity
>   The front of heaven was full of fiery shapes,
>   Of burning′cressets; and at my birth
>   The frame and huge foundation of the earth
>   Shaked like a coward
> HOTSPUR: Why, so it would have done at the
>   same season if your mother's cat had but kitten'd though
>   yourself had never been born.
> GLENDOWER: I say the earth did shake when I was born.
> HOTSPUR: And I say the earth was not of my mind,
>   If you suppose as fearing you it shook.

3.1.13–23

The straight, down-to-earth Hotspur has no time for Glendower's mysticism:

> GLENDOWER: I can call spirits from the vasty deep.
> HOTSPUR: Why, so can I, or so can any man;
>   But will they come when you do call for them?

3.1.53–5

There is another humorous scene when Hotspur returns home
after plotting the campaign against Henry. He won't tell his wife,
Lady Percy, where he's been all this time and where he proposes
to go off to in a hurry. He abruptly says 'Kate, in an hour or two I
must leave thee', or words to that effect, and the rest of the scene
shows her coaxing, begging, threatening him to find out what
he's doing and why he won't tell her. He finds it amusing to tease
her, but it's no laughing matter for her if he leaves her for any
length of time as she's passionately in love with him. She
threatens to break his finger if he doesn't tell her where he's
been all these weeks. It's what we would call a sex-comedy today.
When I played Hotspur at Stratford for the Festival of Britain
celebrations, Lady Percy chased me round the stage in an effort
to get hold of me:

> LADY: But hear you, my lord.
> HOTSPUR: What say'st thou, my lady?
> LADY: What is it carries you away?
> HOTSPUR: Why, my horse, my love, my horse.
> LADY: Out, you mad-headed ape!
>   A weasel hath not such a deal of spleen
>   As you are toss'd with. In faith,

I'll know your business, Harry, that I will.
I fear my brother Mortimer doth stir
About his title and hath sent for you
To line his enterprise; but if you go –
HOTSPUR: So far afoot, I shall be weary, love.
LADY: Come, come, you paraquito, answer me
Directly unto this question that I ask.
In faith, I'll break thy little finger, Harry,
An if thou wilt not tell me all things true.

2.3.70–85

The man pitted against Hotspur in character, life-style and
political aims is Prince Hal. We see him carousing with Falstaff
and his crew in the Boar's Head Tavern for most of the early
part of the play. He drinks, jests and plays practical jokes on
Falstaff. Yet this is the same man who is to become the great and
glorious Henry V, who defeats the French at Agincourt. Hal's a
splendid part to play, but a difficult one because of the contra-
diction between what he says and does. He is not, however, a
hypocrite, but a young man who knows exactly what he's doing.
His actions are those of a practical joker. Unexpected things are
bound to happen in his scenes with that other great practical
joker, Falstaff. These scenes make the play the comic masterpiece that it is. In one such scene at the Boar's Head, messengers arrive to tell Prince Hal that he's got to go to the court
next morning to discuss important matters of state with his father
and, of course, to answer for his riotous living as well. Falstaff
persuades him to practise his answer there and then. A play
within a play is set up in which Falstaff pretends to be King
Henry calling his son to task. Hal responds by reversing the role.
He plays his stern father to Falstaff's wayward son:

PRINCE: Now, Harry, whence come you?
FALSTAFF: My noble lord, from Eastcheap.
PRINCE: The complaints I hear of thee are grievous.
FALSTAFF: S'blood my lord, they are false. Nay, I'll tickle ye
    for a young prince, i'faith.
PRINCE: Swearest thou, ungracious boy? Henceforth ne'er
    look on me. Thou art violently carried away from grace;
    there is a devil haunts thee in the likeness of an old fat man;
    a tun of man is thy companion. Why dost thou converse with
    that trunk of humours, that bolting-hutch of beastliness,
    that swoll'n parcel of dropsies, that huge bombard of sack,

that stuff'd cloak-bag of guts, that roasted Manningtree
ox with the pudding in his belly, that reverend vice, that grey
iniquity, that father ruffian, that vanity in years? Wherein is
he good, but to taste sack and drink it? wherein neat and
cleanly, but to carve a capon and eat it? wherein cunning,
but in craft? wherein crafty, but in villainy? wherein villainous, but in all things? wherein worthy, but in nothing?

FALSTAFF: I would your Grace would take me with you; whom
means your Grace?

PRINCE: That villainous abominable misleader of youth,
Falstaff, the old white-bearded Satan.

2.4.425–47

It's a wonderful, if not particularly original, technique for allowing the speaker to speak his mind while attributing the actual
words to somebody else.

The political theme running throughout the play is the contrast between Hotspur, the hot-headed man of single purpose
who is totally convinced that it is right to rebel, and Prince Hal of
the taverns, later to reject Falstaff and become a great national
hero. Shakespeare does not necessarily suggest that justice has
been done at the Battle of Shrewsbury. It's certainly a good clean
fight, which is fought with a good deal of gallantry on both sides.
Yet it's partly through accident that Hotspur loses, since Glendower and his army don't get to the battle in time and the Earl of
Northumberland is too ill to be present. There is a complex web
of loyalties operating within the play. Many of the rebels who
opposed King Henry at Shrewsbury had assisted him to gain the
crown. It is often difficult to remember who's on which side,
who's turned against whom and exactly why Henry is supported
or rebelled against. It's just like real life in fact. One of the
driving forces of the play is that Shakespeare takes both sides
and by doing this he is able to show how ephemeral and relative
political loyalties can be and were.

2 HENRY IV
Fred Emery

Fred Emery was the chief Washington correspondent for The Times *from 1970–77. He returned to become Political Editor of the paper and a regular presenter on* Panorama. *He made this programme at the Palace of Westminster, Chipping Campden and Westminster Abbey.*

The problem of succession has once again become a crucial one. These past years we've all had time to reflect on changes in government and leadership. Our leaders believe and try to persuade us that the right succession might stop the decline of Britain. *2 Henry IV* is a play which personalises this problem. We may be a democracy, but our age can still produce party upheavals to match those experienced by the Yorkists and Lancastrians 500 years ago. Thorpe is succeeded by Steel, Heath is deposed by Thatcher who succeeds Callaghan, himself unexpectedly advanced by Wilson. Or consider the consequences of Kennedy's assassination in America. LBJ succeeds Kennedy, but is forced to step down by public pressure. He is succeeded by a resurgent Nixon, who eventually resigns in deep disgrace.

I must confess that, as a political journalist covering wars and elections abroad before coming back home to cover politics here, it's these political twists and turns that excite my interest in *2 Henry IV*. I'm in almost daily contact with politicians and their minions. Lobby correspondents at Westminster have good access to them, provided of course it's on a 'not for attribution' basis. We're often privy to their inner hopes, fears and ambitions. This play captures such emotions by dealing with the eternal preoccupation with both public and private succession. Henry IV worries himself sick, finally to death at the age of only forty-six, that all will turn to dust after he's gone. His heir, the wayward Prince Hal, is the disappointment of his life:

> Most subject is the fattest soil to weeds;
> And he, the noble image of my youth,
> Is overspread with them; therefore my grief

Stretches itself beyond the hour of death.
The blood weeps from my heart when I do shape,
In forms imaginary, th' unguided days
And rotten times that you shall look upon
When I am sleeping with my ancestors.
For when his headstrong riot hath no curb,
When rage and hot blood are his counsellors,
When means and lavish manners meet together,
O, with what wings shall his affections fly
Towards fronting peril and oppos'd decay!

4.4.54–66

From this dissolute son who is the despair of his father, Shakespeare builds up the myth of reformed youth in the character of the regenerate Prince Hal who will later flourish as Henry V. But Shakespeare keeps a very dry and unsentimental eye. As the master of all political journalists, he hints from the beginning of the play that Hal is every bit as devious and cunning a politician as his father. Indeed, it's only some rather frantic political advice on the deathbed that brings any sort of reconciliation into this rather strained father-son relationship. It's this problem of father-son communication, which baffles many middle-aged parents today, that will concern us throughout the play every bit as much as the futile longings of politicians to master events.

While these public and private pressures of life at the top take centre stage in the play, the scenes set away from Westminster form an important backcloth. Shakespeare shows us both in Eastcheap in London and in Gloucestershire the other end of the political spectrum. He shows us the life of the common people in England, who wouldn't be that concerned with power politics at Westminister, unless, as today, either their pockets or their lives were directly affected.

Henry IV had gone out of his way to seek a popular following. When he was, before this play, acting like a rival candidate to Richard II, whose crown he eventually usurped, he played the arch-populist with considerable success. The people liked him, but then as now, new and heavier taxes had brought very swift disenchantment. Things had turned very sour by the time of our play. There is, nevertheless, some marvellous comedy when the tavern folk and country people exhibit much generosity of spirit amidst all their adversity.

Some commentators have suggested that this other England is

the real hero of the play. Well, I don't know about that, but Shakespeare certainly shows, behind the laughter, the common folk getting shabby treatment. We see the funny side of a very nasty business in the famous recruiting scene, when Falstaff press-gangs soldiers for the civil war and pads his muster and payroll with shadow soldiers, or 'phantom' soldiers as they were called in our own time in Vietnam and Cambodia. Elizabethan audiences knew that the prisons got emptied and that those who couldn't afford to pay bribes were swept up into the press-gangs. They didn't like this practice any more than we should. Incidentally, one of the characters in this recruiting scene, Thomas Wart, may have been based on a real person named Thomas Warter. He was a carpenter who lived and died in Chipping Campden, which is only a few miles away from Stratford. We find him in 1608 on a list of men deemed fit, if unwilling, for military service:

FALSTAFF: Is thy name Wart?

WART: Yea, sir.

FALSTAFF: Thou art a very ragged wart.

SHALLOW: Shall I prick him, Sir John?

FALSTAFF: It were superfluous; for his apparel is built upon his back, and the whole frame stands upon pins. Prick him no more.

SHALLOW: Ha, ha, ha! You can do it, sir; you can do it, sir; you can do it. I commend you well. Francis Feeble!

FEEBLE: Here, sir.

FALSTAFF: What trade art thou, Feeble?

FEEBLE: A woman's tailor, sir.

SHALLOW: Shall I prick him, sir?

FALSTAFF: You may; but if he had been a man's tailor, he'd ha' pricked you. Wilt thou make as many holes in an enemy's battle as thou hast done in a woman's petticoat?

FEEBLE: I will do my good will, sir; you can have no more.

FALSTAFF: Well said, good woman's tailor! well said, courageous Feeble! Thou wilt be as valiant as the wrathful dove or most magnanimous mouse. Prick the woman's tailor – well, Master Shallow, deep, Master Shallow.

3.2.138–159

If the people of Gloucestershire submit with resignation, other parts of the country are in open revolt. The English regions, Scotland and Wales provide a sub-plot which is central to the problems bearing down on King Henry. The action opens with the Earl of Northumberland hearing at last that his son, Hotspur, has been killed at the Battle of Shrewsbury by Prince Hal. Old Northumberland is overcome with grief and guilt and swears a terrible vow of revenge. He prepares at York to renew rebellion against the King. It looks like a pretty mighty confrontation with about 25,000 men on each side. The rebels are led by Scroop, the Archbishop of York, a priest in armour, who is at the head of rather a dangerous sort of domestic crusade against the King's repressive and wasteful policies. In order to hold on to power, King Henry has had to deal with uprisings from the Welsh and the Scots, not to speak of fighting off the French, and all this has led to a drain on the country's men and money. Scroop paints a picture of a country racked with civil violence and fratricide:

> we are all diseas'd
> And with our surfeiting and wanton hours
> Have bought ourselves into a burning fever,
> And we must bleed for it; of which disease
> Our late King, Richard, being infected, died.

4.1.54–8

It's a pretty dicey business trying to divine what Shakespeare thought about either Elizabethan or medieval politics. Suffice it to say that he, along with most of his contemporaries, abhorred civil wars. The infighting that led to the Wars of the Roses was, for the Elizabethans, still very much a live topic, in the same way that the Irish problem and its continuation is for us.

Along with this sense of political unrest, Shakespeare establishes right from the start of the play a preoccupation with ageing and the accompanying nostalgia for a lost golden age. As Archbishop Scroop puts it rather pessimistically: 'Past and to come seems best; things present worst'. Even Falstaff becomes increasingly reprehensible and pitiful. Despite the victory at the Battle of Shrewsbury, there's a sense of let-down. Prince Hal seems weary, lacklustre and prone to bouts of Hamlet-like self-disgust. King Henry has turned into a man disfigured by disease, hiding himself away from all but his closest advisers. Some have said that he had leprosy, but it might have been a nervous complaint, for this King was not merely a worrier, he was hounded by a sense of his own guilt at the deposition and murder of Richard II. His great soliloquy provides three reasons for his sleeplessness: remorse, worry over the State and, a bit like Henry Kissinger this, railing at his inability to foresee and manage events. And yet the King tries to justify everything by what Shakespeare calls necessity, which we would probably recognise as 'national security' or 'national interest'. I am reminded of LBJ sleepless, with the boys not back from bombing Vietnam, going off to see a Catholic priest; or Nixon, after having been up all hours, venturing out for some small talk with Cambodian war protesters. He is reported to have muttered to the pictures on the walls of the White House during the night watches in the final days of his Watergate disgrace. Like Henry IV, he justified his crimes on the grounds of national security. And nearer home, didn't Anthony Eden fret away his health in Downing Street during the Suez crisis? Henry explains why the head that wears the crown is so uneasy:

How many thousands of my poorest subjects
Are at this hour asleep! O sleep, O gentle sleep,
Nature's soft nurse, how have I frighted thee,
That thou no more wilt weight my eyelids down,
And steep my senses in forgetfulness?
Why rather, sleep, liest thou in smoky cribs,
Upon uneasy pallets stretching thee,
And hush'd with buzzing night-flies to thy slumber,
Than in the perfum'd chambers of the great,
Under the canopies of costly state,
And lull'd with sound of sweetest melody?
O thou dull god, why liest thou with the vile
In loathsome beds, and leav'st the kingly couch
A watch-case or a common 'larum-bell?

3.1.4–17

Even though the King himself is obviously in decline at Westminster, up North at Gaultree, outside York, all the cunning and expediency of his reign are crystallised in the way in which his men score a near bloodless victory over Archbishop Scroop's rebellious forces. It all turns on a con trick. Having assembled his forces outside Gaultree, the Archbishop, all piety, tells the King's emissary that he's really a man of peace, who wants only that grievances be settled amicably. The King's men promise such cordial negotiations suggesting that both armies be stood down. The gullible Archbishop agrees, but, as soon as his men are disbanded, he and his co-conspirators are arrested. There was a catch. The King's men may have promised that the grievances would be settled, but nothing was said about sparing the rebel chiefs, who are subsequently beheaded. Shakespeare appears to believe that all's fair in dealing with rebels who threatened a generation of civil war, just as we today might believe all's fair in dealing with, say, terrorists or hijackers.

When the news of Gaultree reaches the King in London, instead of buoying him up, it rather perversely sends him nearer to death. He is brought to the Jerusalem Chamber in Westminster Abbey to die. A callous-seeming Hal, in vigil at the deathbed, solemnly assumes the crown. There's an echo here of his own father's seizure of the crown from Richard II:

> Lo where it sits –
> Which God shall guard; and put the world's whole strength
> Into one giant arm, it shall not force
> This lineal honour from me. This from thee
> Will I to mine leave as 'tis left to me.

4.4.43–7.

There are plenty of parallels here for modern audiences: Napoleon crowning himself, or, more recently, younger contenders in the Labour Party reaching for the leader's crown. I find all this gripping in the extreme, especially as we, the audience, don't know for a second or two whether the King is dead or alive, until he suddenly awakes:

> PRINCE: I never thought to hear you speak again.
> KING: Thy wish was father, Harry, to that thought.
> I stay too long by thee, I weary thee.
> Dost thou so hunger for mine empty chair
> That thou wilt needs invest thee with my honours
> Before thy hour be ripe? O foolish youth!
> Thou seek'st greatness that will overwhelm thee.

4.4.92–8

The momentary disappearance of the crown produces that understandable, bitter, Lear-like outpouring of fatherly wrath, which undoubtedly hastens the King's demise. Hal's reply, which is part sincere, part panicky, is surely also calculating in the best Lancastrian tradition. All along, we've heard him claim that he's following a plan of reform, as if his riotous youth has been a pre-plotted course of political education. I find this 'a likely story'. Hal is also altogether too glib when he tries explaining away his seizure of the crown. He persuades the King, however, by telling him what he wants to hear. But then, instead of any personal reconciliation, we hear the most coldly calculating deathbed advice. A crusade to the Holy Land, which King

Henry himself apparently desperately wanted to make, is now urged on the son as the foreign diversion beloved of all rulers down the ages:

> Therefore, my Harry,
> Be it thy course to busy giddy minds
> With foreign quarrels, that action, hence borne out,
> May waste the memory of the former days.

4.4.213–6

There are no fond farewells. It's politics to the death in the House of Lancaster. Prince Hal, who has been weeping, weeps no more.

There is now a change of power. A new King is in and all the old King's men go in fear for their jobs. The repercussions from such a change, then as now, echo swiftly down the corridors of power. Who'll get what? Who'll keep what? Is it like that in the higher Civil Service today, I wonder? It's at this point that Shakespeare returns to his secondary theme: the education of a prince. The Lord Chief Justice is in the singularly precarious position of having committed Prince Hal to prison earlier in the action for striking a judge (himself) in court. He challenges the newly crowned Henry V to play the father and imagine that his son had struck a judge, thereby flouting the King's own law. Shakespeare shows in Henry's reaction to the Lord Chief Justice's argument that the new King is a new man. Henry shows wisdom, responsibility and balance, not without a slight touch of pleasure at routing his critics, and also that old Lancastrian self-congratulation. He even claims that in the Lord Chief Justice he has found a new father-figure: 'You shall be as a father to my youth'. The finale is the fall-out of the change of power. The Lord Chief Justice, an expected reject, is retained and honoured, whilst Falstaff, the Prince's friend and mentor who vainly expects to gain the world, is cruelly cast off:

FALSTAFF: My king! my Jove! I speak to thee, my heart!
KING: I know thee not, old man.

5.5.47–8

It's a rough end, a wry one, not at all a happy one.

2 HENRY IV
Anthony Quayle

Anthony Quayle played Falstaff in the BBC TV
*Shakespeare productions of 1 and 2 Henry IV.
Although better known amongst my generation for
his film performances, he was the Director of Shakespeare Memorial theatre from 1948–56 and has produced and/or played in most of Shakespeare's plays.*

Have you ever turned on the radio and listened to Prime
Minister's Question Time in the House of Commons? There
is such a ferocious baying and snarling from the opposition
Members of Parliament that you'd think they were about to
spring at the Prime Minister's throat. Have you ever watched
one of the 'demos' in our streets when the extreme Right and
extreme Left manage to come to blows and the long-suffering
police have to act like shock-absorbers in the middle? Worse
still, have you ever been caught in one? If you have, I'm sure you
thought that England was on the brink of civil war. I am glad to
say that you would have been quite wrong. We have a lot of
differences, some of them strongly held, but we still manage to
hang together because of a deep, underlying unity. I don't
exactly know where this unity comes from. Perhaps it is the
result of living together on a small island, or perhaps it comes
from sharing a lot of history. We may take this unity almost for
granted, but it was barely established in the reign of the first
Queen Elizabeth. It was only a 100 years since the end of the
Wars of the Roses when Shakespeare wrote his cycle of history
plays. It was only Queen Elizabeth's grandfather who had put an
end to the civil wars by winning the Battle of Bosworth. The
wars between the great houses of York and Lancaster were as
vivid in the minds of the Elizabethans as the Boer War is in ours.
If you say that that isn't very vivid anymore, I will reply with

> Goodbye, Dolly, I must leave you
> Though it breaks my heart to go.
> Something tells me I am needed
> At the front to fight the foe.

We are still singing, or humming, the songs of the Boer War. Queen Elizabeth's own grasp of the crown was not wholly secure, however much she may have been adored. The great Spanish Armada had been defeated only ten years before this play was written and Essex's rebellion was yet to come. Men still lost their lives through religious persecution. The times were very uncertain and the unity of the country could by no means be taken for granted. It is small wonder that a man like Shakespeare was concerned with order.

Shakespeare was interested most of all in the workings of men's hearts and in this he was a psychologist to rank with Jung and Freud. At the same time, he was endlessly questioning the more abstract problems of government and order. He was particularly interested in the consequences of the breakdown of the relationship between ruler and ruled. Although he never actually states his conclusion, or forces it down our throat, his view is pretty clear. He believed that what we call history springs simply from the nature and actions of powerful individuals and that, if order is destroyed, then chaos will automatically follow. He showed that it took a mighty effort to clean up this chaos. That is roughly the lesson to be learned from the cycle of plays that starts with *Richard II* and ends with *Henry V.* The theme of these plays is the search for order amidst threatening anarchy. The central character is that of England itself, a prostrate England, bleeding to death from self-inflicted wounds.

It is baffling that so little is known about Shakespeare's own life, but hardly a mystery. He must have been a very private man just to write out in longhand his enormous volume of work, let alone conceive and shape it. Scholars go on hunting for clues that might shed light on the identity of the Dark Lady and perhaps, one day, some yellowing, long-forgotten paper will make all clear. Yet Shakespeare had one great love that does not have to be researched as he wore it on his sleeve, or, rather, wrote about it on page after page. This was his love for England. He loved English trees, flowers, rivers, hills, birds and even English weather. Above all, he loved the English people and the lower they came on the social scale, the more he loved them. He has collected some very rich specimens indeed: Henry IV himself, Hal, Hotspur, Falstaff, the ineffectual country justice Shallow and Feeble, the woman's tailor who is not afraid to die in battle:

> a man can die but once; we owe God a death. I'll ne'er bear a base mind. An't be my destiny, so; an't be not, so. No man's too good to serve's Prince; and, let it go which way it will, he that dies this year is quit for the next.

3.2.228–32

These histories are a very ambitious piece of writing, so ambitious in fact that I can think of no other playwright who has attempted it, let alone pulled it off. They present a cross-section of British life from the very top to the very bottom of the social ladder. Shakespeare spreads before us the whole country: king and commoner, churchman and cut-throat, ploughman and pimp. They are all caught in the murderous, wasteful trap of the civil war, which threatens to destroy Shakespeare's beloved country.

Shakespeare's genius reaches out to two extremes: at one extreme are the misty, bloodshot tragedies of *King Lear* and *Macbeth;* at the other are the elegant, enchanting comedies of *As You Like It* and *Twelfth Night. Henry IV,* both parts of it, lies between these two extreme views of life. Although these two plays are shot through with magnificent poetry, they are the nearest that Shakespeare came to realism. Their characters are of ordinary, recognisable human size. Their passions are of a scale, and of a kind, that we can understand only too well today. These two plays represent Shakespeare's heartland. They may not be his greatest plays, but they are my favourites.

Although they are really two halves of one great play, each of them has a very different atmosphere. The landscape of Part One may be blood-spattered, but it is bathed in the sunlight of courage and chivalry. There is also gaiety and confidence in the friendship between Falstaff and Hal. King Henry himself, though sick and troubled, is not yet dying. Shakespeare drains all the sunlight away in Part Two, leaving us a bitter and wintry landscape to look at. The King, more and more estranged from his son, is indeed dying a lingering death. He is tormented by his own past actions and by forebodings about the future. Hal and Falstaff hardly meet throughout the play and, when they do, Falstaff's wit doesn't flow as readily as it used to. He seems to be straining to be funny and his best efforts bring no more than a frosty smile to the Prince's lips. The rebels do not meet an honourable death, as Hotspur did in Part One, but are tricked into dispersing their army, then grabbed and put to death. Disease stalks or scuffles, ratlike, through the play. Death and decay are hovering over all. The whole of the country is diseased and it must get sick to death before it can be restored to health again. *2 Henry IV* is full of comedy and humour, but it is a black, morbid kind of comedy.

The grotesque form of Sir John Falstaff still waddles and rumbles through this landscape of corruption. He's still fertile in wit, still the enemy of law and order and still pricking every balloon of pomposity that comes within his reach. He's therefore still vastly attractive even in his most cynical, and sometimes downright cruel, moments. We can still laugh at him and with him. We can delight in his scheme to fleece Master Robert Shallow, but, increasingly, we are also made aware that Hal must rid himself of this dangerous friend if England is to survive. Falstaff begins to emerge as the figure of Vice from an old morality play, so it is inevitable tht Hal should eventually reject him. To say that the Elizabethans worshipped Queen Elizabeth for providing them with order and stability is hardly an exaggeration. So when Shakespeare looked back into history and came up with a cycle of plays that ended with *Henry V,* it is unthinkable that he, a working playwright whose living depended on the box office, would conceive the young Henry or Hal as anything but an ideal King in the making. Shakespeare was, however, well acquainted with the stores and legends of this ideal King's youth. He had struck the Lord Chief Justice and been friends with all the riff-raff of London. Shakespeare therefore had to show that Hal only went about with the equivalent of the Kray gang in order to fit himself the better for kingship. If he was to govern England, he must get to know all sides of her society. This was easy enough to achieve, but it was much harder to present the inevitable break with Falstaff, for Shakespeare had created in Falstaff one of the most joyous, fascinating characters ever written. He had to hold back the final scene of rejection till the very end of the play, so that his true hero could shine forth, untrammelled and untarnished, in *Henry V.*

When we first meet Falstaff in Part One he seems to be compounded of nothing but wit and good fellowship. He's the most glorious companion you could wish for. He has his faults and failings, but he makes no secret of them. Indeed, he turns them to advantage by making fun of his cowardice, lechery, addiction to drink and tendency to lie. These are all very human failings, so it is easy to forgive him and hard not to love him. There is a great deal of Falstaff in all of us, except the capacity to be so witty. Then slowly, glimpse by glimpse, we are shown a more unappetising side of him. His amusing cynicism imperceptibly hardens into ruthlessness and his comical, harmless bombast turns into dangerous egotism. I think that this process of disenchantment starts at the Battle of Shrewsbury. Men are preparing to face death on both sides of the field for a point of honour. Yet for Falstaff honour is just a word to be joked about. He is brilliantly funny about it, but our laughter begins to curdle. Are the Cenotaph and the man who lies in the Unknown Soldier's grave really that meaningless? Falstaff also does something appalling during the battle itself. He creeps up to the body of Hotspur, makes sure that there is no life left in it and then drives his sword into the dead man's thigh. A moment later he is claiming that he killed Hotspur in single combat. There is something quite dangerous lurking behind the wit, jocularity and Father Christmasish aspect of Falstaff.

When we come to Part Two we find that Falstaff has undergone the same wintry transformation as the rest of the play. His treatment of Mistress Quickly, who obviously dotes on him, is positively mean. He is utterly callous in his treatment of the recruits. His plan to squeeze Justice Shallow between his finger and thumb has a cruel ring to it:

> Well, I'll be acquainted with him if I return; and 't shall go hard but I'll make him a philosopher's two stones to me. If the young dace be a bait for the old pike, I see no reason in the law of nature but I may snap at him. Let time shape, and there an end.
>
> 3.2.308–12

Falstaff is also preoccupied with thoughts of disease and death from his first entrance:

> FALSTAFF: Sirrah, you giant, what says the doctor to my water?
> PAGE: He said, sir, the water itself was a good healthy water; but for the party that owed it, he might have moe disease than he knew for.
>
> 1.2.1–3

He also appears to be lame, for he is soon cursing his gout:

> A pox of this gout! or, a gout of this pox! for one or the other plays the rogue with my great toe. 'Tis no matter if I do halt; I have the wars for my colour, and my pension shall seem the more reasonable. A good wit will make use of anything. I will turn diseases to commodity.
>
> 1.2.228–32

We have an even better insight into Falstaff's mental and physical state later on at the Boar's Head, a kind of tavern-cum-brothel. Doll Tearsheet, the draggled little whore who is the old knight's bedfellow, presumably when he can afford it, says to him:

> Thou whoreson little tidy Bartholomew boar-pig, when wilt thou leave fighting a days and foining a nights, and begin to patch up thine old body for heaven?
>
> 2.4.223

Falstaff replies 'Peace, good Doll! Do not speak like a death's-head; do not bid me remember mind end'. A few moments later he is confessing 'I am old, I am old'. Disease and old age, to which he never gave a thought in the past, have got him in their grip. That giant vitality of his is at last under deadly siege, and he knows it.

Yet it is only towards the very end of the play, when he hears of Hal's succession to the throne, that he finally over-reaches himself:

> I am Fortune's steward. Get on thy boots; we'll ride all night. O sweet Pistol! Away, Bardolph! . . . I know the young King is sick for me. Let us take any man's horses: the laws of England are at my commandment. Blessed are they that have been my friends; and woe to my Lord Chief Justice!

> 5.4.129–37

Riding day and night, stained with travel and sweating with a desire to see his Prince, Falstaff arrives at Westminster just as the newly-crowned King is emerging from the Abbey. Falstaff hails him as his old crony in front of the whole crowd, which includes the Lord Chief Justice. There is only one thing for Hal to say and he says it:

> I know thee not, old man. Fall to thy prayers.
> How ill white hairs become a fool and jester!
> I have long dreamt of such a kind of man,
> So surfeit-swell'd, so old, and so profane;
> But being awak'd, I do despise my dream.

> 5.5.48–52

He then banishes Falstaff, on pain of death, 'Not to come near our person by ten mile'. The royal procession moves on and Falstaff is left, braving it out to the end, inviting his friends to dine with him, though he has no money, and insisting that the newly-crowned King will send for him soon. He must know that he will never be sent for again. The last we see of him is being bundled away to prison by the officers of the Lord Chief Justice. There is nothing for him to do but die and pass into immortality.

Shakespeare's plays may seem to us to have been written a long time ago. Actually, we are only separated from him by some fifteen generations. Has he anything to say in this, one of the most English of all his plays, that is relevant today? I think that there are three things. Firstly, there is the belief that though the order of things must and should change, the change of this order needs to be orderly. Secondly, there is the conviction that, whatever our differences, an underlying unity is our most previous possession. Finally, there is advice that, to retain health and sanity, we must throw out Falstaff's vices but hold fast to his redeeming sense of humour.

HENRY V
Lord Chalfont

Lord Chalfont served in Burma during the Second World War and was Minister of State at the Foreign and Commonwealth Office from 1964–70. He has written and broadcast extensively on foreign and defence policy and has also published in the field of military history. He made most of this programme on location in Northern France.

*H*enry V has always seemed to me to be one of the really great English plays. It depicts a king of England in his historic role as commander-in-chief, organising and planning a great military campaign and then commanding his soldiers personally on the battlefield. But what is more remarkable is Shakespeare's skill through his dialogue in conveying the ebb and flow of a battle and the confusion and fear of soldiers in combat.

Henry was crowned King of England at the age of twenty–five in Westminster Abbey on a cold spring Sunday in 1413. Henry IV, his father, had died in the Abbot's house three weeks earlier, leaving to his son the dangerous inheritance of a bitter and unresolved quarrel with France. It was a quarrel about the vast stretches of French territory which had been acquired for England through the accession to the throne of William of Normandy and then almost entirely lost by the beginning of the fourteenth century. Henry at once determined to renew England's claim to them. He demanded the return of the territories in the south-west and the north of France that had been captured by Edward III. He opened negotiations with the Duke of Burgundy and with the followers of his great rival, the Duke of Orleans, and at the same time he began to make preparations for war. It was at this time that the immature and foppish extravagances of his early days began to give way to a new sense of resolution and patriotism:

> Now all the youth of England are on fire,
> And silken dalliance in the wardrobe lies;
> Now thrive the armourers, and honour's thought
> Reigns solely in the breast of every man;

They sell the pasture now to buy the horse,
Following the mirror of all Christian kings
With winged heels, as English Mercuries.
For now sits Expectation in the air,
And hides a sword from hilts unto the point
With crowns imperial, crowns and coronets,
Promis'd to Harry and his followers

2. Prologue 1–11

From his headquarters at Porchester Castle, Henry began to organise his invasion force with all the tireless attention to detail without which no commander can ever hope for success in battle. Throughout the summer the army had been mobilised – the miners and the gunners, the fletchers and bowyers, the heralds and armourers and all the great royal retinue were now joined by men-at-arms with their axes and their heavy armour, and by the more lightly equipped archers from the villages of England and Wales, armed with the longbow that had made such a fearsome reputation at Crécy and Poitiers. Siege guns came from Bristol and the Tower of London and by the beginning of August, the great army of 8,000 archers and 2,000 men-at-arms was ready to embark. While all these preparations were going on, Henry discovered a plot against his life by the Earl of Cambridge, Lord Scroop, who was the King's Treasurer, and Sir Thomas Grey. He moved with ruthless speed. The three men were tried by a commision under the Earl Marshal and executed within a week. It was afterwards alleged, although it's never been conclusively proved, that the whole assassination plot had been financed by the French. Certainly, when it was discovered, it provided some useful propaganda for Henry's warlike plans. Meanwhile, the soldiers and the ships were being assembled along the Hampshire coast. The King's flagship, *La Trinité Royale*, was off Spithead with the golden crown at its masthead. On 10 August, having prayed in St Paul's Cathedral and incidentally having made his will, Henry went on board. All day the great convoy of ships, 1,500 of them, took up their stations, and on the following day, Sunday, with drums beating and trumpets sounding on the crowded decks, they set off for France.

In the early morning of 14 August 1415 the invasion began when hundreds of small boats began to put the English soldiers ashore, about three miles to the west of the town of Harfleur. The docks of Le Havre have now grown up where the salt flats and the beaches were at the time of the invasion. For the next three days Henry concentrated on consolidating his position and making his tactical plan. On 18 August, he sent the Duke of Clarence over to the high ground to the east of the town and when that had been occupied, he called upon the surrounded garrison to surrender. But by now the garrison of Harfleur, which had numbered no more than 100 men when the English landed, had been substantially reinforced and the fortifications, too, had been improved by the addition of earth-works and moats and great wooden fortified towers called barbicans. The River Lezard, running through the town, had been blocked with chains and great wooden stakes with sharpened ends, rather like the under-water tank obstacles of World War II. Henry was now faced with a difficult tactical problem. He tried sapping and mining, tunnelling under the French defences, but the French countermining was too good. So in the end he hit on the bright idea of bringing up his artillery pieces under the cover of great heavy wooden shields and for over a week the walls of Harfleur were were battered with great stones, some of them weighing over 500 pounds. Eventually, on 17 September, a desperate French sortie from the south-west barbican was defeated. Henry was now able to bring up all his guns and his other siege instruments and he subjected the town to a bombardment which reduced most of its houses and churches to rubble. On the following day he demanded the unconditional surrender of the garrison and he did it in terms which left little doubt of the alternative:

> How yet resolves the Governor of the town?
> This is the latest parle we will admit;
> Therefore to our best mercy give yourselves
> Or, like to men proud of destruction,
> Defy us to our worst; for, as I am a soldier,
> A name that in my thoughts becomes me best,
> If I begin the batt'ry once again,
> I will not leave the half-achieved Harfleur
> Till in her ashes she lie buried.
> The gates of mercy shall be all shut up,
> And the flesh'd soldier, rough and hard of heart,
> In liberty of bloody hand shall range
> With conscience wide as hell, mowing like grass
> Your fresh fair virgins and your flow'ring infants.

3.3.1–14

The keys of Harfleur were handed over to Henry on 22 September in a ceremony which was calculated to inflict the maximum humiliation on the French. With characteristic piety, he gave thanks in the Church of St Martin. Of the 10,000 men who had sailed with him from England, many were now dead of wounds or disease and others were too ill to continue the campaign, so the great design of a march on Paris and then on to Bordeaux seemed out of the question. But Henry was determined not to turn back in spite of all the efforts of his Council of War to persuade him to do so. He decided instead to march north to Calais where the British enclave was established. Right from the beginning of the march, Henry left no doubt about the kind of discipline he expected from his heterogeneous and somewhat battered little army. He issued proclamations reminding them of the severe punishments for rape and looting and especially for sacrilege, for which the punishment was not only hanging but drawing and quartering as well. By the standards of the day Henry moved fast. After six days the army had covered eighty miles, but there were still ninety miles to go to Calais.

Soon after dawn on 13 October, they reached the valley of the Somme. The French had reached there first and established a defence force of 6,000 men covering the ford at Blanche-Taque, exactly where Henry had planned to cross the river. The English were forced to turn east and march inland down the south bank of the river with the French watching them from the other side and so they marched on, cold and hungry, through a countryside that had been stripped of its provisions. They were now a long way from their intended route. On 18 October Henry made a significant tactical decision. When he reached the village of Fouilloy, near Amiens, where the river goes around in a bend, he decided to strike across country to the ford at Voyennes, hoping to reach there before the French who would have to go the long way round. The plan was successful. He crossed the river at the ford and then turned north again towards Calais. But by now the French were across his path and on 20 October three heralds were sent to the King to challenge him to battle, but Henry decided to continue his march to the north, challenging the French in their turn to stand in his way. In fact, the two armies did not meet until 24 October, about sixty miles south of Calais, at the village of Maisoncelles.

It rained all night before the battle. English morale was at a very low ebb. It was at times like this that Henry's own endurance and powers of leadership were displayed at their best. He would walk around the encampment, talking to the soldiers, inspiring them with his own determination to defeat the enemy, renewing their courage and their loyalty, and offering them something which is very precious to a soldier on the eve of battle – the sense that he will not fight and perhaps die in vain, that his exploits will become a part of history:

> This story shall the good man teach his son;
> And Crispin Crispian shall ne'er go by,
> From this day to the ending of the world,
> But we in it shall be remembered –
> We few, we happy few, we band of brothers;
> For he today that sheds his blood with me
> Shall be my brother; be he ne'er so vile
> This day shall gentle his condition;
> And gentleman in England now a-bed
> Shall think themselves accurs'd they were not here,
> And hold their manhoods cheap whiles any speaks
> That fought with us upon Saint Crispin's day.

4.3.56–67

After spending a miserable night in and around the village of Maisoncelles, Henry's army began to take up positions for the battle that was now inevitable. They moved out north of the village towards the ground which the French had chosen for their position between Tramecourt and the village which has to give its name to the battle, Agincourt. The English position was a defensive line, designed to inflict maximum casualties on the French once they had been provoked into attack. It consisted of three detachments of mounted men-at-arms drawn up in four ranks. Henry himself commanded the centre detachment and he positioned on either side of him a wedge-shaped detachment of archers. Outside them were the two other detachments of men-at-arms, the right under the Duke of York and the left under Lord Camoys. On the extreme flanks were two more detachments of archers, this time inclined slightly towards the centre. The English army in all was not more than 6,000 strong. Meanwhile, between the villages of Agincourt and Tramecourt, were the French forces, 20 or 30,000 of them, drawn up in three great phalanxes of men-at-arms, the first two lines were dismounted, with detachments of archers in between. The third line consisted of mounted men-at-arms and on the flanks were smaller detachments of gunners and more mounted men-at-arms.

The ground, although it had been chosen by the French, in fact favoured the English. The French had denied themselves room for manoeuvre by placing themselves between two heavily wooded areas which created a funnel between them and the English, so that even if the French had attacked, their front would have become progressively more congested and confused. They did not, however, attack first. At eleven o' clock, the whole of the British line began to move forward, slowly but firmly, with drums beating and colours flying. They halted about 300 yards from the French lines. The French men-at-arms from the flanks charged the English lines, many of them impaling themselves on the sharpened stakes, thrust into the ground by the English archers. The dismounted men-at-arms turned into line in order to avoid the arrows from the front, but immediately became vulnerable to the bowmen from the flanks. As the gap narrowed, the pace quickened and soon the two armies were locked in hand-to-hand combat. It was ancient battle of the bloodiest kind with men hacking and stabbing and slashing at each other until the piles of dead and dying were packed so high that, according to one historian, they were higher than the heads of the living. For two hours the battle went on and as well as inflicting heavy casualties on the French, the English took a number of prisoners. Meanwhile, the third line, the mounted men-at-arms, had remained in position while the other two lines were now dispersed around the battlefield. At this point Henry made a decision that has been the cause of great controversy amongst historians. Fearing that the third line of French troops might come into the battle and that the dismounted men-at-arms might re-group and come to support them, he thought that the English soldiers would be so obsessed with guarding their prisoners, who were worth a great deal to them in ransom money, that they might be overwhelmed. So he ordered all the prisoners to be killed immediately. The counter-attack, which Henry had expected, never took place. The French lost 10,000 killed, the English casualties were no more than 500. Indeed, some historians say as few as 100.

It had been a glorious triumph for Henry and the archers of England and Wales. The way to Calais now lay open, thanks to divine intervention:

KING: ... O God, thy arm was here!
And not to us, but to thy arm alone,
Ascribe we all. When, without stratagem,
But in plain shock and even play of battle,
Was ever known so great and little loss
On one part and on th'other? Take it, God,

> For it is none but thine
> EXETER: 'Tis wonderful!
> KING: Come, go we in procession to the village:
> And be it death proclaimed through our host
> To boast of this or take that praise from God
> Which is his only.

4.8.104–14

Many historians have clearly shared the view of Henry's own contemporaries that he was a King of great intellectual and moral stature, a noble soldier and a great military commander. Shakespeare and his contemporaries tended to endorse much of this uncritical adulation. In modern times, however, the judgement on Henry has been somewhat cooler. There was something unscrupulous about the way he went on making preparations for war while continuing to negotiate with his French adversaries. His judgement and his tactics at Agincourt were beyond reproach, but much of his success was undoubtedly due to the French choice of a battlefield which handed the tactical initiative to the English. And there are still many people who regard his decision to have the prisoners at Agincourt put to death as the cold-blooded act of a commander who would prefer to order a massacre rather than take a risk in battle. When all this had been said, however, it's success in battle that counts, and there's no doubt that somewhere around 6,000 Englishmen had defeated 30,000 Frenchmen in a pitched battle on French soil. Of course, it can be argued that the battle was in strategic terms irrelevant and that the campaign was, in fact, a failure, but Henry had revived the pride of Englishmen in being English and had by his own example inspired them to believe that there are still values worth fighting for and worth dying for.

Henry V
Robert Hardy

Robert Hardy played Sir Toby Belch in the BBC TV
*Shakespeare production of Twelfth Night. He is an
expert on the longbow, as well as being a Shakespearean, film and television actor.*

The plot of Shakespeare's play is straightforward enough: the
new young King, Henry V – he was twenty five at his accession –
is determined to invade France, and he seeks the financial and
moral backing of his most important subjects. From the church
he gets both, and both from the nobility, too. Having satisfied
himself of the legality of his claim to the French crown, the
Ambassadors from the Dauphin of France are called in. Henry
has already determined on invasion, but he uses the Dauphin's
insulting gift of tennis balls to threaten France with the dreadful
volleys of war. The young Henry was unsure of the loyalty of his
subjects but he hoped the revived idea of a war of conquest
against France would, like the contemplation of death, marvellously concentrate the mind of the nation.

The play is introduced and shaped by the Chorus, not a group
of intoning observers, but really Shakespeare himself, openly
admitting the appalling difficulties of putting on the stage such a
story of war, and danger, and death, and intrigue:

> O for a Muse of fire, that would ascend
> The brightest heaven of invention,
> A kingdom for a stage, princes to act,
> And monarchs to behold the swelling scene!
>
> Prologue 1–4

That was the very opening. After the dismissal of the French
Ambassadors, the Chorus describes the preparations for war –
'Now all the youth of England are on fire'. And so, no doubt, they
were, and not only the youth; large numbers of men-at-arms and
archers in the pay, or worse, out of the pay of their military em-
ployers were making the countryside dangerous. There'd been no
foreign loot, no prisoners' ransoms for a generation, and they were
avid for another go at the old enemy across the Channel. But

. . . three corrupted men –
One, Richard Earl of Cambridge, and the second,
Henry Lord Scroop of Masham, and the third,
Sir Thomas Grey, knight of Northumberland,

2 Prologue 23–6

have conspired to kill the King, all ready to embark with his army at Southampton. The insecurity of Henry's throne is very apparent. Shakespeare sticks closely to history in this episode; Henry confronts the traitors with their guilt, they condemn themselves out of their own mouths, then beg for mercy. Cambridge's letter of confession, and another for clemency can still be read today.

The conspiracy behind him, Henry sets sail for France. He did so in truth in *La Trinité Royale*, with at least 10,000 men in 1500 little ships, on his great expedition to Harfleur. Before we join the fleet, we bid farewell to Falstaff, the Great, the leader of the young Prince astray, the other side of Henry's life. Shakespeare could not let Falstaff survive to mock the gallantry and the pain across the Channel as he mocked the courage of the men who fought at Shrewsbury. Then: away with the fleet to France, where the play leaps straight into the siege of Harfleur. In fact, the fleet anchored offshore for several hours before a landing was attempted, and I love the *immediacy* of this: they were off the *Quai de Caux*, and the lads in the ships soon cockneyed the French name into a London version: 'kidcocks', they called it.

The siege goes badly, as indeed it did, for all Henry's brave rallying:

Once more unto the breach, dear friends, once more;
Or close the wall up with our English dead.

3.1.1–2

One of the most difficult tasks confronting the actor in the whole of the play, that speech. You are in full armour, apparently shouting at thousands – when I did it in Chicago, I was indeed shouting to an audience of 2,500: the speech starts at the top, then you have to change down to first, up to second, to third, to fourth, to overdrive and at the end still have trumpet and clarion left on top thirty three lines with:

Follow your spirit; and upon this charge
Cry 'God for Harry, England, and Saint George!

3.1.33–4

The soldiers – Pistol, Nym, Bardolph and their boy – expose a little of the seamy side of war, when the thunder of the guns and the gleaming chivalry pass on; and then the incomparable Welsh captain, Fluellen, and his English, Scots and Irish fellow soldiers are caught up in the difficulties of siege warfare. Fluellen helps to fill the aching gap left by Falstaff, and remains a wonderfully sharp portrait not only of a Welshman but also of a devoted and professional soldier. Eventually Harfleur falls, and we encounter two aspects of the French court: the delicious Princess Katherine having an English lesson, just in case; and then the French royals and nobles, summoning up their spirits to resist.

The real story of the English march from Harfleur is a grim and gallant one and was long drawn out, and full of hardships and mistakes. Shakespeare whisks us through it in a trice and it is only from Henry's answer to Mountjoy, the French Herald, when the long march is nearly over that we learn anything of the English plight:

> My people are with sickness much enfeebled;
> My numbers lessen'd; and those few I have
> Almost no better than so many French;

3.6.140–2

Then we are close to a little village called Agincourt. We see the high spirits of the French, and the awful plight of the English – a little 6,000 against the might of a whole nation.

The night before the battle, Henry goes among his army, in disguise, gets into an awkward altercation with some soldiers, is left alone, prays for victory against insupportable odds, and goes off to arm for the battle. Shakespeare's version of it includes carnage, cruelty, hysteria, comedy, pathos and horror. He writes of war as one who must have known it, of armies as one who seems to have been in them.

The Chorus wafts us through time and space, from Agincourt, to Calais, to London and back again to France. The main business of the end of the play is to think about treaties, and peace, marriage. Henry will wed the lovely Kate, the French King's daughter, or know the reason why: 'Yet leave our cousin Katherine here with us; She is our capital demand . . .'. 'She hath good leave', says her mother, who could hardly say anything else, things being as they are. At the end, all is sweetness and light – or is it? This is from the last speech of the Chorus:

Small time, but, in that small, most greatly lived
This star of England. Fortune made his sword;
By which the world's best garden he achieved,
And of it left his son imperial lord.
Henry the Sixth, in infant bands crown'd king
Of France and England, did this king succeed;
Whose state so many had the managing
That they lost France and made his England bleed;

5–12

Henry's conquests came to nothing within a few years; his dynasty ended in a saintly, useless son; his nation fell into the horrors of an appalling civil war. He got, as some are pleased to recall, his come-uppance!

The play has come in for a lot of criticism over the years, and many people writing about it or simply reacting to it, for generations now have called it a dismissable piece of chauvinism, a charade of militarist patriotism. They have also said that as the third part of the Hal trilogy, it founders. Indeed, coming after both parts of *Henry IV*, the two great panoramas of English life, low and high, and the wonderfully subtle portrait of a rakehell youth progressing towards kingship, the gear is changed. But the changing of a man into a king requires a gear-change; it is inevitable. The forces acting on him are different; his stance must be a different one. I believe there is nothing in the character of Henry that isn't presaged in Hal, and that Henry the King is both a likely and an accurate outcome of the promises in the preceding plays. You may or may not *like* the result, but it is the *true* result.

'Day after day we are witnessing the building of a nation's unity', said the BBC's Teheran correspondent from among the banners and shouting there on 29 November 1979. That building of a nation's unity, out of the chaos of rebellion and civil war, was exactly what the real Henry was after, and a hell of a task he set himself. We may quite properly judge his motives and his actions now, but it is silly to let disappointment, if we find Henry less than an ideal leader, warp our judgement either of the historical King, or Shakespeare's picture of him.

The Prince turned to us in *I Henry IV* and revealed his attitude to the world and the values of Falstaff and Poins and their companions:

I know you all, and will awhile uphold
The unyok'd humour of your idleness;
Yet herein will I imitate the sun,

And he went on:

> And, like bright metal on a sullen ground,
> My reformation, glitt'ring o'er my fault,
> Shall show more goodly and attract more eyes
> Than that which hath no foil to set it off.
> I'll so offend to make offence a skill,
> Redeeming time when men think least I will.

1.2.188–210

The boy who said that becomes the man who plans the invasion of France before the Ambassadors have delivered their scornful insult. And that early Hal becomes the King who sends the traitors, after he has tricked them into condemning themselves out of their own mouths, to their deaths. In any case, what possible hope is there for a leader who is not ruthless with traitors?

> old Jack Falstaff – banish not him thy Harry's company, banish not him thy Harry's company. Banish plump Jack, and banish all the world

cries Falstaff at the Boar's Head. Hal, *playing* at being King, replies with chilling accuracy 'I do, I will'. And yet we worry when he does as he promised. And we worry when he gives the order at Agincourt to kill the prisoners. But it's worth remembering that no contemporary voice, either French or English, was raised against that action. It is we who deplore it. The values and attitudes were a great deal harder in the late Middle Ages, *and* in the age of Elizabeth, than they are today. And, in any case, is cruelty gone from the world today – butchery and inhumanity in the name of some *right* or other? Shakespeare shows us a man who grew to power and becomes a successful leader; he does not take up a moral posture.

Did Shakespeare admire the man whose portrait he painted so clearly? In many ways, I think he did, and was able to put in his mouth some of the best patriotic and warlike exhortations ever written. But he also saw the other, darker side, as he had, quite clearly, ever since he started to create the young Hal. Incidentally, Hal was very much Shakespeare's creation. He had little else to go on but legends of Henry's riotous youth. The real young Prince was a hardened sailor by the time he was sixteen, conducting his father's campaigns against the Welsh, and writing clear and precise despatches back to London. In one of them, after defeating a larger force than his own, he wrote: 'It is well seen that victory does not lie in the multitude of people, but in the power of God'. Shakespeare may or may not have read that despatch – he got the man right, though! In between the gruelling times of action in those border wars, it's highly likely that Hal drank and drabbed and let off steam. Think of the prayer of young St Augustine: 'O God, give me purity and continence, but not yet'. Shakespeare's genius in the two Hal plays was to show all the sides of the developing man. One side leaned to the delights and temptations that are Falstaff – that side must be eliminated in the end; another side rebelled against the authority of his father, and against his own future; another side showed real sorrow at his father's illness, genuine grief at his death; another showed his icy determination to turn himself into a great leader of men.

Yet another side of Henry's character which comes out more strongly in *Henry V* than in the earlier plays is his devout belief in his God and his Destiny. When still Prince, it was once his duty in 1410 to attend at Smithfield the burning to death in a barrel of a man condemned for religious heresy, a tailor called John Badby. When Henry heard the piteous cries from the fire, he ordered the half-burnt creature to be removed, and promised him pardon and a life pension if he would recant. With incredible courage, Badby refused the offer. Henry displaying his own courage and convictions ordered the fearsome execution to go on. A Frenchman, Jean Fusoris, meeting Henry for the first time in Winchester in 1415, said afterwards of Henry 'though he had a lordly manner and a fine appearance, he seemed to be more suited to the church than to war'.

This was the man with whom Shakespeare had to deal. He also had to show a man who *could* lead his army from Harfleur to Agincourt against appalling ill chances and the gravest dangers, and keep that army as it were moulded, in his hand. The real man did it. Shakespeare shows us how, like other great leaders in times of war, he can raise his men's spirits, and defy all dangers, even when his soul is in torment:

> Not to-day, O Lord,
> O, not to-day, think not upon the fault
> My father made in compassing the crown

4.1.288–90

he cries in anguish on his knees, alone in the night, before battle. And then, within an hour or two before his army:

> This day is call'd the feast of Crispian.
> He that outlives this day, and comes safe home,
> Will stand a tip-toe when this day is nam'd,
> And rouse him at the name of Crispian.

4.3.40–3

There are two crucial scenes I'd like to glance at, because to me they're proof positive that *Henry V* is a worthy, indeed the right and logical third play of a trilogy, and a trilogy which hangs wonderfully together. The first is the night scene, when Henry goes among his army in disguise. Incidentally, there's no absolute proof he did go, on the night before Agincourt, among his men camped about the orchards and paddocks of Maison-celles in the pouring rain; but it *is* extremely likely. It was his general practice at Harfleur, and years later on those long, arduous campaigns that led to his death. The soldier Williams, whom I always think of as being, like Fluellen, a Welshman, thinking Henry is a man in Sir Thomas Erpingham's company, asks him what his commander thinks of their chances. Henry replies 'Even as men wreck'd upon a sand, that look to be wash'd off the next tide'. Another soldier, Bates, says 'He hath not told his thought to the King':

> HENRY: No; nor it is meet he should. For though I speak it to you, I think the King is but a man as I am: the violet smells to him as it doth to me; . . . his ceremonies laid by, in his nakedness he appears but a man. . . . Therefore, when he sees reason of fears, as we do, his fears, out of doubt, be of the same relish as ours are; yet, in reason, no man should possess him with any appearance of fear, lest he, by showing it, should dishearten his army.
>
> BATES: He may show what outward courage he will; but I believe, as cold a night as 'tis, he could wish himself in Thames up to the neck; and so I would he were, and I by him, at all adventures, so we were quit here.

4.1.99–116

Henry replies that 'methinks I could not die anywhere so con-tented as in the King's company, his cause being just and his quarrel honourable', but Williams responds

> But if the cause be not good, the King himself hath a heavy reckoning to make when all those legs and arms and heads, chopp'd off in a battle, shall join together at the latter day and cry all 'We died at such a place'–

Henry has to reply and put a good face on it:

> So, if a son that is by his father sent about merchandise do sin-fully miscarry upon the sea, the imputation of his wickedness, by your rule, should be imposed upon his father that sent him; . . .

and he goes on, after pressing that point, arguing very speciously, and when he stops, Williams says' 'Tis certain, every man that dies ill, the ill upon his own head – the King is not to answer for it'. Henry breathes a sigh of relief. His sleight of mind is not taken up by these honest straightforward men, though a nasty argument develops on another point and Williams and the King give and take up a witnessed challenge to fight, when the French quarrels are over, which emerges later in the play.

Thus far, Shakespeare exposes Henry to the most ordinary fears and doubts of his men, and Henry cannot honestly answer them; he bluffs his way out, and there is exposed the weakness of the man in power. He has changed the point of the argument and left *us* wondering if we have not witnessed a killing weakness in a hero. I say hero, because that is what the objectors always say – this man is presented as a hero and look, he has feet of clay. Shakespeare doesn't present a hero; he presents Henry V without judging him, and leaves it to us, to be the judges. Henry, then is left alone, and speaks, in soliloquy, an almost Hamlet-like, bitter series of thoughts about the *fact* of kingship of leadership:

> Upon the King! Let us our lives, our souls,
> Our debts, our careful wives,
> Our children, and our sins, lay on the King!
> We must bear all. . . .
>   What infinite heart's ease
> Must kings neglect that private men enjoy!
> And what have kings that privates have not too,
> Save ceremony – save general ceremony?
> And what art thou, thou idol Ceremony?
> . . .
> 'Tis not the balm, the sceptre, and the ball,
> The sword, the mace, the crown imperial,
> The intertissued robe of gold and pearl,
> The farced title running fore the king,
> The throne he sits on, nor the tide of pomp
> That beats upon the high shore of this world –
> No, not all these, thrice gorgeous ceremony,
> Not all these, laid in bed majestical,
> Can sleep so soundly as the wretched slave
> Who, with a body fill'd and vacant mind,
> Gets him to rest, cramm'd with distressful bread;

> . . . but in gross brain little wots
> What watch the king keeps to maintain the peace
> Whose hours the peasant best advantages.

4.1.226–80

Critics have been swift to seize on that *cri du coeur* about *peace*, when the crier is intent upon a bloody war of conquest. Their answer lies about us: out of peace comes war, out of war peace – that is the shape of *all* history, in all lands, until we learn better; until we want to find out follow leaders towards real peace, who have the sort of charismatic appeal that has until now only seemed to appear in the gravest crises of internal or external WAR. It can be argued that the real Henry as well as being the last of the great medieval Paladins, was also ahead of his time, in looking towards a united Christian Europe to stand against the Infidel. You will recall that the present battle cry in Islam is 'Stand together against the Infidel!'. It must be admitted that this vision of Henry's did assume that England, and Henry, would lead that united Christendom.

The other scene which has come in for a good deal of battering is the wooing scene: 'Henry is no more than a coarse boor!' they say. 'He's a schoolboy athlete with great big initials on his chest!' My advice is to look at the care with which the playwright gets exactly the degree to which Henry play-acts knowingly before the girl he woos. There's a particular *Englishness* in the way he plays himself down, even mocks himself – but his purpose is quite clear – it's to excite her interest in what he really is. He's a man who knows exactly what he's doing:

> I'faith, Kate, my wooing is fit for thy understanding: I am glad thou can'st speak no better English; for if thou couldst, thou wouldst find me such a plain king that thou wouldst think I had sold my farm to buy my crown. I know no ways to mince it in love, but directly to say 'I love you'. Then, if you urge me farther than to say 'Do you in faith?' I wear out my suit.

5.2.121–7

Certainly there is *double-entendre*, and bawdy, in what he says:

> If I could win a lady at leap-frog, or by vaulting into my saddle with my armour on my back, under the correction of bragging be it spoken, I should quickly leap into a wife.

5.2.135

But that also harks back to the picture of the Renaissance prince described by an enemy in *1 Henry IV*:

I saw young Harry with his beaver on,
His cushes on his thighs, gallantly arm'd,
Rise from the ground like feathered Mercury,
And vaulted with such ease into his seat
As if an angel dropp'd down from the clouds
To turn and wind fiery Pegasus,
. . .
4.1.104–9

That was the Prince, and *is* the King, who in truth could out-run a buck on his own two legs, could play the lute, and write songs, and despatches full of observation from the battlefield, and who was also the first English king to issue all his army ordinances in *English* rather than Norman French! And of course he leans on his position of the moment as conqueror:

No, it is not possible you should love the enemy of France,
Kate, but in loving me you should love the friend of France;
For I love France so well that I will not part with a village
of it; I will have it all mine. And, Kate, when France is
mine and I am yours, then yours is France and you are mine.
5.2.169–73

How the audiences at the Globe must have loved that. France was still the old enemy 400 years later in the Crimea, when France was our ally and Russia the enemy, our commander-in-chief, Lord Raglan, kept talking of the enemy as 'the French', even to the French. It was a very long, old enmity, France and England – not like today!

Have we arrived anywhere? It's only been a cursory glance at this and that, but I've arrived where each acting of the play, confirms or reaffirms that *Henry V* can be interpreted in many different ways, just as any episode in history. Yesterday's great achievement becomes today's shoddy deception, perhaps tomorrow's glory again. Yesterday's great leader is soon thrown down and judged a villain, perhaps one day to be re-pedestalled. I've seen the play done boorishly, subtly, as a patriotic extravaganza, and a strongly anti-war play. All the elements are there; it is as broad as life itself because the playwright saw life whole, and in the round. Here is a play which tells us of a nation in its youth, a nation full of inconsistencies, led by a unique man, who stood for centuries as the archetypal English hero, who for many years has been attacked as no hero. But try not to be prejudiced either way – because Shakespeare wasn't. He looked at the man, and at history, in the chronicles that he read (and don't forget he only wrote about 180 years after Henry's death, and we're judging it nearly 400 years after that) and he looked at *war*, and at our nations and there they all are for us to see. And watch how Shakespeare puts his finger on the very pulse of leadership, knowing that men will only follow a leader who can be ruthless, and yet whose common touch will melt their hearts:

O, now, who will behold
The royal captain of this ruin'd band
Walking from watch to watch, from tent to tent,
Let him cry 'Praise and glory on his head!'
For forth he goes and visits all his host;
Bids them good morrow with a modest smile,
And calls them brothers, friends, and countrymen.
. . .
A largess universal, like the sun,
His liberal eye doth give to every one,
Thawing cold fear, that mean and gentle all
Behold, as may unworthiness define,
A little touch of Harry in the night.

4 Prologue 28–47

TWELFTH NIGHT
David Jones

David Jones was Editor of BBC TV's Monitor *programme, before becoming an Associate Director with the Royal Shakespeare Company. He made this programme at Packwood House.*

Peter Brook starts his famous book *The Empty Space* with this remark: 'I can take any empty space and call it a bare stage'. And by definition you can take any bare stage and move it on to become exactly the place you want it to be. In a few days' time I start rehearsal at The Other Place in Stratford-upon-Avon for an early play of Brecht's called *Baal*. It's got to have twenty-one scenes ranging from sleazy little brown bars to the wind and the rain of the Black Forest and we'll be doing it with an absolute minimum of scenery. Any act of theatre really has to be that kind of collaboration between the imagination of the people who make it and the people who are coming to watch it. *Twelfth Night* begins in what is sometimes called Orsino's palace. What do you need? A candelabra, a chair, music and the play can begin. The heroine, Viola, is shipwrecked on a strange shore in the second scene of the play. Add the sound of waves, bring your characters on out of the darkness, salt-stained and weary, and Shakespeare's words will do the rest:

> VIOLA: What country, friends, is this?
> CAPTAIN: This is Illyria, lady.
> VIOLA: And what should I do in Illyria?
>   My brother he is in Elysium.

1.2.1–4

Well, you won't find Illyria in the atlas, although there are some scholars who like to say that it's Yugoslavia. In a sense Illyria's simply a country of the mind, it's a charmed, timeless land where an anthology of lovers can pursue their passions without any kind of interference from real life. But somehow the story doesn't feel at all escapist. Partly because, like all good fantasies, Shakespeare's has a great deal of concrete detail built into it. Viola's arrival in Illyria is a little bit like Alice in Wonderland.

Aguecheek, Feste, and Belch are certainly unpredictable and fantastic characters, but they're as solidly there as the Mad Hatter or the White Rabbit are to Alice. Shakespeare, in fact, had been a good deal bolder than that. Having set off with the lyric keynote in the first two scenes, he moves us on into the world of Olivia's household where most of the play is going to take place. And there we're in for a surprise because what we find, in full documentary detail, is the life and atmosphere of an Elizabethan country house.

Twelfth Night was written in 1601. In one way you can see it as a celebration of the golden days of the Elizabethan country house, but behind that celebration there's always a sense that somehow those days are numbered. With all the leisure in the world to enjoy their loves and their jokes and their revenges, the characters in the play are still obsessed with time. They're surrounded by clocks, sundials and watches, all of which 'upbraid them with the waste of time'. Beauty, Shakespeare seems to be saying in the play, only lasts for a very short time, lives can easily remain unfulfilled and joy is often mixed with sadness:

> What is love? 'Tis not hereafter;
> Present mirth hath present laughter;
>   What's to come is still unsure.
> In delay there lies no plenty,
> Then come kiss me, sweet and twenty;
>   Youth's a stuff will not endure.

> 2.3.46–51

Shakespeare was never a scenic photographer. He wrote for bare boards and the minimum of scenery. Each play in a sense carries unspoken that request by the Prologue to *Henry V* for the audience to use their 'imaginary forces'. But I think it's fair to suppose that Shakespeare's own imagination, as well as that of his audience, would have continually referred back to something as English as country houses while he was building up the world of Olivia's household.

Now that's a very formal world where everybody knows, or at least ought to know, their exact position and the flow of the comedy should not blind us to the fact of just how rigid that social framework was, every bit as rigid, for instance, as the social ladder in *Upstairs Downstairs*. You'll remember that Olivia, the mistress of the house, has lost both her father and her brother within a year just before the play begins. Her excessive grief is a kind of mirror to Orsino's excessive passion. She falls in love with the idea of mourning just as he's fallen in love with the idea of being in love. She decides she's going to lock herself away in the house for the next seven years, but even if she wasn't obsessed with grief, she'd expect the running of that house to be totally organised for her. What we see is a very efficient domestic machine designed to ensure elegant living and leave her all the time in the world to pursue her own emotional life. Maria would be Olivia's personal waiting gentlewomen. She'd look after the bedroom and Olivia's wardrobe, as well as carrying out a lot of the duties which later on in Victorian times we'd associate with the lady companion. Fabian's job is never really specified in the play, but it seems to have something to do with outside the house. Perhaps he was the head groom or the master of the stables before Malvolio brought him out of favour.

The role of Feste is perhaps a little bit more foreign to us as he was the household jester, a form of living-in home entertainment long before the days of television. He would be expected to be able to tell stories, sing songs, make jokes and it is interesting that he would be allowed to sail really close to the wind in his efforts to lift the bad moods of his employer:

CLOWN: The lady bade take away the fool; therefore, I say again, take her away.

OLIVIA: Sir, I bade them take away you.

CLOWN: Misprison in the highest degree! . . . Good madonna, give me leave to prove you a fool.

OLIVIA: Can you do it?

CLOWN: Dexteriously, good madonna.

OLIVIA: Make your proof.

CLOWN: I must catechize you for it, madonna. Good my mouse of virtue, answer me.

OLIVIA: Well, sir, for want of other idleness, I'll bide your proof.

CLOWN: Good madonna, why mourn'st thou?

OLIVIA: Good fool, for my brother's death.

CLOWN: I think his soul is in hell, madonna.

OLIVIA: I know his soul is in heaven, fool.

CLOWN: The more fool, madonna, to mourn for your brother's soul being in heaven. Take away the fool, gentlemen.

1.5.48–66

The family jester was beginning to disappear from the Elizabethan house by around 1600. It's significant that there's a lot of talk in the play of Feste being turned away. Probably he's only kept on because he was a particular favourite of Olivia's father.

His position in the household would have been a humble one. When he wasn't required to entertain in the Big Hall, he probably wouldn't aspire above the kitchen. But he's got a really sharp professional pride as a comic, which never forgets Malvolio's taunt that he is a 'barren rascal'.

We're all familiar with dependent relatives forming a permanent part of the household in the way that Sir Toby does. He's of a rank with Olivia and could live quite peaceably in his own wing of the house without interfering with her life. But, alas, like other dependent relatives, he has unfortunate habits. He thinks that he can run the house himself, keeps late hours, invites cronies for unlimited stays and is always hobnobbing with the servants as drinking companions. Generally, he's spreading anarchy wherever he goes. His attitude to life is quite clear from his first appearance:

> SIR TOBY: What a plague means my niece to take the death of her brother thus? I am sure care's an enemy to life.
> MARIA: By my troth, Sir Toby, you must come in earlier o' nights; your cousin, my lady, takes great exceptions to your ill hours.
> SIR TOBY: Why, let her except before excepted.
> MARIA: Ay, but you must confine yourself within the modest limits of order.
> SIR TOBY: Confine! I'll confine myself no finer than I am. These clothes are good enough to drink in, and so be these boots too; an they are not, let them hang themselves in their own straps.

1.3.1–13

Incidentally, the knighthoods of Sir Toby and Sir Andrew don't bear quite the weight they would nowadays. It was very easy to purchase a knighthood or simply to adopt it without much question. To be called 'sir' simply meant that you were a gentleman. As one contemporary observer drily comments:

> Whosoever shall live idly and without manual labour and will bear the port, charge and countenance of a gentleman, he shall be called master.

Significantly, Fabian, Feste and Sir Toby all know that their positions are threatened by the most important person in this household and that's the steward, Malvolio. His responsibilities would have been very wide-ranging. He's a kind of mixture of estate manager, head butler and bailiff all rolled into one. He'd be responsible for all the domestic arrangements in the house, for keeping the accounts and for the hiring and the payment of servants. He could fire them too, once he got the ear of his mistress, Olivia, as to their unsuitability. Malvolio is really into business efficiency in a big way. He's got an absolute passion for neatness, order and decorum. If he had his way, there'd be no more parties in the world, the drinks cupboard would be always locked tight, subversive employees like Feste would be given their cards and all sponging relatives sent packing. It's the conflict between Malvolio and the lesser servants, 'the lighter people' as he likes to call them, who gang up with Sir Toby, that provides one of the liveliest strands of the play. War is declared very early on when Malvolio bursts into the kichen to break up a late-night drinking party:

> My masters, are you mad? Or what are you? Have you no wit, manners, nor honesty, but to gabble like tinkers at this time of night? Do ye make an ale-house of my lady's house, that ye squeak out your coziers' catches without any mitigation or remorse of voice? Is there no respect of place, persons, nor time, in you?

2.3.85–9

Two philosophies of life are in open conflict here: the wild against the prim, the cavalier in its widest sense against the puritan principle. In all his comedies Shakespeare, however lightly, deals with the question of what's the best way to live and in this play there's no doubt that for most of the time the cakes-and-ale boys carry the day. Perhaps it's in that that we can find the secret to the riddle of the play's title, because Twelfth Night was traditionally the final fling of the Christmas festivities, a last chance for celebration and excess before returning to the sober working pattern of the year. The figure of the Lord of Misrule was closely associated with these festivities. He was a kind of anarchical figure who was allowed to flout all authority publicly, to invade churches and to indulge in excesses of eating and drinking. So the success of the plot against Malvolio in a sense is the victory of misrule, idleness and folly against the imposing figure of virtue and authority which is Malvolio. Mind you, Shakespeare's pretty certain that he wants our sympathies to be on the side of the unruly. It's hard to feel a lot for Malvolio when he's so busy in his denigration of the domestic staff to Olivia. He's always treating Maria like a kitchen servant and he kicks Fabian out for bear-baiting. He claims that Feste is no good at all at jokes, the ultimate insult, and it's pretty certain that he delivers a daily list to Olivia of Toby's drinking habits and exactly what he had the night before. So it's really no surprise when this lot decide to band together and make Malvolio himself ultimately ridiculous in Olivia's eyes. The way they decide to do this is by persuading him that his mistress is in love with him. Shakespeare points out that what's really open to mockery is not the puritan side of him but the lunatic scale of his ambition, the fact that he has such a high opinion of himself.

There's a sense of carnival confusion at the heart of the serious love plot of the play as well. Orsino imagines that he's in love with Olivia, although he doesn't really know her at all well. Olivia falls in love with Viola, not realising that, in fact, she's a girl disguised as a boy. Viola, disguised as a boy, can't tell Orsino she's in love with him or explain to Olivia why it is that she can't love her. It's all rather like the comic misunderstandings of a masked ball, but there are no masks in this play, simply the blindness of love which makes the characters comically incapable of seeing what's sitting there under their own noses. You can see the play, too, in a sense of Shakespeare's own personal Twelfth Night. It's his farewell to festive comedy, to the world of high spirits and of happiness. Soon he's going to be moving on to other things, to the bitterness of the cynicism of his problem comedies and then on into the darkness of the great tragedies. Malvolio's final cry of 'I'll be reveng'd on the whole pack of you' casts an even longer shadow over the play as it is going to have its answer forty years down the line when the Puritans come to power in England and every theatre in London is shut down. But Malvolio's behaviour isn't unique within the world of the play. His part of the story certainly gets pushed out to farcical limits, but it still remains a kind of comic mirror for what you could call the more serious side of the play. Now there we've got two characters, Orsino and Olivia, who, like Malvolio, are very fond of their own performance. Like him, they're absolutely deluded as to the object of their love and so passionate in its pursuit that they come near to the borders of sanity. They, too, have been touched with midsummer madness just like Malvolio. For Olivia, falling in love has been like catching the plague. For Orsino, his desires savage him like a pack of hunting dogs that have caught a deer. You've got to remember that both these two are really great self-dramatisers. The more Orsino talks about the size of his passion, the less he talks about the girl he's supposed to be in love with. All his talk of love is in terms of taking, of insatiable appetite, but you get the feeling that what he really wants is to be left on his own, hugging his fantasy of an unobtainable mistress. It's a familiar emotional pattern and not just in adolescence. It's one that Shakespeare knows inside out and he outlines it for us with deadly precision.

Now Olivia's more touching in her delusions than Orsino. At least she deals with the object of her passion face to face. But she, too, is a great role-player. We see her first as the 'sad little mourner', then it's the 'coquette playing hard to get', then it's the 'girl breathlessly in love'. She's a lot more vulnerable and more seductively insistent in her love suit than Orsino, but every bit as blind. She just can't see that that beloved page is a girl disguised as a boy. 'Poor lady', says Viola, 'she were better love a dream'. It's the kind of riddling confusion that Shakespeare really enjoys. And centrally, of course, there's Viola herself who throughout the play, hiding behind the disguise she has as a boy, watches Orsino with patience, understanding and an ever-increasing love. This love of hers is probably the truest and the deepest thing in the play because it knows that it can't expect any reward and it doesn't ask for any either:

> A blank, my lord. She never told her love,
> But let concealment, like a worm i' th' bud,
> Feed on her damask cheek. She pin'd in thought;
> And with a green and yellow melancholy
> She sat like Patience on a monument,
> Smiling at grief. Was not this love indeed?
> We men may say more, swear more, but indeed
> Our shows are more than will; for still we prove
> Much in our vows, but little in our love.

2.4.109–17

The discovery of the true nature of love is one of the vital themes of Shakespearean comedy. He takes his characters on a journey towards emotional maturity and a real discovery of relationships that deserve to be crowned with marriage. The women always lead the way.

Why is *Twelfth Night* the best loved and perhaps the most often performed of all Shakespeare's comedies? It's got tremendous comic energy and it's full of fun and high spirits that are shared with the audience. But I think there's something more elusive about its quality, something more haunting. It's a bittersweet feeling that is summed up in that phrase of Viola's 'smiling at grief'. Chekhov said of the characters in his comedies that they ought to be played as if they were laughing through tears, 'and I don't mean that literally', he added. And in that sense *Twelfth Night* is a deeply Chekhovian play. Yes, it is golden and festive. There's plenty of sunlight in it and 'matter for a May morning'. But, at the same time, underneath all that there's always an undertow of unrequited love, of old injuries, of jobs lost and dignities about to be destroyed. Like the sound of the sea outside that country of Illyria, always reminding us of the real world, these moments of shadow also tell us that life can't be all joy and fulfilment. They add a very real dimension to what could be the easy fantasies of a comic world. Their spirit is summed up in the character of Feste, wry, impenetrable, sharp as a knife. He's the outsider to whom Shakespeare gives the last moments of his play while everyone else goes off to enjoy their newfound happiness:

> But when I came to man's estate,
>> With hey, ho, the wind and the rain,
> 'Gainst knaves and thieves men shut their gate,
>> For the rain it raineth every day.

5.1.379–82

TWELFTH NIGHT
Dorothy Tutin

Dorothy Tutin's Shakespearean roles, apart from Viola in Twelfth Night, *include Juliet, Ophelia, Portia, Rosalind and Cleopatra.*

It's surprising how difficult it is to talk about a play which one has appeared in and loved so much. Shakespeare probably wrote *Twelfth Night* in 1601. It comes after the histories and comedies such as *Much Ado About Nothing* and *As You Like It*, but just before the great tragedies. It was probably a commissioned play to be performed at court on Twelfth Night itself, but there's no reference in the play to the Feast of Twelfth Night so perhaps the alternative title of 'What You Will' is just as relevant. When I was at school, I enjoyed Shakespeare's histories and loved the tragedies but I simply couldn't understand *Twelfth Night.* I expect I thought it rather silly. I didn't even know that it was about love, as my idea of that emotional state was so adolescent and intense that I couldn't see the wit and the skill with which it was reflected in perhaps the most loving and lovely play Shakespeare every wrote. But having acted in Peter Hall's production of the play at Stratford in 1958 and now coming to it again for this talk, I'm still amazed by its wit, wisdom and compassion. I'm fascinated by its music, not just the songs, but by its whole form and construction. It seems to me like a concerto for perfectly assorted characters all playing their own tunes, not necessarily to the right person. There is an endless variety of tone and pace, which is finally resolved into a most brilliant collective coda. The play is so well constructed you could hardly cut a line. The characters are exquisitely balanced and the juxtaposition of scenes move the story on a seemingly effortless groundswell of human contradictions.

The principal subject is stated immediately: Love. The Duke Orsino, who perhaps ought to be played as a youthful poet, is in love with love and in love with words. He can thus say the most beautiful, but not necessarily the most sensible, things in the play with a passion and intensity of language which gets matters off to a very good start. He also tells us a good deal about two of the main characters. He is in love with the Countess Olivia, who is in love with grief and determined to mourn an excessively long time for her brother's death. Then Viola comes into this hothouse of fastidious and extreme emotion. She's shipwrecked, destitute and a realist. She takes refuge in the Duke's court and, disguising herself as a boy and calling herself Cesario, gains the Duke's confidence and is used by him as a sort of go-between to deliver his declaration of love to Olivia. Unfortunately, Viola has fallen in love with Duke Orsino, 'a barful strife!/ Who'er I woo, myself would be his wife'. When pressing Orsino's suit to Olivia, Viola reveals something of her own passions, which immensely excites Olivia, who immediately falls in love with Cesario-Viola. That's the triangle of emotion that runs through the play: Orsino loves Olivia, Olivia loves Viola and Viola loves Orsino, even though she can't tell him.

We are then introduced to the older but no less excessive characters, such as Sir Toby Belch, Olivia's uncle, who's like one of those guests that settle in and never leave, a heavy drinking gentleman and lover of jests and japes. Then there's Sir Andrew Aguecheek, a highly unlikely suitor to Olivia, who is foolish to the point of being a danger to himself and others. They are both in a precarious and transitory position in Olivia's household. Feste the clown is also in fear of his livelihood. He's conscious of everything that is happening, perhaps too clever to be funny, a shrewd and bitter thread in the play's tapestry. The one seemingly impregnable character in Olivia's household is the steward, Malvolio, who knows his place and wishes others knew theirs. He's self-satisfied, arrogant, self-regarding, pompous and humourless. The exposition of situation and character is extraordinarily swiftly completed by Shakespeare and the ground is economically laid for the numerous misunderstandings and complications that arise. Let's take Malvolio for a moment. His self-righteousness and pomposity become so tiresome to the other members of Olivia's household that they decide to play a trick on him. Goaded on by Maria, Olivia's maid, they write a letter which looks as though it was written by Olivia herself. It insinuates that Olivia is in love with Malvolio. He's naturally thrilled to think that he's got the chance of a wife way above his station. One day he might even become Count Malvolio. Whilst Sir Toby and company remain hidden behind box-trees in Olivia's garden to see the effect of their trick, Malvolio reads the letter and acts upon it:

I will be proud. I will read politic authors, I will baffle Sir Toby, I will wash off gross acquaintance, I will be point-devise the very man. I do not now fool myself to let imagination jade me; for every reason excites to this, that my lady loves me. She did commend my yellow stockings of late, she did praise my leg being cross-garter'd; and in this she manifests herself to my love, and with a kind of injunction drives me to these habits of her liking. I thank my stars I am happy. I will be strange, stout, in yellow stockings, and cross-garter'd, even with the swiftness of putting on. Jove and my stars be praised! Here is yet a postscript.

'Thou canst not choose but know who I am. If thou enter-tain'st my love, let it appear in thy smiling; thy smiles become thee well. Therefore in my presence still smile, dear my sweet, I prithee.'
Jove, I thank thee. I will smile; I will do everything that thou wilt have me.

2.5.142–60

Malvolio isn't the only one deceived. Everyone, it seems, is part of a deception in the play at some time or another. Even towards the end Viola's brother, Sebastian, who was also shipwrecked, appears and is immediately mistaken by Olivia for Cesario. She takes him into her house – to his great delight and surprise! The dénouement, of which this is a part, is a marvel. One after another, all the protagonists appear on stage until suddenly there is the exquisite moment when the brother and sister, Sebastian and Viola, meet one another much to the amazement of the others. 'Most Wonderful!' says Olivia, seeing two of a good thing! This discovery is deliberately drawn out by Shakespeare to make the most of the meeting between them. Viola has already surmised that Sebastian is alive, so she's not surprised when she sees him. Sebastian is surprised, though, and they have this marvellous moment of total joy, happiness and wonder at seeing one another, which neither of them wants to spoil by hurrying it. It's a very human thing to do, but so often people just fall into one another's arms and it's all over! But here they want to keep all that for the future. I find the time and placing of that scene wonderful:

SEBASTIAN: Were you a woman, as the rest goes even,
    I should my tears let fall upon your cheek,
    And say 'Thrice welcome, drowned Viola!'
VIOLA: My father had a mole upon his brow.

SEBASTIAN: And so had mine.
VIOLA: And died that day when Viola from her birth
  had numb'red thirteen years.
SEBASTIAN: O, that record is lively in my soul!
  He finished indeed his mortal act
  That day that made my sister thirteen years.
VIOLA: If nothing lets to make us happy both
  But this my masculine usurp'd attire,
  Do not embrace me till each circumstance
  Of place, time, fortune, do cohere and jump
  That I am Viola; . . .

5.1.231–45

There is such a range of human emotions in *Twelfth Night* but I think it is essentially a play about youth and love. *Romeo and Juliet* may be Shakespeare's great romantic tragedy, but I think there is more said about love in *Twelfth Night* than in any other play he ever wrote. It deals with the pains, foolish fantasies and excesses of love. It shows, above all, the way in which the centre of your being can be misled by love. All the 'romantic' parts need to be played young. If Olivia is in any way mature, then it becomes very hard to believe in her infatuation with Viola. Olivia may have delusions of grandeur and self-awareness, yet she's silly, poised and almost pathetic, a rather infanta–like creature. Viola is also young, but she has a certain sort of inner depth and maturity. She is thus capable of a deep, true and unselfish love. Apart from frequent revelling in their own sufferings, all these ill-matched lovers, as in other Shakespeare plays, make a journey by way of experience into maturity. When we are young we are perhaps too close to the passions that Shakespeare so delicately mocks to appreciate the grace of his irony. The young generally want to have very passionate feelings and can force them on the wrong object or even the wrong idea. Shakespeare shows all the paradoxes and dangers of love. He illustrates the heartache of truth that must be denied and the dangers of extreme and passionate feelings.

Feste is very important to the development of this theme. The bitter-sweet, wise fool is a moral guide who visits both houses. He may appear to be enigmatic, isolated and strange, but he says some very pertinent things to both Olivia and Orsino, who are not capable of taking them in. The audience long for Feste and Viola to meet because they have both, in their different ways, a mature attitude towards love. Yet they only meet once in a very transitory scene which has no weight, even though it reverberates with a sense of danger. Viola feels for the first time that someone actually knows who she is. They exchange witty wordplay, dallying with the meaning and non-meaning of words in a very Elizabethan way. The intensity with which they do this shows that language itself is dangerous. If you are too clever with words, you can actually talk yourself out of anything:

> VIOLA: Save thee, friend, and thy music!
>   Dost thou live by thy tabor?
> CLOWN: No, sir, I live by the church.
> VIOLA: Art thou a churchman?
> CLOWN: No such matter, sir; I do live by the church; for I do live at my house, and my house doth stand by the church. . . .
> VIOLA: Art thou the Lady Olivia's fool?
> CLOWN: No, indeed, sir; the Lady Olivia has no folly; she will keep no fool, sir, till she be married; and fools are as like husbands as pilchers are to herrings – the husband's the bigger. I am indeed not her fool, but her corrupter of words.

3.1.1–34

Viola is left musing aloud about the nature of folly. Perhaps Shakespeare was using her to deliver his own message to that very first night audience:

> This fellow is wise enough to play the fool;
> And to do that well craves a kind of wit.
> He must observe their mood on whom he jests,
> The quality of persons, and the time;
> And, like the haggard, check at every feather
> That comes before his eye. This is a practice
> As full of labour as a wise man's art;
> For folly that he wisely shows is fit;
> But wise men, folly-fall'n, quite taint their wit.

3.1.57–65

There is another scene which is also perhaps personal to Shakespeare himself. He was constantly sending up the academic and had a great hatred of pedagogues and puritans. Malvolio is, of course, a perfect example of the latter. Olivia banishes him to a dark room because she thinks that he's mad. Feste baits him there, blinding him with science so that it is impossible for him to answer for his own sanity. It's a cruel scene, and Shakespeare meant to be cruel when he wrote it, but he leaves Malvolio unrepentant, which oddly enough makes him more sympathetic.

Through all this drama the frustrations of Viola are extreme. When she is with Olivia, she often has difficulty in not giving herself away. Her scenes with Orsino are different. They are subtle and deliciously erotic, but also painful. Orsino talks to Viola about his passion for Olivia and she has to listen to him, whilst at the same time, because of her own deep love for him, trying to persuade him that he might be mistaken, not because she thinks he could ever love *her* but because she cannot bear to see him hurt:

VIOLA: But if she cannot love you, sir?
DUKE: I cannot be so answer'd.
VIOLA: Sooth, but you must.
 Say that some lady, as perhaps there is,
 Hath for your love as great a pang of heart
 As you have for Olivia. You cannot love her;
 You tell her so. Must she not then be answer'd?
DUKE: There is no woman's sides
 Can bide the beating of so strong a passion
 As love doth give my heart; no woman's heart
 So big to hold so much; they lack retention.
 Alas, their love may be call'd appetite—
 No motion of the liver, but the palate—
 That suffer surfeit, cloyment, and revolt;
 But mine is all as hungry as the sea,
 And can digest as much. Make no compare
 Between that love a woman can bear me
 And that I owe Olivia.
VIOLA: Ay, but I know—
DUKE: What dost thou know?
VIOLA: Too well what love women to men may owe.
 In faith, they are as true of heart as we.
 My father had a daughter lov'd a man,
 As it might be perhaps, were I a woman,
 I should your lordship.

            2.4.86–108

Perhaps what gives *Twelfth Night* its extra dimension is the sense of mortality and time passing: 'the clock upbraids me with the waste of time'. Pleasure will have to be paid for at one time or another as 'youth's a stuff will not endure'. After the lovers have rejected either self-denial or self-destructive passion in favour of a joyful affirmation of love and life, they are able to rearrange their hearts and lives. Yet there is still Feste to sing a wild, sad and almost nihilistic song to remind us that youth does not endure:

When that I was a little tiny boy,
   With hey, ho, the wind and the rain,
A foolish thing was but a toy,
   For the rain it raineth every day.

But when I came to man's estate,
   With hey, ho, the wind and the rain,
'Gainst knaves and thieves men shut their gate,
   For the rain it raineth every day.

But when I came, alas! to wive,
   With hey, ho, the wind and the rain,
By swaggering could I never thrive,
   For the rain it raineth every day.

5.1.375–86

THE TEMPEST
Laurens van der Post

*Laurens van der Post is a South African writer and
explorer whose publications include The Dark Eye
in Africa, The Lost World of the Kalahari and
A Story Like the Wind. He made this programme
on the Island of Porquerolles.*

For more than fifty years now, whenever I've thought of *The
Tempest*, the island of Porquerolles has flashed into my mind. It's
done this for many reasons. I think, first of all, because insofar as
The Tempest represented an island in the external world, this for
me was it. Obviously it had to be a Mediterranean island because
the voyage on which the tempest occurred was on a voyage by the
King of Naples from Tunisia back to Italy. After my disillusionment with all that scorched earth of Greece, this island seemed to
have all the physical attributes of what the Classical world meant
to Renaissance man. Here were the ilexes, the asphodel, the
myrrh and the pine trees walking down to the edge of the sea, so
that one could easily imagine it full of magic, nymphs and cen-
taurs, with the goddess Artemis herself hunting in the woods.
When I came to the island as a boy of twenty to write my first novel,
I found myself reading *The Tempest* again. I suddenly realised in
the isolation of the place how much I had been pre-conditioned
and that really to understand Shakespeare I had to treat him as a
strange kind of new music and to know him as one knows music
through the impact he makes on all one's senses. And I came to
see the island as Shakespeare saw it: an image of enduring
achievement of man's spirit. The island represents that area of life
in which the individual has to work to contribute something of
himself in the oceans and seas of space and time.

Scholars are inclined to think that the story has a great deal to do
with the Virginia expedition of 1609, in which a ship called the *Sea
Venture* was thought lost, but was miraculously preserved and run
ashore on an island in the Caribbean. Shakespeare obviously knew
this story, but shipwrecks were normal occurrences in the Elizabethan world. The sea to Renaissance man was what space is to us
today. The story of the *Sea Venture* was no more than the grit on
which the oyster of his imagination formed this great pearl of *The*

Tempest. So on one level *The Tempest* is a popular story of an Elizabethan shipwreck, but of course it is much more than that. On a deeper level, it is profoundly autobiographical because we find that, as Shakespeare grew older, more and more he explored his own inner nature through personifications in the plays that he wrote. Patterns, mirror patterns that we call Hamlet, Macbeth, Othello, Lear, Coriolanus or Prospero, all reflect efforts at self-exploration by Shakespeare. That is why Wordsworth could refer so movingly to *The Tempest* as a 'journey of the mind'.

All good stories, whether told as music, drama, fiction, fairy tales or parables, would seem to operate on two levels. There is the obvious everyday level in which they make sense in terms of people's here and now, but there is a deeper level of the imagination where they seem to carry the seeds of a new kind of awareness. Now mothers, in telling their children fairy tales, seem to know this. Christ, in telling people parables, obviously knew that this was a means of heightening spiritual perception. The Elizabethans had no difficulty in understanding magic. They believed in it, just as they believed in witchcraft, in the miraculous and in alchemy. In experiencing Shakespeare, they used him as a gateway to an increase of their own awareness. Even to this day, when Shakespeare seems almost too profound for us, we also experience this deeper level of meaning when we are exposed to him, whether we like it or not:

> Full fathom five thy father lies;
> Of his bones are coral made;
> Those are pearls that were his eyes;
> Nothing of him that doth fade
> But doth suffer a sea-change
> Into something rich and strange.

1.2.396–401

Now we who find Shakespeare so complex may doubt the Elizabethan capacity for understanding him. But one very convincing example occurs to me. In 1607 a certain Captain Keeling sailed from Southampton for India, and, when his ship was off Sierra Leone, his sailors performed *Henry V.* When they were near the Cape of Good Hope they performed *Hamlet,* its first performance in the outside world. *Hamlet* is described in the ship's log as 'this popular play now running in London'. So even the Elizabethan sailor was wide open to all levels of Shakespeare.

The play begins with Shakespeare as Prospero, master of the island, in total command of his island self. With him is his daughter Miranda, his own soul as it were, who represents all the loving, feeling, caring values of Shakespeare's life, and on this island for some twelve years now he's educated her for this crisis, away from the contamination of the world which has failed him. As a result, these values are so firmly integrated in Propero that when the tempest is let loose against the island, the storm remains on the fringe and he and his soul, his daughter, remain at the still centre of it:

MIRANDA: If by your art, my dearest father, you have
Put the wild waters in this roar, allay them.
The sky, it seems, would pour down stinking pitch,
But that the sea, mounting to th' welkin's cheek,
Dashes the fire out. O, I have suffered
With those that I saw suffer! A brave vessel,
Who had no doubt some noble creature in her,
Dash'd all to pieces! O, the cry did knock
Against my very heart! Poor souls, they perish'd.
Had I been any god of power, I would
Have sunk the sea within the earth or ere
It should the good ship so have swallow'd and
The fraughting souls within her.

PROSPERO: Be collected;
No more amazement; tell your piteous heart
There's no harm done.

MIRANDA: O, woe the day!

PROSPERO: No harm.

1.2.1–15

Shakespeare says quite firmly that Ariel had been on the island with Caliban for twelve years before Prospero arrives there. He then goes on to make it quite clear that Prospero spent another twelve years on the island before the tempest. These two periods of twelve years are profoundly significant. The first period roughly represents the time it took Shakespeare from his beginning as a playwright to arrive at the Hamlet in himself. This Hamlet turning point was a great crisis in the mind of Shakespeare as it was in the mind of this time. When Prospero arrives on the island, he finds Ariel imprisoned in a cloven pine:

PROSPERO: This dam'd witch Sycorax,
For mischiefs manifold, and sorceries terrible
To enter human hearing, from Argier
Thou know'st was banish'd; for one thing she did
They would not take her life. Is not this true?

ARIEL: Ay, sir.
PROSPERO: This blue-ey'd hag was hither brought with child,
    And here was left by th' sailors. Thou, my slave,
    As thou report'st thyself, wast then her servant;
    And, for thou wast a spirit too delicate
    To act her earthy and abhorr'd commands,
    Refusing her grand hests, she did confine thee,
    By help of her more potent ministers,
    And in her most unmitigable rage,
    Into a cloven pine; within which rift
    Imprison'd thou didst painfully remain
    A dozen years; . . .

1.2.263–79

Now the pine is a natural image of the growth of the spirit of man and it's split because, up to the time he wrote *Hamlet*, Shakespeare was divided against himself. The progression from *Hamlet* to *The Tempest* is Shakespeare's means of finding his own individual island self.

Caliban is perhaps the most important element of all in *The Tempest*. He introduces something entirely new in Shakespeare. Now scholars argue that Caliban was inspired by the discovery of primitive man in the great new world opened up during the Renaissance and, of course, Shakespeare may well have been stimulated by all this. But ultimately there is no anticipation of a colonial subject in Caliban. There is no political point to be made about him. He is, in fact, Shakespeare's first recognition of the debt which he owes to his own instinctive self. Caliban is a personification of the dark animal side of his nature, the raw material, the natural instinctive sources out of which the artist creates. Prospero declares 'this thing of darkness I/Acknowledge mine'. Caliban is no monster. He is simply a creature of Nature with all the qualities of the natural world. Shakespeare doesn't pass moral judgement on him as he's concerned with understanding rather than condemning the totality of human nature. He recognises a certain dark, earthy, poetic quality in Caliban and so makes him speak the most moving and beautiful lines about the natural things of the island: the water, the woods, the sources of fire and, ultimately, the strange sound of music that fills the island night and day:

Be not afeard. The isle is full of noises,
Sounds, and sweet airs, that give delight, and hurt not,
Sometimes a thousand twangling instruments
Will hum about mine ears; and sometimes voices,

167

That, if I then had wak'd after long sleep,
Will make me sleep again; and then, in dreaming,
The clouds methought would open and show riches
Ready to drop upon me, that, when I wak'd,
I cried to dream again.

3.2.130–8

Meanwhile, on the other side of the island, there is the person of Ferdinand. Through shipwreck and suffering, he has redeemed the sin of his father against Prospero. Purified, the masculine in man is now ready at last to join the feminine in the person of Miranda. The marvellous, accident-proof imagination of Shakespeare chooses a game of chess to illustrate this. He chooses chess because it's perhaps the most symbolic of all games. Every piece on the board is symbolic and constitutes the totality of the heraldic quality of Renaissance life. It's not an artistic piece of chi-chi because chess was to Renaissance man what dancing was in my own day. It was the natural means of communication between young men and young women and it was quite normal for young men to go into the rooms of young women to play a game of chess with them. So, through this demonstration of chess, Shakespeare introduces us to the union of two of the most evocative characters he ever created, created with the utmost economy. He introduces us to his sense of the future, to his hope of a brave, new world. It's not only his hope, it remains ours:

MIRANDA: Sweet lord, you play me false.
FERDINAND: No, my dearest love,
    I would not for the world.
MIRANDA: Yes, for a score of kingdoms you should wrangle,
    And I would call it fair play.
ALONSO: If this prove
    A vision of the island, one dear son
    Shall I twice lose.
SEBASTIAN: A most high miracle!
FERDINAND: Though the seas threaten, they are merciful;
    I have curs'd them without cause.
ALONSO: Now all the blessings
    Of a glad father compass thee about!
    Arise, and say how thou cam'st here.
MIRANDA: O, wonder!
    How many goodly creatures are there here!

How beauteous mankind is! O brave new world
That has such people in't!

5.1.172–84

When the reconciliation between Prospero and Antonio takes place, which is one of the great points of cathartic resolution in *The Tempest*, there follows something which has always annoyed and puzzled scholars. Why, they ask, was it necessary to introduce another conspiracy to kill royalty? But for me this is one of the most significant and moving things about *The Tempest*. Shakespeare demonstrates that in dealing with Prospero's own sense of injury he was dealing with something which was not just subjective, but which was profoundly objective. As it is in the nature of man to be negative, there is always a tendency in human beings to pull down and kill what is good and great. We must all learn, as Shakespeare did, to come to terms with this without turning sour in the process ourselves. Shakespeare has come at home to himself at last. He's arrived at the final destination of one of the greatest journeys ever undertaken by human imagination. Through the exploration of the light and dark in himself and shirking nothing, however unpleasant, in his own character, he's constituted an extraordinary resolved world in space and time. And he knows that art cannot carry the human spirit further and that it needs something else than the great gift that has brought it there, to carry it on beyond:

Our revels now are ended. These our actors,
As I foretold you, were all spirits, and
Are melted into air, into thin air;
And, like the baseless fabric of this vision,
The cloud-capp'd towers, the gorgeous palaces,
The solemn temples, the great globe itself,
Yea, all which it inherit, shall dissolve,
And, like this insubstantial pageant faded,
Leave not a rack behind. We are such stuff
As dreams are made on; and our little life
Is rounded with a sleep. . . .

4.1.148–58

What that something is, we don't know precisely. There's a brief hint of it in the Epilogue where Shakespeare says 'And my ending is despair/Unless I be reliev'd by prayer'. But what we do know is that everything that he's ever written has grown naturally out of itself to constitute one of the richest worlds of art ever created. He broke through into his greatest poetic self in *A Midsummer Night's Dream*, giving us a dream of one summer of increase. He carried on to fulfil a great dream for all seasons and for all times in *The Tempest*.

THE TEMPEST
Michael Hordern

Michael Hordern played Prospero in the BBC TV
Shakespeare production of The Tempest, *as well as*
Capulet, in Romeo and Juliet *and Lafeu in* All's
Well That Ends Well.

It's some thirty years now since I played Caliban in *The Tempest*
at Stratford-upon-Avon. The following year I played Prospero at
the Old Vic. I played Prospero again at Stratford throughout the
1978 season and on into 1979. Altogether I suppose that I must
have played in *The Tempest* well over 200 times. During last year
at Stratford I begged from the Local Education Authority an 'A'
level, perhaps it was only an 'O' level, paper on *The Tempest*,
which was a set book for the year. I honestly reckon that I would
have scraped no more than a pass. I mention this because, even
after all these years, there are still more questions than answers in
my mind about the play. On that first occasion when I played
Caliban I confessed that I was totally ignorant about the play to
Glen Byam Shaw, the greatly respected Artistic Director of the
Royal Shakespeare Theatre. My contract had already been safely
signed. 'Splendid', he replied, 'read the play as often as you like,
but promise me not to read any "prefaces". Come to the first
rehearsal in February with the script as if it had been written
yesterday'. I have gone into this personal preamble in some detail
because I would wish an audience watching *The Tempest* just to
let the delight, the beauty, the language, the music and the magic
of it wash over them. I want them to feel the play. The thinking
about it is best left till afterwards. *The Tempest* will only take off if
you don't worry it to death.

The story concerns an elderly Duke of Milan who, with his
three year old daughter, has been cast ashore on an almost
deserted island through the machinations of his wicked younger
brother, who thereby supplanted him in his Dukedom. Unfortunately for this wicked brother, the Duke was also a magician.
He had in fact been studying magic, his 'art' as he calls it, at the
expense of the art of government. He had certainly neglected to
keep an eye on his brother. When the brother and his fellow

plotters are blown off course in their ship by 'accident most strange', they are wrecked on the self-same island by a tempest which had been conjured up by the magician Duke. This takes place twelve years after his own confinement on the island, which makes his daughter now fifteen. The only other beings they found on the island were Caliban, 'a savage and deformed slave' as the cast list has it, and Ariel, 'an airy spirit', both in their separate ways to become the Duke's servants. This magician Duke is, of course, Prospero, his daughter is Miranda and his wicked brother is Antonio.

This is the point at which the play proper begins. Among those wrecked in the ship with Antonio are Alonso, the King of Naples, who knows about the original plot against Prospero, and his son Ferdinand, who does not. Prospero's actions are motivated by a desire to bring Ferdinand and Miranda together and through their union to reconcile the factions. Prospero and Ariel see to it that no lives are lost in the shipwreck:

> ARIEL: Not a hair perish'd;
>   On their sustaining garments not a blemish,
>   But fresher than before; and, as thou bad'st me,
>   In troops I have dispers'd them 'bout the isle.
>   The King's son have I landed by himself,
>   Whom I left cooling of the air with sighs
>   In an odd angle of the isle, and sitting,
>   His arms in this sad knot.

I.2.217–24

Prospero needs them all alive to show them the error of their ways and, up to a point, to have his revenge on them. Twelve years of banishment have left him a very angry man. Ariel disperses the various people from the wrecked ship about the island. Alonso, Antonio and various attendant lords are sent off in one direction, whilst Ferdinand heads off by himself in another, to meet Miranda in a fairy tale courtship. Alonso's jester, Trinculo, and his drunken butler, Stephano, go off in yet another direction to team up with Caliban. They get involved in a hopeless plot to murder Prospero, during which they teach Caliban the pleasures and remorse of alcohol. Sherry was their tipple, incidentally; fancy being permanently drunk on sherry – almost punishment enough I would have thought. I used to get very cross when I was rehearsing as Caliban for the first time when the producer used to refer to Caliban, Trinculo and Stephano as the 'three comics'. Caliban is the catalyst in their scenes together, which are indeed splendidly funny, but he must never be a figure of fun or a 'comic' himself.

Why does Prospero conjure up the tempest in the first place? We learn in the first scene between him and Miranda of his warmth and tremendous love for her. It is this which largely motivates his actions throughout the play:

> I have done nothing but in care of thee,
> Of thee, my dear one, thee, my daughter, who
> Art ignorant of what thou art, nought knowing
> Of whence I am, not that I am more better
> Than Prospero, master of a full poor cell,
> And thy no greater father.

1.2.16–21

As an actor one often finds a line early on, a text you might almost say, on which to hang one's characterisation and performance. 'I have done nothing but in care of thee' is, for me, just such a line. It is interesting to note how often Shakespeare presents a strong father-daughter relationship: Capulet and Juliet, Shylock and Jessica, Polonius and Ophelia, Lear and Cordelia as well as Prospero and Miranda. I have played all these fathers and there's a tremendous warmth coupled with a firm sense of discipline in all of them:

> PROSPERO: Here in this island we arriv'd; and here
> Have I, thy schoolmaster, made thee more profit
> Than other princess' can, that have more time
> For vainer hours, and tutors not so careful.

1.2.171–4

Shakespeare certainly had no time for parental permissiveness.

The fact that we are on an island immediately adds the essential quality of mystery to the play. This is wonderfully portrayed for us in one of Caliban's speeches:

> The isle is full of noises,
> Sounds, and sweet airs, that give delight, and hurt not.
> Sometimes a thousand twangling instruments
> Will hum about mine ears; and sometimes voices,
> That, if I then had wak'd after long sleep,
> Will make me sleep again; and then, in dreaming,
> The clouds methought would open and show riches
> Ready to drop upon me, that, when I wak'd,
> I cried to dream again.

3.2.130–8

Where is Prospero's island? It's quite fun to puzzle out some of the references to space, time and distance. Prospero and Miranda were taken from their home in Milan to somewhere on the Italian coast. I'd suggest that this would have been the nearest point, which would be on the Gulf of Genoa. Prospero takes up the story:

> In few, they hurried us aboard a bark;
> Bore us some leagues to sea, where they prepared
> A rotten carcass of a butt, not rigg'd,
> Nor tackle, sail, nor mast; the very rats
> Instinctively have quit it.

1.2.144–8

I don't see that 'rotten carcass of a butt' making the Straits of Gibraltar, so the island must be somewhere in the Mediterranean. Yet I wonder where you would have found, even in those days, an island perfectly capable of supporting life but, except for Caliban, unoccupied. The island is really where you imagine it to be because it is nowhere except in the mind. It means just what you and the characters in the play make of it. It is such stuff as dreams are made on. Everybody in the play has a different conception of it. As just mentioned, it is a place full of 'Sounds, and sweet airs, that give delight, and hurt not' to Caliban before his fall from grace. The evil Antonio believes that the air is foul 'as 'twere perfum'd by a fen'. The good Lord Gonzalo, on the other hand, sees the island as containing 'everything advantageous to life'. Life is in fact what the good or bad in you makes of it. So is Prospero's island as far as any audience is concerned.

How are we to handle the magic in *The Tempest?* This is one of the great difficulties in presenting the play and in playing Prospero. A Jacobean audience would have been steeped in superstition, magic and the supernatural and so would have been in complete accord with Prospero's conjuring. Yet no amount of abracadabra, clever lighting effects and crystal balls is going to carry a modern audience to the suspension of disbelief. It is better by far just to try to accept the fact that Prospero has learned the art and can therefore summon up spirits to enact his fancies when he entertains the young lovers to a masque. He can command Ariel

> to tread the ooze
> of the salt deep,
> To run the sharp wind of the north,
> To do me business in the veins o' th' earth
> When it is bak'd with frost.

1.2.252–6

The magic is surely in the words –' to tread the ooze of the salt deep' or 'the veins of the earth when it is baked with frost'. So I would say cut the wand-waving to a minimum and rely on those words.

What about Ariel? He was rescued by Prospero's magic after twelve years of confinement in the cleft of a cloven pine tree. He was quite rightly thankful to be set free and so became Prospero's 'industrious servant'. Though Shakespeare does call him Ariel, he's no Tinkerbell. He's rather reluctant to do Prospero's bidding and is forever reminding him of the promised and approaching termination of this servitude. Although Prospero has to ride Ariel on a very tight rein, their relationship is one of the beauties of the play and their parting at the end is deeply moving. Your examination paper may ask you what Ariel represents. I don't know but I don't think that I need to know. To me as Prospero he is my 'brave spirit', 'my chick', 'my Ariel' and I am his 'noble master', his 'grave sir' to whom he comes to answer my 'best pleasure; be't to fly,/ To swim, to dive into the fire, to ride/ On the curl'd clouds'. That's us and that's how we shall be together, as Shakespeare means us to be.

Just as Ariel is no Tinkerbell, so Caliban is no noble savage. Just as it is hard for a modern audience to take the magic in *The Tempest*, so it is hard for them as well to take Prospero's ill-treatment of Caliban. A Jacobean audience would have been as sympathetic to such treatment of what they considered a lower form of humanity as they would have been to, say, the anti-semitism of *The Merchant of Venice*. There are those who read anti-colonialist sentiments into *The Tempest*. I can't go along with that, although Shakespeare does present Caliban's side of things with some sympathy. Prospero attempts to educate him and takes him to live in his own cell. Yet Caliban attempts to violate Miranda's virginity. Shakespeare does not, however, crudely present this in terms of 'give the natives and inch and they'll take an ell'. For there's a line of Caliban's which stays with me as much as any in the play: 'You taught me language, and my profit on't/ Is, I know how to curse'

Miranda and Ferdinand are ecstatically betrothed and Prospero is reconciled to the King of Naples and reunited with his good Lord Gonzalo. Trinculo, Stephano and Caliban suffer from imperial hangovers, but appear to be repentant at the end of the play. The ending is not altogether happy for my Prospero. He has lost his beloved daughter to Ferdinand, loosed his beloved Ariel to the elements and his brother has not spoken one word of contrition. He is returning to Milan where, he says, 'Every third thought shall be my grave'. He has recently seen an apocalyptic vision of the fate awaiting humanity. My Prospero saw the mushroom cloud as he spoke one of the most famous speeches in the play:

> The cloud-capp'd towers, the gorgeous palaces,
> The solemn temples, the great globe itself,
> Yea, all which it inherit, shall dissolve,
> And, like this insubstantial pageant faded,
> Leave not a rack behind. We are such stuff
> As dreams are made on; and our little life
> Is rounded with a sleep.

4.1.152–8

I found myself repeating these lines when I was at Hiroshima a few weeks ago on the exact spot where the first atom bomb fell. There are those for whom this speech refers only to the transient quality of theatrical presentation. I don't want to turn *The Tempest* into an anti-nuclear tract any more than I want it to be seen as an anti-colonialist one. I am just underlining Ben Jonson's words on Shakespeare: 'He was not of an age, but for all time'. That applies to the future as well as to the past.

When Prospero speaks of breaking his staff and drowning his book, are we to take this as Shakespeare's own farewell to the theatre? Such a question may be asked in the study, but must not be considered on the stage. The actor playing Prospero must only be concerned with Prospero. The text he speaks must mean no more and no less than what it says: he is going to break his magic wand and throw his library into the sea. It's only when he comes to the matchless Epilogue to the play that the actor can allow himself to step outside the character he has been playing. He speaks as Prospero saying goodbye to his island, but also as the actor who has been playing Prospero for the last two hours saying goodbye to the empty stage behind him and the audience in front of him. It is also now, at last perhaps, William Shakespeare saying goodbye to his plays and his public. The magic of *The Tempest* is that all this occurs in one speech. It is in the words themselves:

> Now my charms are all o'erthrown,
> And what strength I have's mine own,
> Which is most faint. Now 'tis true,
> I must be here confin'd by you,

Or sent to Naples. Let me not,
Since I have my dukedom got,
And pardon'd the deceiver, dwell
In this bare island by your spell;
But release me from my bands
With the help of your good hands.
Gentle breath of yours my sails
Must fill, or else my project fails,
Which was to please. Now I want
Spirits to enforce, art to enchant;
And my ending is despair
Unless I be reliev'd by prayer,
Which pierces so that it assaults
Mercy itself, and frees all faults.
As you from crimes would pardon'd be,
Let your indulgence set me free.

HAMLET

Clive James

Clive James was until recently the television critic for The Observer. *He has also published topical satires and autobiography, as well as appearing regularly on television. He made this programme at Cambridge, Berkeley Castle, and the Theatre Royal, Drury Lane.*

I want to start off in familiar surroundings because I'm setting out on a task foredoomed to failure: to sum up Shakespeare's *Hamlet*, one of the supreme achievements of the human imagination. Fifteen years ago I was an undergraduate at Pembroke College, Cambridge University, and then later on I stuck around for a while as a postgraduate. I hope I was too weatherbeaten to fall for the mystique that these old dens of privilege supposedly generate, but I can't deny that I've got the sort of affection for Cambridge that anybody feels for a place where they read a lot and thought a lot and wasted a lot of time.

Hamlet feels the same way about his university, Wittenberg. He has to act out his destiny on the sleet-spattered battlements of Elsinore, while Horatio makes regular trips back to Wittenberg for the port and walnuts and the relative safety of academic intrigue. Many a time in Fleet Street, as I've sat there sucking my typewriter and waiting desperately for inspiration, I've envied those of my contemporaries who stayed on in Cambridge to become academics, the Horatios. In other words, I identify with Hamlet. In my mind's eye, he even looks a bit like me. Perhaps a couple of stone lighter, with blonde hair and more of it: one of those rare Aussies who happen to fence quite well and stand first in line of succession to the throne of Denmark. I don't think this is mad conceit because I think all men and most women who've ever read or seen the play, feel that its hero is a reflection of themselves.

What's more, I think Shakespeare felt the same way. All his characters in all his plays – men or women, heroes or villains – are aspects of himself, because his was a universal self and he knew it inside out. Shakespeare was everybody. But Hamlet is probably the character who comes closest to reflecting Shakespeare's *whole* self. When I think of what Shakespeare was like, I think of Hamlet. Shakespeare probably didn't behave like that, and he almost certainly didn't talk like that. Hamlet talks a great deal and Shakespeare probably spent most of the time listening. At the end of the night's revelry in the tavern, he was probably the only one sober and the only one silent. Nor was Shakespeare famous for being indecisive. From what little we know of him, he was a practical man of affairs in the theatre, which gave unlimited scope to his imagination. He was an art prince, like Michelangelo. If he'd been the other kind of prince, his imagination would have become his enemy, the enemy of action:

> Thus conscience does make cowards of us all;
> And thus the native hue of resolution
> Is sickled o'er with the pale cast of thought,
> And enterprises of great pitch and moment,
> With this regard, their currents turn awry
> And lose the name of action –

3.1.83–8

In Shakespeare's time, the biggest question of the day was how a prince should rule. When *Hamlet* was being written, as the sixteenth century turned into the seventeenth, the stable reign of Queen Elizabeth, amidst universal trepidation, was drawing to its end. The Earl of Essex, 'the glass of fashion and the mould of form, the observ'd of all observers', had dished himself through not knowing how to do what when. Essex died on the block somewhere about the time that Hamlet was being born on the page. Shakespeare was a keen student of these weighty matters. He was a keen student of everything. Not that he ever went to university as his university was the theatre. The same has held true for a lot of our best playwrights right down to the present day. John Osborne, Harold Pinter, Tom Stoppard were all educated in the university of life. Shakespeare was a gigantic natural intellect who had no more need of a university that Einstein did, who didn't go to one either. But Shakespeare did have a contemplative mentality. We know that much for certain because we've heard so little about him. Only in the theatre did Shakespeare create experience. In the outside world, he was content to reflect upon it. Shakespeare knew that he was a man of outstanding gifts. Talent of that magnitude is never modest, although it's almost always humble. Shakespeare knew that he could dream up a whole kingdom and breathe so much life into it that it would live in men's minds, perhaps for ever. But he also knew that he didn't have what it took to rule a real kingdom for a week. He lacked the limitations; he wasn't simple enough; and it was out of that realisation that he created Hamlet, who was really a changeling. Hamlet is what would happen if a great poet grew up to be a prince. He might speak great speeches, but the native hue of resolution would be . . . well, let's hear him tell it:

> To be, or not to be – that is the question;
> Whether 'tis nobler in the mind to suffer
> The slings and arrows of outrageous fortune,
> Or to take arms against a sea of troubles,
> And by opposing end them? To die, to sleep –
> No more; and by a sleep to say we end
> The heart-ache and the thousand natural shocks
> That flesh is heir to. 'Tis a consummation
> Devoutly to be wish'd. To die, to sleep;
> To sleep, perchance to dream. Ay, there's the rub;
> For in that sleep of death what dreams may come,
> When we have shuffled off this mortal coil,
> Must give us pause.

3.1.56–68

'To be, or not to be' – I wish I'd said that. By now that speech has been translated into every major language on earth and most of the minor ones, and it's remarkable how the first line always seems to come out sounding the same. 'Sein, oder nicht sein', runs the German version,' das ist die Frage'. Which perhaps lacks the fresh charm of the English subtitle in the recent Hindi film version: 'Shall I live, or do myself in? I do not know'. Today Hamlet belongs to the world. He's come a long way from Elsinore, and there's no reason why not. After all, Shakespeare not only didn't go to university, he didn't go to Denmark either. He got his idea of what Elsinore should look like from local rock piles like Berkeley Castle. It's got battlements outside and arrases inside. There's a graveyard next door and the sea's not far away. If you happen to be William Shakespeare, that's all you need to go on for a Danish setting.

He inherited the plot from a Scandinavian scholar called Saxo Grammaticus, who wrote an early version of the play. Hamlet was called Amleth and his wicked uncle Claudius was called Fang, who sounds like the leading heavy in *Flash Gordon Conquers Denmark.* Saxo's story was the basis for a later English stage version by Thomas Kyd of *Spanish Tragedy* fame. Shakespeare took over the property and transformed it out of all comparison, although not out of recognition. That old warhorse of a plot is still there inside it. So – what happens in *Hamlet?* Well, the old King dies and the Queen marries his brother with indecent haste. The fretful Prince is told by his father's ghost that murder most foul has occurred. Hamlet feigns madness, gives Ophelia a thin time, casually rubs out her father Polonius and waits for the right moment to act. But he waits too long. Things get out of hand. The story ends with Hamlet being carried up to lie in state on the battlements. Before Shakespeare got hold of it, the old plot was pretty barbaric stuff. He civilised it by moving it inside the mind and inside the house.

One of the things that makes Shakespeare a great man of the theatre is that he knew the real thing when he saw it. He knew that power couldn't be wished out of the world. If power were used wisely and firmly, then everyone might thrive. If it were mismanaged, corruption ensued as surely as rats brought plague, and the whole state went rotten. Shakespeare believed in order and degree. He believed in justice, too, but he didn't think there was any hope of getting it unless the civil fabric was maintained. The idea of social breakdown was abhorrent to him. He knew that he was a kind of prince himself, but he had no illusions about how long his own kingdom would last if the real one fell into disarray. To Shakespeare, Hamlet's tragedy was not just personal but political. Like Prince Hal in an earlier play and indeed like Mark Antony in a later one, or even King Lear, Hamlet has responsibilities. And because Hamlet can't meet those responsibilities, he gets a lot of good people killed for nothing and loses his kingdom to the simple but determined Fortinbras.

Nowadays we tend to see Hamlet's blonde head surrounded by the flattering nimbus of nineteenth century Romanticism, which held that Hamlet was a sensitive plant with a soul too fine for the concerns of this world. But Shakespeare was too realistic to be merely Romantic. And, of course, he was too poetic to be merely realistic. He knew that there was more in this world than the mere exercise of power. He could feel it within himself – imagination, the supreme power. But even that had its place. In the wrong place it could have tragic consequences. The first reason Hamlet hesitates is dramatic. If Fortinbras were the play's hero, it would be all over in five minutes instead of five acts, with Fortinbras heading for the throne by the direct route, over Claudius's twitching corpse. But the second reason Hamlet hesitates is that he has puzzled his own will by thinking too precisely on the event:

How all occasions do inform against me,
And spur my dull revenge! What is a man,

If his chief good and market of his time
Be but to sleep and feed? A beast, no more!
Sure he that made us with such large discourse,
Looking before and after, gave us not
That capability and god-like reason
To fust in us unus'd. Now, whether it be
Bestial oblivion, or some craven scruple
Of thinking too precisely on th' event –
. . .   I do not know
Why yet I live to say 'This thing's to do',
Sith I have cause, and will, and strength, and means,
To do't.

4.4.32–46

Throughout history, the thoughtful onlooker has been astonished at the man of action's empty head. Napoleon and Hitler, to take extreme examples, did the unthinkable because they lacked the imagination to realise that it couldn't be done. With Hamlet it's the opposite. More than 300 years before Freud, Montaigne, a great student of the human soul, whose essays Shakespeare knew intimately, identified the imagination as the cause of impotence. Because Hamlet can't stop thinking, he can't start moving. Hence his melancholy. Happiness has been defined as a very small, very cheap cigar named after him, but really Hamlet is as sad as a man can be. He's doubly sad because of his capacity for merriment. Clowns don't want to play Hamlet half as much as Hamlet wants to play the clown, but always the laughter trails off. He loses his mirth and the whole world with it. But he does this with such marvellous words that he stuns us into admiration. No actor can resist turning Hamlet's defeat into a victory.

From the moment the part was there to be played, every important actor has looked on his interpretation of Hamlet as defining him, not just as a talent but as a human being. And every Hamlet has studied the Hamlet before him in an almost unbroken succession from that day to this. Richard Burbage, the original Hamlet, gave way to Joseph Taylor, Taylor gave way to Thomas Betterton. Samuel Pepys saw Betterton play Hamlet in Lincoln's Inn Fields in 1661 and said that he played the Prince's part beyond imagination, 'the best part, I believe, that ever man played'. Pepys spent a whole afternoon learning 'To be, or not to be' by heart. And as the seventeenth century became the eighteenth, Betterton was still playing Hamlet in his seventieth year when Richard Steele saw him and said that for action, he was perfection. Hamlet was at centre stage all over the world. In London he was at Covent Garden, he was in the Haymarket, but above all he was at the Theatre Royal, Drury Lane, where great actor after great actor strove to convince the audience that to play Hamlet stood as far above ordinary acting as Hamlet in the play stands above the Players. In the early eighteenth century, the great tragedian Robert Wilks played Hamlet here. According to contemporary accounts, when the Ghost came on, Wilks climbed the scenery. When he climbed back down again some time later, he used his sword not to fend off his companions who were trying to keep him from the Ghost but to attack the Ghost. In other words, he tore a passion to tatters. And he did so while wearing a complete tragedian's outfit of full-bottomed wig, plumes and a cape. The outfit was the only complete thing about his performance because, like most of his successors, he cut the text drastically. When David Garrick came on, he wore elevated shoes and stole one of the Ghost's best lines, 'O, horrible! O, horrible! most horrible!'. Dr Johnson thought Garrick was over the top, but most of the playgoing public concurred in the opinion that Garrick was unbeatable in the role. Garrick agreed with them and played it every season of his career.

As the eighteenth century gave way to the nineteenth, John Philip Kemble arrived and the Romantic interpretation of Hamlet began to arrive with him. William Hazlitt didn't think much of Kemble in the role. He thought he played it with a fixed and sullen gloom, but I think we recognise that gloom as the beginning of the Romantic interpretation of Hamlet, which has persisted almost down to our own day. Hazlitt didn't think much of Edmund Kean either. He thought Kean's performance was a succession of grand moments, but had no real human shape. Everybody else thought Kean was marvellously natural, especially in his appearance, and he *looked* like the Hamlet we know today – short hair, white lace collar. And on they came: William Charles Macready, Barry Sullivan, Edward Booth – who some people thought was the ideal Hamlet but who had his thunder stolen by Henry Irving. The total effect of the nineteenth century actor-managers was to establish Hamlet as the Romantic, alienated outcast, the poet who perhaps couldn't write poetry but could certainly speak it, the man who was just too good for this world.

As the nineteenth century gave way to the twentieth, a truly revolutionary actor-manager arrived on the scene, Johnston

Forbes-Robertson. Revolutionary because he widened the focus of attention from the central character to the whole play, so that never again was it possible to argue plausibly that the play was anything less than the miraculous sum of its parts. Nowadays we never think of any interpretation of the central character, no matter how brilliant – John Gielgud's vividly mental, Laurence Olivier's vividly physical – as anything more than a contribution to the total character, just as we never think of any cut version, no matter how consistent within itself, as anything more than a contribution to the total play.

I live and work in the part of London that's still called the City, even though the old City in which Shakespeare ruled as a prince of the theatre is long gone. The ground clearance around here was done by the German air force. Even from the top of one of the tower blocks you still can't see the edge of modern London. I suppose the day is coming when all the cities on earth will join up. And yet the world could go on changing unimaginably and Hamlet would still have everything to say to us. Whenever we hear of some new atrocity and wonder impotently what life is for, we always find that he got there ahead of us. Hamlet poses the eternal question of whether life is worth living. The answer that he appears to arrive at is that it isn't, but the way he says so makes us realise that it is. Hamlet has been given the creative vitality of Shakespeare himself. Even though robbed of will, he's still the embodiment of individuality. Hamlet it what it means to be alive. So all those actors were right, after all. Hamlet's tragedy really is a triumph. A prince of the imagination, he inherits his kingdom in eternity, even if Fortinbras inherits it on earth.

Boris Pasternak, who translated *Hamlet* into Russian, also wrote a famous poem in which Hamlet faces something even worse than his own doubts – a world in which his doubts are not permitted:

> Yet the order of the acts is planned
> And the end of the way inescapable.
> I am alone;

Pasternak wasn't the first, and probably won't be the last, to see Hamlet as the supreme symbol of liberty. As the doomed Prince of Denmark, Hamlet must act out his tragic fate, but as a mind he remains free. He fails in the outer world only because his inner world is so rich. Scorning necessity, he reflects upon his own existence. 'In my mind's eye, Horatio'. Hamlet is the human intelligence made universal, so he belongs to all of us. 'For which of us', wrote Anatole France, addressing Hamlet, 'does not resemble you in some way?' We're all like him because we all think, and it's because, on top of all its other qualities, that its hero incarnates the dignity of human consciousness, that *Hamlet* is the greatest play by the greatest writer who ever lived.

HAMLET

Derek Jacobi

Derek Jacobi played Hamlet in the BBC TV *Shakespeare production, as well as Richard II. Other television roles include the Emperor Claudius in* I, Claudius.

*H*amlet has probably been performed more times than any other drama ever written. It has certainly attracted more attention. A Polish critic called Jan Kott has estimated that a bibliographical catalogue of works about *Hamlet* is longer than the Warsaw telephone directory. If you were to ask people who haven't read or seen the play about it, they would probably tell you Hamlet dresses in black, has Scandinavian fair hair, says 'To be, or not to be' and holds up the skull of somebody called Yorick. Those who have read or seen the play obviously have their own conception of it. Audiences for *Hamlet* are, in my experience always bristling with preconceptions and prejudices. They come knowing what Hamlet should look, sound and behave like. If he doesn't live up to their expectations, the actor has the difficult task of trying to win them by the end of the evening. Failure means that they won't accept him as their Hamlet.

So much has happened in *Hamlet* before the play starts. The obvious thing is that Hamlet's father, the King of Denmark, is dead. His mother has remarried his uncle Claudius with seemingly indecent haste. This is causing Hamlet a great deal of anguish at the beginning of the play. There is no question of murdering Claudius at this stage. Hamlet just dislikes and distrusts him. He also has a complicated love-hate relationship with his mother. The other aspect of Hamlet's pre-play life we need to know about concerns his relationship with Ophelia. We are told that he and Ophelia are in love, but not whether they have actually consummated their love affair or are still idyllic, romantic lovers. Whichever one you choose, of course, makes a tremendous difference to the way both the parts are played. Ophelia has been played pregnant with Hamlet's child, although she is more conventionally represented as the virginal, pale, weak, romantic lover and obedient child.

Hamlet meets the Ghost of his father, who claims to have been murdered by Claudius:

> Sleeping within my orchard,
> My custom always of the afternoon,
> Upon my secure hour thy uncle stole,
> With juice of cursed hebona in a vial,
> And in the porches of my ears did pour
> The leperous distilment; whose effect
> Holds such an enmity with blood of man
> That swift as quicksilver it courses through
> The natural gates and alleys of the body;
> And with a sudden vigour it doth posset
> And curd, like eager droppings into milk,
> The thin and wholesome blood. So did it mine;
> And a most instant tetter bak'd about,
> Most lazar-like, with vile and loathsome crust,
> All my smooth body.
> Thus was I, sleeping, by a brother's hand
> Of life, of crown, of queen, at once dispatch'd;
> Cut off even in the blossoms of my sin,
> Unhous'led, disappointed, unanel'd;
> No reckoning made, but sent to my account
> With all my imperfections on my head.
> O, horrible! O, horrible! most horrible!

1.5.59–80

Hamlet's immediate reaction is to revenge his father. His problems begin after the Ghost has gone and he begins to realise the implications of this vow of revenge. He wonders whether the Ghost is a good spirit or the Devil in disguise and thus whether Claudius really is a murderer. In other words, he starts discovering reasons for not carrying out his revenge. Traditionally, of course, Hamlet is a man of great inaction, who, in the opening words of a famous and wonderful film version, cannot make up his mind. Despite the welter and weight of scholarly tradition, I firmly believe Hamlet to be a man of great and diverse action and enormous energy too. Consider, for instance, what happens when the strolling players turn up at the court. A moment before they come, Hamlet is brooding about the frailty of man:

> What a piece of work is a man! How noble in reason! how infinite in faculties! in form and moving, how express and admirable! in action, how like an angel! in apprehension, how like a god! the beauty of the world! the paragon of animals! and yet, to me, what is this quintessence of dust? Man delights me not – . . .

2.2.302–8

A moment later he hears the players are coming and he's transformed. He's immediately energised, formulating his plan to 'catch the conscience of the King' by getting these players to perform a play within a play:

> I'll have these players
> Play something like the murder of my father
> Before mine uncle. I'll observe his looks;
> I'll tent him to the quick. If 'a do blench,
> I know my course. The spirit that I have seen
> May be a devil; and the devil hath power
> T'assume a pleasing shape; yea and perhaps
> Out of my weakness and my melancholy,
> As he is very potent with such spirits,
> Abuses me to damn me. I'll have grounds
> More relative than this. The play's the thing
> Wherein I'll catch the conscience of the King.

2.2.590–601

Hamlet may have doubts about the identity of the Ghost, but he's in his element actively plotting a solution to the problem.

The one action he cannot perform, however, is the anachronistic act of vengeance. It's his duty to kill Claudius, but he feels unable to do it because he doesn't really believe in the revenge code. When he does finally kill Claudius, it's almost as if he does so on the basis of an instant, split-second decision. He leaves himself an element of choice, which would have been unthinkable to a revenger pure and simple, and then makes a quick, intense emotional decision. The Player King says in the play within the play:

> What to ourselves in passion we propose,
> The passion ending, doth the purpose lose.

3.2.189–90

Hamlet makes decisions in moments of great passion and emotional upsurge. Perhaps this is why he ends the play as a mass murderer. He certainly kills far more people than Claudius ever killed. He personally kills three and is directly responsible for the deaths of Rosencrantz and Guildenstern as well. He's probably indirectly responsible for the death of Ophelia, as she would not have died if Hamlet had not killed her father. His mother would have survived if she had not drunk the poison intended for her son.

Are these the actions of a sane man? I don't think that Hamlet is ever quite mad. He initially assumes an 'antic disposition' to cloak his detective work on Claudius. There are, however, three moments when he gets himself into a dangerously traumatic state, in which he at least approaches real madness, teetering on the edge of insanity without quite going over it. The first of these moments is with the Ghost of his father. The other two are the nunnery scene with Ophelia and the closet scene with his mother. But, for the rest of the time, he is eminently sane. He has a razor-sharp mind and a very clear appreciation of what is going on around him. His black, sardonic, sarcastic, ironic humour often steers him away from insanity. He uses his humour throughout the play as a method of both attack and defence. As he cloaks his actions with his defensive kind of humour, as well as with an 'antic disposition', you never actually see the man properly. It is as if he's constantly out of focus both to himself and to the spectator. You never really see all the bits come together at the same time until perhaps the latter half of the play when the dust begins to settle.

One of the main tragedies of Hamlet as a man is that he is not allowed to fulfil the qualities and talents that he has been given. In the normal course of events he would have become King on the death of his father. Although Denmark is an elective monarchy, Hamlet gives a clear indication that he hoped to be King when he accuses Claudius of popping 'in between th' election and my hopes'. I doubt that he was an introverted, depressive character before the play started. He's in a state of deep shock at the speed with which his mother has married his uncle. Yet it is not a melancholic, introverted, passive disgust. He's very, very angry and he wants everybody to know about it. He can hardly bear to talk to his mother:

Seems, madam! Nay, it is; I know not seems.
'Tis not alone my inky cloak, good mother,
Nor customary suits of solemn black,
Nor windy suspiration of forc'd breath,
No, nor the fruitful river in the eye,
Nor the dejected haviour of the visage,
Together with all forms, moods, shapes of grief,
That can denote me truly. These, indeed, seem;
For they are actions that a man might play;
But I have that within which passes show –
These but the trappings and the suits of woe.

1.2.76–86

This is a very aggressive kind of sadness. Hamlet is a young man studying at Wittenberg, who, like the other students, loves the theatre. I can't say that he's just an ordinary young man, but he's certainly not a great tragic figure from curtain up. He's more like a thorn in everybody's flesh: truculent, rude and selfish. Ophelia suggests that, far from being melancholy and introverted, Hamlet is in the mould of the great Renaissance men like Sir Philip Sydney, Sir Walter Raleigh and the Earl of Essex:

> O, what a noble mind is here o'erthrown!
> The courtier's, soldiers, scholar's, eye, tongue, sword;
> Th' expectancy and rose of the fair state,
> The glass of fashion and the mould of form,
> Th' observ'd of all observers – quite, quite down!
> And I, of ladies most deject and wretched,
> That suck'd the honey of his music vows,
> Now see that noble and most sovereign reason,
> Like sweet bells jangled, out of time and harsh;
> That unmatch'd form and feature of blown youth
> Blasted with ecstasy. O, woe is me
> T'have seen what I have seen, see what I see!

3.1.150–61

He could do it all, but it all went wrong for him. Ophelia thinks that he has become mad, but indicates that he's not naturally more depressive than anyone else. The capacity for depression is part of the human condition, inherent in all of us, not particularly so in Hamlet. We can all be nudged towards it, like Hamlet, given the circumstances.

All plays are journeys and Hamlet's journey is chartered through every conceivable terrain. There's a curious double time sequence for this journey: the logical and, let's say, the poetical. The logical is certainly no more than two or three months, whereas the poetical is spread over anything up to twelve years. Hamlet changes attitude, direction and personality constantly during this time. If, as Ophelia suggests, he was once idealistic, he loses this by the end of the play. Just before he goes to England, he says 'from this time forth,/ My thoughts be bloody, or be nothing worth!' He has already hardened and become more realistic. By the time he comes back from England, he's gone beyond even this position into one of pre-destination. He believes that there is 'a divinity that shapes our ends,/ Rough-hew them how we will'. When the challenge to the duel comes, his great friend Horatio offers to make his excuses, but Hamlet replies:

> Not a whit, we defy augury: there is a special providence
> in the fall of a sparrow. If it be now, 'tis not to come;
> if it be not to come, it will be now; if it be not now, yet
> it will come – the readiness is all. Since no man owes of
> aught he leaves, what isn't to leave betimes? Let be.

5.2.207–210

He believes that you've got to be prepared for the moment and be able to recognise it. He had the time, place and opportunity to kill Claudius earlier on in the play, when the King was praying. Hamlet argued that to have done so under these circumstances would have sanctified the murder and sent Claudius's soul straight to heaven. It is, perhaps, a reason which is really an excuse. This time it is action first, with no time for words afterwards:

> I am dead, Horatio. Wretched queen, adieu!
> You that look pale and tremble at this chance,
> That are but mutes or audience to this act,
> Had I but time, as this fell sergeant Death
> Is strict in his arrest, O, I could tell you –
> But let it be. Horatio, I am dead:
> Thou livest; report me and my cause aright
> To the unsatisfied.

5.2.325–33

Hamlet may well be right about the futility of existence. Nearly everyone's dead or dying and he doesn't have time to explain what the point was.

Playing Hamlet is often thought to be the acme of an actor's career. That's both good and bad news. The good news is that Hamlet is the most wonderful part to play. It calls on an actor's full armoury of craft: vocal, physical, mental and emotional. It is also a canvas that can be painted in so many ways and with so many different colours. The fact that many questions are posed in *Hamlet* and very few answers given makes the title role one of the greatest acting parts. You are allowed to attempt to give some of the answers through the performance. They can never be definitive answers, but they can always be different ones. The bad news is that the part has become a hoop through which aspiring classical actors have to jump. It is the part you are going to be judged on. If you are seen to succeed as Hamlet, then you may be allowed to join the ranks of established classical actors. If you don't, then your report may say 'A good effort, but must try harder next term'. In the end, of course, the play itself *is* the thing.

THE TAMING
OF THE SHREW

Penelope Mortimer

Penelope Mortimer's publications include The
Pumpkin Eater *and* About Time. *She made this
programme in and around her home at Chastleton.*

Everybody knows that *The Taming of the Shrew* takes place in
Padua. But many people forget, if indeed they ever knew, that
Shakespeare's story of Petruchio's outrageous courtship is a
'play within a play', performed by a troupe of touring actors in an
English country house for the benefit of Christopher Sly, a
drunken tinker. Sly lived and probably died in a Warwickshire
village rather than on the plains of Lombardy. For some reason,
perhaps tidiness, this Prologue, which is known as the Induction,
is frequently omitted. Some bardologists doubt its authenticity.
Others, like Robert Atkins, believe that it's the only part of *The
Taming of the Shrew* to be written entirely by Shakespeare. 'The
play within a play', he says, 'is part Shakespeare, part anyone,
with perhaps a few lines thrown in by the actors'. William Hazlitt
compares Christopher Sly with Sancho Panza and Frederick
Schlegel thought that the Induction was far more remarkable
than the play proper: 'the whole is but a light sketch, but in ex-
cellence and nice propriety, it will hardly ever be excelled'.

Why did Shakespeare bother to set *The Taming of the Shrew* in
remote Padua when there were chauvinist husbands and nagging
wives nearer home? Probably because the Mediterranean was for
Elizabethan audiences what the 'wild west' was for moviegoers in
the great days of the cinema, or what 'outer space' is now. Love
stories in particular became more dramatic and romantic in an
Italian setting. Foreigners, then as now, were always permitted to
behave more outrageously than the stodgy British. But, apart
from a smattering of phrasebook Italian and a bit of name-
dropping, there's no attempt to make the location realistic. The
countryside is as cold and muddy as Warwickshire and
Petruchio's servingmen are called Nathaniel, Philip, Walter and

Sugarsop – there's not a Giovanni among them. Sly could have conned a pot of small ale off any of them at the local. Whatever the reasons some directors have for leaving out the Induction, to me it has the warmth of a family joke, the magic of something that's not quite a fairy story. Sly may have had his head in the clouds but, like Shakespeare, his feet, and very often the rest of him, were firmly in the Warwickshire mud.

The play opens with Sly staggering out of the local alehouse, pursued by the Hostess demanding payment for the glasses he's broken. He falls into a drunken sleep by the side of the road. The local squire comes along on his way home from the hunt. He tells his huntsmen to carry the insensible Sly into the house and put him in the best bedroom. When he wakes up, they must treat him like 'a mighty Lord'. It will be 'pastime passing excellent' to see what he makes of it:

> Carry him gently to my fairest chamber
> And hand it round with all my wanton pictures;
> Balm his foul head in warm distilled waters,
> And burn sweet wood to make the lodging sweet;
> Procure me music ready when he wakes,
> To make a dulcet and a heavenly sound;
> And if he chance to speak, be ready straight,
> And with low submissive reverence
> Say 'What is it your honour will command?'

Scene 1, 44–52

Those are the orders, but when Sly comes round and finds himself in the lap of luxury he's extremely fractious:

> Am not I Christopher Sly, old Sly's son of Burton Heath; by birth a pedlar, by education a cardmaker, by transmutation a bear-herd, and now by present profession a tinker. Ask Marian Hacket the fat ale-wife of Wincot, if she know not me; if she say I am not fourteen pence on the score for sheer ale, score me up for the lying'st knave in Christendom.

Scene 2, 17–22

Shakespeare's uncle, Edmund Lambert, lived at Barton-on-the-Heath and his mother came from Wilmcote. There were Hackets in the parish at that time, perhaps there still are. It's more than likely that Shakespeare, like Sly, owed fat Marian fourteen pence for sheer ale.

The Squire, for some reason, disguises himself as a messenger and the scene is set for the swapping of identities and the change of personalities that is what *The Taming of the Shrew* is all about. A fanfare of trumpets and Sly's bedroom becomes a street in Padua . . .

Old Baptista Minola has two daughters, Katherina and Bianca, whom he's anxious to sell on the marriage market. Bianca, the younger of the two, appears to be a docile, sweet little thing and has three eager suitors. Katherina appears to be, in modern parlance, a right bitch. No sensible man would touch her with a bargepole. She makes life very difficult for her family:

> BAPTISTA: Why dost thou wrong her that did ne'er wrong thee?
> When did she cross thee with a bitter word?
> KATHERINA: Her silence flouts me, and I'll be reveng'd.
> BAPTISTA: What, in my sight? Bianca, get thee in.
> KATHERINA: What, will you not suffer me? Nay, now I see
> She is your treasure, she must have a husband;
> I must dance bare-foot on her wedding-day,
> And for your love to her lead apes in hell.
> Talk not to me; I will go sit and weep,
> Till I can find occasion of revenge.

2.1.27–36

When Shakespeare wrote *The Taming of the Shrew*, he seemed impatient with the whole business of romantic love, as though he felt that the sighing and swooning, the protestations, the lutes, handkerchiefs, potions and tokens wasted a lot of time. Bianca's suitors appear to have nothing to do but plot to out-manoeuvre each other, like a bunch of silly schoolgirls. Lucentio only has to see Bianca in the street to be burning, pining and perishing with passion. Gremio, who is old enough to be her father, querulously bids for her with his herd of dairy cows and his two houses. Hortensio postures as a music teacher in order to speak a word to her, although he's obviously known the family for years. Shakespeare appears to be saying that men, far from being the superior sex, behave far more foolishly than women when they're in love:

> LUCENTIO: Tranio, I burn, I pine, I perish, Tranio,
> If I achieve not this young modest girl.
> Counsel me, Tranio, for I know thou canst;
> Assist me, Tranio, for I know thou wilt.

1.1.150–3

Petruchio bursts in on all this sentimental rubbish like a high-powered hustler with no time to waste. He's come to Padua to find a rich wife and no nonsense about coral lips and perfumed breath:

> Signior Baptista, my business asketh haste,
> And every day I cannot come to woo.
> You knew my father well, and in him me,
> Left solely heir to all his lands and goods,
> Which I have bettered rather than decreas'd.
> Then tell me, if I get your daughter's love.
> What dowry shall I have with her to wife?

2.1.113–9

He's a practical, down-to-earth man, who refuses to let anything stand in his way:

> I am as peremptory as she proud-minded;
> And where two raging fires meet together,
> They do consume the thing that feeds their fury.
> Though little fire grows great with little wind,
> Yet extreme gusts will blow out fire and all.
> So I to her, and so she yields to me;
> For I am rough, and woo not like a babe.

2.1.130–6

My guess is that he's bored with suitable women. Any woman renowned for her 'beauteous modesty' is suspect to this man of the world. If it's a choice between a scolding tongue and a sly minx, he has no doubt at all which he's going to choose. He senses in Katherina a challenge, a sport, a 'pastime passing excellent'. She doesn't disappoint him. Their first conversation is worthy of an early Frank Capra movie, in which wisecrack for wisecrack, she gives as good as she takes:

> PETRUCHIO: Hearing thy mildness prais'd in every town,
>   Thy virtues spoke of, and thy beauty sounded,
>   Yet not so deeply as to thee belongs,
>   Myself am mov'd to woo thee for my wife.
> KATHERINA: Mov'd! in good time! Let him that mov'd you hither
>   Remove you hence. I knew you at the first
>   You were a moveable.
> PETRUCHIO: Why, what's a moveable?
> KATHERINA: A join'd-stool.

PETRUCHIO: Thou hast hit it. Come, sit on me.
KATHERINA: Asses are made to bear, and so are you.
PETRUCHIO: Women are made to bear, and so are you.
KATHERINA: No such jade as you, if me you mean.
PETRUCHIO: Alas, good Kate, I will not burden thee!
 For, knowing thee to be but young and light –
KATHERINA: Too light for such a swain as you to catch;
 And yet as heavy as my weight should be.

2.1.190–204

Now, in his odd way, Petruchio respects her and the marriage deal he proposes, while it may not be very elegantly phrased, is scrupulously fair. But things were changing. Poets, playwrights and balladmongers were coming out against arranged marriages. Admittedly their love matches usually ended in tears, but as women kicked over the pedestals on which they'd been uncomfortably perched since the Age of Chivalry and demanded to be treated as creatures of flesh and blood, parents had to realise that their daughters were rather more than commodities.

What was Shakespeare's opinion? He seems to be saying in this play at least that a sensible deal between equals is a lot more satisfactory than a short-lived honeymoon, however ecstatic. When it came to marrying off his own daughters, Shakespeare was an old man in his early forties who found himself in something like Baptista's predicament. Susanna, 'witty above her sex', married the admirable Dr Hall and lived happily ever after. Judith romantically married Thomas Quiney, a ne'er-do-well four years her junior, and came to grief. I'm sure that Dr Hall behaved impeccably at the wedding, but I wonder whether Shakespeare would have preferred a less austere son-in-law for his favourite daughter's bridegroom. Although perhaps not quite as outrageous as Petruchio:

PETRUCHIO: And wherefore gaze this goodly company
 As if they saw some wondrous monument,
 Some comet of unusual prodigy?
BAPTISTA: Why, sir, you know this is your wedding-day.
 First were we sad, fearing you would not come,
 Now sadder, that you come so unprovided.
 Fie, doff this habit, shame to your estate,
 An eye-sore to our solemn festival!

3.2.90–7

The play has, predictably enough, outraged many sensibilities over the years. Samuel Pepys called it 'a mean play'. Frank

PENELOPE MORTIMER

Harris wondered how Shakespeare could ever have put his hand
to such a paltry subject. Liberated women rioted in Central Park
during Joseph Papp's production a few years ago. No other play
has touched so many sore spots or raised such a furore of criticism. On the other hand no other play has been such a popular
success. You just have to think of Richard Burton taming Elizabeth Taylor, or Howard Keel belting out 'I come to wive it
wealthily in Padua'. Petruchio's certainly a cad, but most male
sex symbols are. Like it or not, very few women are turned on by
saints and gentle reason seems to be more appreciated when it
comes, however infrequently, from an apparent bully. This is the
nature of the sexual game, if you're the sort of person who's good
at it. Petruchio and Katherina are experts:

> KATHERINA: Gentlemen, forward to the bridal dinner.
> I see a woman may be made a fool
> If she had not a spirit to resist.
> PETRUCHIO: They shall go forward, Kate, at thy command.
> Obey the bride, you that attend on her;
> Go to the feast, revel and domineer,
> Carouse full measure to her maidenhead;
> Be mad and merry, or go hang yourselves.
> But for my bonny Kate, she must with me.
> Nay, look not big, not stamp, nor stare, nor fret;
> I will be master of what is mine own –
> She is my goods, my chattels, she is my house,
> My household stuff, my field, my barn,
> My horse, my ox, my ass, my any thing,
> And here she stands; touch her whoever dare;
> I'll bring mine action on the proudest he
> That stops my way in Padua.

3.2.216–31

Of course the fun gets out of hand. That's why the average
Elizabethan audience would have enjoyed it so much. But why
take it so seriously? It provides laughs for a lot of neglected libi-
dos, just as Punch and Judy did in the bad old days before the
moralists banned it. Everything's got so glum. We're not supposed to laugh at the shortsighted, or the hard of hearing or
drunks. The Irish and the Scots are getting touchy, possibly on
behalf of the Jews, who have their own jokes. The curious notion
of blasphemy has been revived. It won't be long before the
Association of Mothers-in-Law starts lobbying for protection.

If Shakespeare were asked to write a play for the Royal

Shakespeare Company with its reverent middle-class audiences, he probably wouldn't be able to write a word. He set out to antagonise just such an audience in *The Taming of the Shrew:*

> PETRUCHIO: This is a way to kill a wife with kindness,
> And thus I'll curb her mad and headstrong humour.
> He that knows better how to tame a shrew,
> Now let him speak; 'tis charity to show.

4.1.192–5

So let's try to think of the play as Shakespeare intended it. In Sly's words, it is a 'Christmas gambold or a tumbling-trick'. If some women are still offended by it, they show a great deal less sense than Katherina. I wonder how many wives, or husbands for that matter, are skilled in the use of the magic phrase 'Yes, dear'. It doesn't imply agreement and should never be used when you're actually listening to something. But it does produce an affirmative atmosphere. If you're an expert like Katherina, you can use it as a very effective weapon. It deflates all pompous announcements: 'I've made up my mind to leave you'. 'Yes, dear'. It answers the unanswerable: 'Shall I shave now and bring the coal in later, or shall I bring the coal in before supper and shave while you're watching Robin Day?'. 'Yes, dear', murmurs the modern Katherina, without so much as glancing up from her Open University textbook. If we must look for a moral, it's not so much peace at any price as peace with a kind of devious honour. We know that Petruchio will become the kind of husband who roars a great deal, but, when it comes to the crunch, always has to ask the wife. Katherina, a cat with a lifetime's supply of cream, will adore him, humour him and go her own sweet way regardless. When he dies, thrown on the hunting field or from apoplexy after reading a leader in *The Times,* she will mourn him deeply and take to gardening and good works. If anyone asks her what Petruchio was really like, she'll say 'Impossible!' and laugh, fondly remembering the curious collusion that was her marriage.

THE TAMING
OF THE SHREW
Paola Dionisotti

Paola Dionisotti played Isabella in Measure for
Measure *at the Royal Shakespeare Company in
1978, as well as Katherina in* The Taming of the
Shrew.

My first connection with *The Taming of the Shrew* was when I
was at school. I had to find a big Shakespearean speech at the
last minute for some competition which a celebrity was coming
to adjudicate. I flipped desperately through the complete works
and lighted on this enormous two and a half page speech. I had
no time to read it, but a friend told me that the play had a
wonderful story and was very funny. It was, apparently, about a
rich, spoilt, wild-cat girl who gets married off by her long-
suffering father to a clever, strong young man. He knows she is
just the girl for him and proceeds to show her how stupid and
childish she is in a series of very funny and sexy rough and
tumble scenes. He wins her over and, at the end of the play, she
turns round and scolds the other women for standing up to their
husbands in that big speech. She says that all the husbands want
from their wives is love, fair looks and true obedience. If they get
this, then they will look after their wives properly and fight for
them if necessary. The rich girl and the strong young man fall
desperately in love and live happily ever after. Great stuff, I
thought! This was after all the favourite theme of every novel and
woman's magazine story I was reading and of every film I was
seeing. I was invited to play the part of Katherina at Stratford in
1978 and became intimately involved with it for the next fourteen
months of my life. They said to me that it was a great play which
always works with an audience. I went home and read it through
very slowly. I was appalled. I didn't find it in the least bit funny.
In fact I thought it was downright nasty. I suddenly got
frightened that audiences might feel the same way as me about it.
I was told not to worry as it was a sure-fire winner. Shakespeare was
definitely after a winner when he wrote it sometime between 1592

and 1594. The Earl of Pembroke's men, the company he probably wrote it for, were in dire financial straits. A play about the power, money and sex games of wealthy men, then as now, would have made compulsive viewing.

Baptista Minola is a wealthy merchant of Padua. He has two daughters both of marriageable age. He also has a problem, for whereas everybody seems to want to marry Bianca, his younger daughter and obviously his favourite, nobody seems to want to marry Katherina, his elder daughter. Being a canny gentleman who does not wish to be saddled in his old age with a financial burden with whom he so blatantly does not get on, he announces to Bianca's suitors that they don't stand a chance until Katherina has been married. Furthermore, he stipulates that until that takes place the only men to be allowed access to Bianca are 'schoolmasters . . . fit to instruct her youth'. The Minolas exit, leaving the financially precarious Hortensio and the wealthy but elderly Gremio in a state of great frustration. They decide on a two-pronged course of action. Firstly, they must join forces and find a husband for Katherina. Secondly, each privately determines to carry on wooing Bianca willy-nilly despite her father's edict. But unbeknownst to them, and indeed at this stage to Bianca herself, a third suitor has come on the scene, the undoubtedly handsome Lucentio, the son of an extremely wealthy man from Pisa. He has just arrived in Padua with his manservant Tranio. He witnesses by chance Baptista Minola's treatment of the suitors, falls head over heels in love with Bianca and promptly joins the fray. There we have it. The plots concerning both Katherina and Bianca are set up in one impressive stroke.

There is, however, another plot. The story of the Minolas is a play within a play. *The Taming of the Shrew* has the peculiarity of beginning with a so-called Induction. It's a rather unpleasant, flimsy storyline, which is frequently omitted. We see a group of noblemen fresh from the hunt, who come across Christopher Sly, a drunkard lying in a stupor. He's a down and out who has just been kicked out of the pub. One of the noblemen suggests playing a trick on him, a kind of power game to entertain themselves. They take him up, bathe him, clothe him, perfume him, titillate him with dirty pictures, flatter him, get a page-boy to dress up as a woman and pretend to be his wife and finally persuade him that he is really a nobleman who quite simply has been mad for the last fifteen years and has now finally recovered his wits. Then they sit him down and he, they and we all watch *The Taming of the Shrew*. This Induction seems to me to set up very clearly the underlying social ethos of the world in which the Minolas lived and indeed the world in which Shakespeare lived and wrote as well.

I recently started a book that I'd just got out of the library. The opening two sentences went as follows: 'It was intended that this should be a book about women in relation to society as a whole, on the traditional role they have played for so long, the reasons for it and the ways in which I think this role should now change. It has turned out to be a book largely about men'. The story that we and Christopher Sly watch unfold is not, as I in my schoolgirl days believed it to be, that of a spoilt girl who grows up and learns to love. For, springing out of this man-filled, man-dominated, man-obsessed world, it is of course the story of Petruchio, the man who tames her. We are told that he succeeds in taming her, but we are not told how or what she feels and thinks about all this. One of the most crucial moments in Kate's life, in any woman's life, is the moment she agrees to marry someone. Kate's father returns to the room where she and Petruchio have been left alone together for a mere five minutes:

BAPTISTA: Why, how now, daughter Katherine, in your
dumps?
KATHERINA: Call you me daughter? Now I promise you
You have show'd a tender fatherly regard
To wish me wed to one half lunatic,
A mad-cap ruffian and a swearing Jack,
That thinks with oaths to face the matter out.
PETRUCHIO: Father, 'tis thus: yourself and all the world
That talk'd of her have talk'd amiss of her.
If she be curst, it is for policy,
For she's not froward, but modest as the dove;
She is not hot, but temperate as the morn;
For patience she will prove a second Grissel,
And Roman Lucrece for her chastity.
And, to conclude, we have 'greed so well together
That upon Sunday is the wedding-day.
KATHERINA: I'll see thee hang'd on Sunday first.

2.1.276–91

It's quite clear what Kate thinks of the idea at this point, but Petruchio and Baptista proceed quite calmly to discuss the arrangements. They do not ask Kate whether she has changed her mind. She, in turn, says nothing.

She is treated just as badly on her wedding night. She and

Petruchio arrive at his house. It is the middle of winter and they have had quite a journey. Here is Grumio's description of it:

GRUMIO: Now I begin: Imprimus, we came down a foul hill, my master riding behind my mistress –
CURTIS: Both of one horse?
GRUMIO: What's that to thee?
CURTIS: Why, a horse.
GRUMIO: Tell thou the tale. But hadst thou not cross'd me, thou shouldst have heard how her horse fell and she under her horse; thou shouldst have heard in how miry a place, how she was bemoil'd, how he left her with the horse upon her, how be beat me because her horse stumbled, how she waded through the dirt to pluck him off me, how he swore, how she pray'd that never pray'd before, how I cried, how the horses ran away, how her bridle was burst, how I lost my crupper – with many things of worthy memory, which now shall die in oblivion, and thou return unexperienc'd to thy grave.

4.1.58–73

Kate must be starving, as Petruchio has dragged her off from the church without hanging around for the wedding feast. In a world where marriage is the most important event in a woman's life, few women that I know would have tucked into a big breakfast prior to the ceremony. Kate's still in her wedding dress, since Petruchio wouldn't give her a chance to change. Imagine what kind of a state it is in after the journey. She enters this strange household which from now on is to be her home and meets the servants: Nathaniel, Gregory, Joseph, Philip, Peter, Walter, Nicholas, Adam, Rafe, Gabriel and Sugarsop. There's not another woman in sight. Meanwhile Petruchio is more interested in the state of his supper:

PETRUCHIO: 'Tis burnt; and so is all the meat.
What dogs are these? Where is the rascal cook?
How durst you villains bring it from the dresser
And serve it thus to me that love it not?
There, take it to you, trenchers, cups, and all;
You heedless joltheads and unmanner'd slaves!
What, do you grumble? I'll be with you straight.
KATHERINA: I pray you, husband, be not so disquiet;
The meat was well, if you were so contented.

PETRUCHIO: I tell thee, Kate, 'twas burnt and dried away,
And I expressly am forbid to touch it;
For it engenders choler, planteth anger:
And better 'twere that both of us did fast,
Since, of ourselves, ourselves are choleric,
Than feed it with such over-roasted flesh.
Be patient; to-morrow 't shall be mended.
And for this night we'll fast for company.
Come, I will bring thee to thy bridal chamber.

4.1.145–62

Petruchio and Kate exit, but we stay with the scene in the dining hall. What's going on in Kate's mind? All Shakespeare gives us is a brief description of what's happening up in the bedroom from the boy Curtis. Grumio asks him where Petruchio is:

In her chamber. Making a sermon of continency to her,
And rails, and swears, and rates, that she, poor soul,
Knows not which way to stand, to look, to speak,
And sits as one new risen from a dream.

4.1.166–9

We are never allowed to get too close to Kate.

Petruchio on the other hand homes right in and, talking directly to the audience with the utter confidence both as character and actor of someone who knows that they are with him 100 per cent, proceeds to lay his cards on the table. Here are some of the images he uses to describe his wife:

Thus have I politicly begun my reign,
And 'tis my hope to end successfully.
My falcon now is sharp and passing empty.
And till she stoop she must not be full-gorg'd,
For then she never looks upon her lure.
Another way I have to man my haggard,
To make her come, and know her keeper's call,
That is, to watch her, as we watch these kites
That bate and beat, and will not be obedient.

4.1.172–80

Petruchio ends this piece of bravado with a supremely arrogant final couplet:

He that knows better how to tame a shrew,
Now let him speak; 'tis charity to show.

194–5

Jonathan Pryce, who played my Petruchio quite magnificently, would at this point wait and wait. It got to be a joke backstage how long he could hold the pause. It's almost four centuries since that play was written and seven nights out of ten nobody said a word!

Where does this utter confidence that Shakespeare had in presenting this moment spring from? First of all, it comes from his ability to create a magnificent character like Petruchio, the loner, gambler, quick-witted, aggressive, plain-speaking and sometimes childish cynic. His bragging competitiveness verges on the ludicrous when the other suitors challenge his ability to take on Kate:

> Why came I hither but to that intent?
> Think you a little din can daunt mine ears?
> Have I not in my time heard lions roar?
> Have I not heard the sea, puff'd up with winds,
> Rage like an angry boar chaf'd with sweat?
> Have I not heard great ordnance in the field,
> And heaven's artillery thunder in the skies?
> Have I not in a pitched battle heard
> Loud 'larums, neighing steeds, and trumpets' clang?
> And do you tell me of a woman's tongue,
> That gives not half so great a blow to hear
> As will a chestnut in a farmer's fire?
> Tush! tush! fear boys with bugs.

1.2.195–207

But, just when you think he might have gone too far, as he does more than once in his taming of Kate, he swings round and disarms you and her pretty thoroughly:

> Well, come, my Kate; we will unto your father's
> Even in these honest mean habiliments;
> Our purses shall be proud, our garments poor;
> For 'tis the mind that makes the body rich;
> And as the sun breaks through the darkest clouds,
> So honour peereth in the meanest habit.

4.3.165–70

He's full of life and energy. He may get bored easily, but he's so unpredictable that you can be sure that an audience never will be.

The second point from which Shakespeare's confidence springs lies in what the term 'shrew' meant to an Elizabethan audience. The dictionary says a shrew is 'a scolding, bad-tempered, mean-spirited woman'. There is no equivalent label for a man, though I'm sure that there were plenty of scolding, bad-tempered, mean-spirited men around. A shrew is obviously a woman who fails to be, or who doesn't enjoy being, what a woman should be. The Elizabethan age represented the flowering and celebration of a social order, which had been created by men, primarily for men. They were the decision makers who had absolute control over the wealth of the country. There was, however, a highly educated woman on the throne. This enabled women in England more access to learning and thus to have more influence and greater freedom of movement that anywhere else in Europe. But independent women who remained outside what was in effect a small, snobbish social clique were despised, pitied, hated or laughed at. Kate comes to see this very clearly by the end of the play:

> Such duty as the subject owes the prince,
> Even such a woman oweth to her husband;
> And when she is froward, peevish, sullen, sour,
> And not obedient to his honest will,
> What is she but a foul contending rebel
> And graceless traitor to her loving lord?

5.2.155–60

She is in fact a very clear thinker. She springs out of the play as a self-contained, quick-thinking woman, clever and funny with words but also utterly direct when she wants to be. She doesn't suffer fools gladly and above all demands instinctively to be treated with respect. She's a threat to her father and the other men in Padua because she's an outsider and a rebel. She's someone who won't be patronised, whereas Bianca will put up with no end of it to get her man to marry her. Kate, who wants to be married just as much as her sister does, can't do this. So she is punished. Petruchio doesn't even question the fact that she is a shrew and will therefore need taming. His reputation depends, after all, on his ability to tame her.

They get very close to falling in love. They certainly recognise in each other a kindred spirit as they are both rebels. Petruchio comes to Padua, the society there uses him and pays him to take Katherina off its hands. He and Kate return to that world for Bianca's wedding. Kate has struggled to work out what Petruchio really wants of her right from the wooing scene. Just before the last scene we feel that she has twigged that it's to do with him being able to trust in her support and alliance both publicly and privately. The restlessness, bragging competitiveness and the desire to stir things up, which are brought out in him by being back in Padua, demonstrate an extraordinary insecurity in him. I always used to feel that, if anyone needed sorting out by the end of the play, it was Petruchio.

THE MERCHANT OF VENICE
Wolf Mankowitz

*Wolf Mankowitz has written plays, novels, short
stories, biographies, poetry and screenplays. He is
also a theatrical producer. He made this programme
on location in Lincoln.*

I am a Jew and a writer, but I am also a man. If you prick me I
bleed, as the author of *The Merchant of Venice* puts it. That blood
colours my perspective towards a work which, more than any
other in the English language, created the image of the Jew. That
image haunts English literature. The eighteenth century stage
Jews fathered the Svengalis and Fagins of the nineteenth
century. Their literary descendants, sinister, comic or merely
vulgar, continue to run through the plays and novels of the early
twentieth century until the Nazis gave Jew-baiting a bad name.

Shakespeare didn't entirely invent Shylock. There is a fourteenth century tale by one Giovanni Fiorentino which tells of a
Jew who demands a pound of flesh from a Christian debtor, who
is eventually saved by the inspired advocacy of a lady from
Belmont. Fiorentino changed the original story by making the
usurer a Jew instead of a Christian. He was writing soon after the
Black Plague had ravaged Europe. It was said that the Jews were
to blame for this because they had poisoned the wells. So
Fiorentino created a Jewish usurer and found a whole new audience, which included Shakespeare, for a tired old story. Now
Shakespeare may have known that in ancient Roman law a
creditor was allowed to claim the flesh of a debtor who was in-
solvent and, says that law, it did not matter if he cut too much or
too little. But Shakespeare could not have known that such
barbaric practices were specifically forbidden in Jewish law.
There is no such episode in the whole of recorded Jewish
history. But in European literature the Jews were forever seduc-
ing nuns and eating children and poisoning wells and carving off
great bloody hunks of flesh off any passing Christian. Now how
can such a man as Shakespeare believe in such a farrago of nonsense? Did he really believe it, or was he simply catering for the
prejudices of his audience?

Another question I always ask myself whenever I see or read *The Merchant of Venice* is did Shakespeare ever meet a Jew? It seems most unlikely for there were no Jews in England at the time except for a few Portuguese converts. But he must have known something about the history of the Jews in England. They came to Britain with William the Conqueror. The Norman kings tolerated them for their financial abilities which, because they were permitted no further functions, they had developed through the centuries following their dispersal from their own country, Israel. It was a convenient arrangement enabling the Normans to lay off such unpopular and un-Christian activities as money-lending upon the Jews. They could then punish these deviators by crippling taxes at regular intervals. If they needed money, they borrowed it from the Jews. If they needed more, then they taxed the Jews. If they were able to allow their debts to continue until the Jew in question died, then they were, under Norman law, free of the debt. It was wiped clean. This represented a sort of licence to kill and many Jews died from it. The technique was perfected by the time that pious and lion-hearted King Richard I began to organise his crusades. London's Jewry was sacked and many Jews murdered to celebrate his coronation in 1189. The religious ardour kindled by this exercise rapidly spread through the country. Jews were forcibly converted at Dunstable. They were exterminated at King's Lynn. Most of them perished in Stamford and Norwich and in York an entire community escaped massacre by committing suicide. In Lincoln, where there was one of the richest and largest Jewish communities in England, the benevolent authorities offered them protection in the fortified bail. They were not, however, to escape punishment for long. A series of ritual murder accusations followed. It was alleged that the Jews used Christian blood for secret purposes. It was claimed that they crucified Christian children, ate their flesh and used their bowels for magic. The body of a boy was said to have been found in a well by the Jew's House in Lincoln in 1255. Chaucer refers to it in *The Canterbury Tales* and there's a ballad which tells how sweet little Sir Hugh lost his ball through the window of the Jew's House. The Jew's daughter wouldn't give it back to him, but used it, like the witch in a fairy tale, as bait. The body of the dead boy was entombed in the choir wall of Lincoln Cathedral where it soon became a popular shrine, supporting the charges of ritual murder against the Jews. Fear and tension grew among the Jewish communities. 994 Lincoln Jews were imprisoned. Their goods were seized and their houses were looted. The story of the ritual slaughter ran through the country like wildfire. Jews were tried on trumped-up charges everywhere and from this time onwards the sacrifice of Jews on Christian high days and holidays became routine. When Edward I acceded in 1272 the Jews were already so poor as to be of no value whatsoever to his Treasury, so he banished them. By All Saints Day, 1 November 1290, 16,000 Jews were refugees, the prey of any alleged Christian who was eager to improve his standard of living with a little sanctified slaughter. England was free of Jews and remained so for nearly 400 years. After the resettlement in 1655, there were only twenty-seven Jewish males in the City of London. Five years later, there were 150 Jewish souls in that town. Shakespeare had been dead for quite some time. So again I ask myself the question, how could Shakespeare have known a Jew?

Shakespeare had some small knowledge of the habits of the Jews, as illustrated by this speech by Shylock:

BASSANIO: If it please you to dine with us
SHYLOCK: Yes, to smell pork, to eat of the habitation which your prophet, the Nazarite, conjured the devil into! I will buy with you, sell with you, talk with you, walk with you, and so following; but I will not eat with you, drink with you, nor pray with you.

1.3.29–32

Yet such knowledge probably came from art rather than life. The first contemptuous reference to a Jew in Elizabethan literature occurs in *Euphues* by John Lyly. That was followed by a popular play called *The Jew*, which produced yet another by Richard Wilson called *The Three Ladies of London* showing the bloodymindedness of Jewish usurers. Finally there was Christopher Marlowe's monstrous *The Jew of Malta*. This revived the slumbering caricature of the Judas Iscariot Jew, the receiver of silver, the betrayer of Christ, the agent of Satan, in all his horror, prancing about the stage gibbering vindictively with his long red beard and grotesque hooked nose. Shakespeare certainly knew Marlowe's play when he wrote his own audience-catching comedy. A fresh wave of anti-semitism had been inspired by the Lopez affair. Roderigo Lopez, a Portuguese Jew who had converted to Christianity, was Queen Elizabeth's physician. He was accused of trying to poison her virgin Majesty, found guilty and taken to Tyburn, where on 7 June 1594 he was hung, drawn, quartered, disembowelled and burnt in public. This produced a great wave of patriotic anti-semitism, but it was terribly frustrating since there were no more Jews to be punished, except, of course, stage Jews like Shakespeare's Shylock:

> Why there, there, there, there! A diamond gone, cost me two thousand ducats in Frankfort! The curse never fell upon our nation till now; I never felt it till now. Two thousand ducats in that, and other precious, precious jewels. I would my daughter were dead at my foot, and the jewels in her ear; would she were hears'd at my foot, and the ducats in her coffin! No news of them? Why, so – and I know not what's spent in the search. Why, thou – loss upon loss! The thief gone with so much, and so much to find the thief; and no satisfaction, no revenge; nor no ill luck stirring but what lights o' my shoulders; no sighs but o' my breathing; no tears but o' my shedding!

3.1.72–83

The ancestor of this Shylock is Judas, who is possessed by the Devil and condemned to wander until the Second Coming. He was the villain in the religious mythology of Shakespeare and his audience and he remained the villain until 1964 when the Vatican blessedly relieved us of the charge of being Christ murderers for eternity. Shakespeare and his audience believed in an actual, physical Hell. It was presided over by the fallen angel, Satan, the anti-God, and he and the Almighty fought for the souls of men. Christ was man's intercessor in this conflict. He was opposed by Satan with his legion of demons and falsifiers, who were eager to perform his behest by betraying Christian souls. Judas Iscariot was a prince among these monstrous beings. He was the Wandering Jew, a strange, bent, bearded figure who used money and magic for the purchase of Christian souls for the use of his diabolic master. Gratiano vents some of these feelings in the play:

> O, be thou damn'd, inexecrable dog!
> And for thy life let justice be accus'd.
> Thou almost mak'st me waver in my faith,
> To hold opinion with Pythagoras
> That souls of animals infuse themselves
> Into the trunks of men. Thy currish spirit
> Govern'd a wolf who, hang'd for human slaughter,
> Even from the gallows did his fell soul fleet,
> And, whilst thou layest in thy unhallowed dam,
> Infus'd itself in thee; for thy desires
> Are wolfish, bloody, starv'd, and ravenous.

4.1.128–38

But what of the non-Jewish characters in this savage comedy? Shakespeare surely intends us to notice that Portia is a cold, snobbish little bitch, that Bassanio is an opportunistic, petty adventurer, that Lorenzo is a common thief and that Antonio, the good merchant of Venice himself, is a lachrymose, doting, gentleman-ninny, more concerned with the loss of the love of his pretty boyfriend, Bassanio, than he ever is with the profits from the business in which he engages:

> Give me your hand Bassanio; fare you well.
> Grieve not that I am fall'n to this for you,
> For herein Fortune shows herself more kind
> Than is her custom. It is still her use
> To let the wretched man outlive his wealth,
> To view with hollow eye and wrinkled brow
> An age of poverty; from which ling'ring penance
> Of such misery doth she cut me off.
> Commend me to your honourable wife;
> Tell her the process of Antonio's end;
> Say how I lov'd you; speak me fair in death;
> And, when the tale is told, bid her be judge
> Whether Bassanio had not once a love.
> Repent not you that you shall lose your friend,
> And he repents not that he pays your debt;
> For if the Jew do cut but deep enough,
> I'll pay it instantly with all my heart.

> 4.1.260–76

So there they are, the gay gentry of Venice, the city that invented the ghetto. Its Jews were confined to an area called the Gaeta, the cannon foundry. The gentry are concerned only with their fun and games, to finance which they occasionally gamble in trade. If they lose, they take the tattered, diseased remnants of their finery to the nearest rich woman stupid enough to be seduced into marriage. Did Shakespeare really intend us to take these characters as embodying the great virtues preached by Christ? I doubt it.

It is thus possible to see *The Merchant of Venice* in a more humanistic way. Actors and directors can go a long way to lighten the darkness of Shylock by emphasising the casual cruelty of the Venetian gentry:

> Signior Antonio, many a time and oft
> In the Rialto you have rated me
> About my moneys and my usances;

Still have I borne it with a patient shrug,
For suff'rance is the badge of all our tribe;
You call me misbeliever, cut-throat dog,
And spit upon my Jewish gaberdine,
And all for use of that which is mine own.

1.3.101–8

Shakespeare may not have known Jews, but Shylock remains the soul of his play. What is he trying to tell us through this strange character, a religious banker who, against the laws of his religion and of banking, would rather accept a bloody sacrifice than a high rate of interest on a short-term loan? The key is in that speech so often quoted as an example of Shakespeare's extraordinary humanity:

Hath not a Jew eyes? Hath not a Jew hands, organs, dimensions, senses, affections, passions, fed with the same food, hurt with the same weapons, subject to the same diseases, healed by the same means, warmed and cooled by the same winter and summer, as a Christian is? If you prick us, do we not bleed? If you tickle us, do we not laugh? If you poison us, do we not die? And if you wrong us, shall we not revenge? If we are like you in the rest, we will resemble you in that. If a Jew wrong a Christian, what is his humility? Revenge. If a Christian wrong a Jew, what should his sufference be by Christian example? Why, revenge. The villainy you teach me I will execute; and it shall go hard but I will better the instruction.

3.1.51–62

What Shakespeare observed, unique in his time, is that Jews are human beings and reflect the societies in which they live. If those societies are vengeful and villainous, then, as Shylock says 'The villainy you teach me I will execute; and it shall go hard but I will better the instruction'. For me this is the burning heart of the anger of Shylock, perceived by Shakespeare to be an integral part of a Christian civilisation which had, from time immemorial, vented its wrath and anger and revenge upon the body and property of the Jew, the descendant of Judas Iscariot, the betrayer of its religious founder. We know at this moment that Shakespeare perceives that men are what they make of themselves and of one another, that there is no Judas without Christ, there is no Shylock without Antonio. Some would say that there is no anti-semitism without Jews. I wonder, since an anti-semitic caricature was written in a country which had been free of Jews for 400 years. Perhaps *The Merchant of Venice* proves that this Christian disease persists whether we are there or not. If so, it is their problem, not Shylock's or mine.

THE MERCHANT OF VENICE

Timothy West

Timothy West played Cardinal Wolsey in the BBC
TV *Shakespeare production of* Henry VIII. *He has
acted in and directed a large number of Shakespeare's plays, as well as making frequent television
and film appearances.*

The courtroom scene is the best known part of *The Merchant
of Venice*. Most of us know about that infamous 'pound of flesh'
bargain between Shylock, the Jewish financier, and Antonio, the
Christian merchant, which is only prevented from reaching its
dreadful conclusion by a neat Shakespearean trick delivered in
the nick of time by the lady Portia. If the confrontation of Jew
and Christian provides an overpowering central theme for the
play, and if it raises questions for us today about its anti-semitic
overtones, it is not *just* the story of Shylock. With modern acting
traditions we may see new and subtle opportunities in the part. It
could be, however, that Shakespeare didn't quite know what he
had created and that the character ran away with him a bit.

Shakespeare based the play on two different literary sources: a
story from an Italian collection called *Il Pecorone* and, for the
casket sub-plot, the *Gesta Romanorum*. But he created a very
individual play out of them. It is possibly the nearest thing he
wrote to a modern fairy story in that the solutions tend to be cut
and dried. There are even echoes of the old morality plays. But
there is also a very dark threat to it, not only in the whole conflict
between Shylock and Antonio, as there are shades of darkness
and bitterness in all the elements of the comedy. Even the
relationship between the Gobbos, father and son, which produces a scene of high comedy, is nonetheless actually based on
dramatic material which is not intrinsically funny. The comedy,
after all, springs from the way in which the son tries to persuade
his father that his son is dead. At a more general level, a lot of the
comedy and a lot of the drama of the story is to do with the
balancing of emotional and material considerations. This is in
fact the bedrock of the play.

We come across three main groups of characters at the
beginning of the play. We hear first from Antonio, who *is* the

Merchant of Venice. He's at the centre of the crowd of hangers-on. He's in the same position as somebody today who runs a salon. He has a lot of money, and we are led to believe, some artistic sensibility. He collects around him quite a lot of attractive young men. He's obviously not a very sexually solved person and we see him in a considerable state of melancholy at the beginning of the play. We then meet Bassanio, who is his great favourite. Bassanio comes and tells him of his love for Portia, who is a 'lady in Belmont richly left', and of his need to get together the financial means to woo her properly. We're left with the feeling that, while Antonio is prepared to advance Bassanio the money needed through an indirect channel, he does it at a certain emotional cost to himself. We start the play in a rather uneasy way, seeing Venice as a place very dependent upon commercial considerations. People juggle between their emotional evaluation and their material considerations. It seems easier to live frivolously than very seriously.

When we get to Belmont, across the sea, we're in a totally different environment, calmer, more serene, but also much lighter. We meet Portia and her 'waiting woman', Nerissa. They are first shown to us as people who enjoy life very much. Even though Portia is wrestling with this horrendous problem of having to pick one of a number of very unpromising suitors to satisfy the terms of her father's will, we feel instinctively that Belmont is a kind of earthly paradise where things are inevitably going to turn out right. We are also made to feel the difference between the security of inherited wealth, which in Portia's case is considerable, and the difficulties and frustrations of living a life where your income is earned. Portia's suitors have to make a correct choice between three caskets of gold, silver and lead to win their prize. This has strong spiritual associations and it also provides an example of the fairy tale qualities of the play I mentioned earlier. After all, it's hardly realistic to imagine that anybody who had the slightest conception of Portia's sensibilities would ever choose the wrong casket.

We then meet Shylock. His conception is an interesting one dramatically, because although there is considerable reason to suppose that he owes some sort of affinity to Barabas in Marlowe's *The Jew of Malta*, I personally don't find the parallels at all strong. An Elizabethan audience nevertheless expected to see Jews portrayed on stage as wicked usurious people who behaved in an extravagant and appalling manner. Shakespeare uses this stereotype, although he manages to excite compassion for Shylock as well. He is therefore a more complex character than Barabas. I expect that Shakespeare, as usual, did a lot of research into the kind of person that he was. It is interesting, for instance, that usury stopped being a punishable crime about the same time that the play was being presented in London. There was, in London as well as in Venice, enormous need for capital investment as huge numbers of ships were being built and enormous trade projects had to be financed very quickly. People didn't mind at all having to pay interest on sums that could be obtained very readily. Therefore, at the start of the play, I believe that you have to see Shylock as a useful member of the community.

The spring begins to wind up when Bassanio goes to Antonio for that loan. Antonio hasn't got the ready money, as he's sunk it in a number of argosies all around the globe. I imagine that he has a number of friends to whom Bassanio would have gone to before he goes to Shylock, but they haven't been able to help him. 3000 ducats or pounds was quite a lot of money in Elizabethan England. He really is asking an awful lot. Bassanio, in many ways a rather ingenuous character, probably came and made the approach to Shylock without quite realising the implications of his action. I believe that when Antonio comes and finds him talking to Shylock he's not awfully pleased about it, but he's rather been landed in the situation where he has to clinch the deal:

ANTONIO: If thou wilt lend this money, lend it not
    As to thy friends – for when did friendship take
    A breed for barren metal of his friend? –
    But lend it rather to thine enemy,
    Who if he break thou mayst with better face
    Exact the penalty.
SHYLOCK: Why, look you, how you storm!
    I would be friends with you, and have your love,
    Forget the shames that you have stain'd me with,
    Supply your present wants, and take no doit
    Of usance for my moneys, and you'll not hear me.
    This is kind of offer.
BASSANIO: This were kindness.
SHYLOCK: This kindness will I show.
    Go with me to a notary, seal me there
    Your single bond, and, in a merry sport,
    If you repay me not on such a day,

In such a place, each sum or sums as are
Express'd in the condition, let the forfeit
Be nominated for an equal pound
Of your fair flesh, to be cut and taken
In what part of your body pleaseth me,

1.3.127–46

This bargain many look vicious on the face of it, but it mustn't be made to seem so. The point is that Shylock offers Antonio the money, to Antonio's great surprise, without asking any interest on it. Therefore, in legal terms, there has to be some condition. Now Shylock is not used to dealing in forfeits, so I don't think he makes this suggestion in any but a rather frivolous, derisory way, and certainly Antonio must take it as frivolous. But as far as Antonio is concerned, his five ships will be home a month before this bond expires, so he'll sign anything. He may not regard it as a very funny joke, but he isn't alarmed by it.

At this point, then, there is no conspiracy or evil intent between the parties to this bargain, although there is a conspiracy close to Antonio's camp, which triggers off a very nasty train of events. We learn that Lorenzo, one of Antonio's many young friends, has somehow attracted the attention of Shylock's daughter, Jessica, and that they have fallen in love. The go-between is Launcelot Gobbo, who starts as Shylock's servant and then leaves his services to go and work for Bassanio. It's very important to notice that, almost from the first time you see Shylock, you see his material possessions dribbling away from him. Launcelot Gobbo is the first to go. Before he does, he delivers a message from Lorenzo to Jessica telling her to be ready to elope. She disguises herself as a boy and leaves Shylock's house with a huge haul of his money and possessions. The first real movement in the play is the departure of all the Christians, together with Jessica, for Belmont.

We're left for a while before we are allowed to see Shylock's reactions. Fate pulls at the trigger of the loaded gun. Antonio suffers losses at sea and quite unexpectedly he is potentially at Shylock's mercy as the bond cannot be kept. It must be said that Shylock, on the first indication that things are not going well for Antonio, does begin to consider arraigning him for the broken bond, but he's not thinking specifically in terms of cutting his heart out. This only occurs to him in the depth of his grief and imbalance of mind after the loss of his daughter. He's certainly quite ready to step in and exact some sort of revenge on Antonio, which indicates that his feelings towards Antonio go beyond a generalised dislike of Christians. He says several times that Antonio 'hates our sacred nation'. There is every reason to suppose that Antonio is, at any rate in Elizabethan terms, a naturally anti-semitic person. But the loss of Jessica is still the watershed as far as Shylock is concerned. He treated her more like his housekeeper than his daughter and that's probably one of the reasons why she's so ready to run off. She has not had much opportunity to meet any young people in Venice as she is not allowed to go out much. She has to stay in keeping Shylock's house, entertaining Tubal and a few other elderly Jews to dinner occasionally. It may be an emotional shock to Shylock when she leaves, but it's also a very deep practical blow which threatens his domestic comfort and well-being. The 'merry bond' begins to turn sour.

> TUBAL: Your daughter spent in Genoa, as I heard, one night, fourscore ducats.
> SHYLOCK: Thou stick'st a dagger in me – I shall never see my gold again. Fourscore ducats at a sitting! Fourscore ducats!
> TUBAL: There came divers of Antonio's creditors in my company to Venice that swear he cannot choose but break.
> SHYLOCK: I am very glad of it; I'll plague him, I'll torture him; I am glad of it.
> TUBAL: One of them showed me a ring that he had of your daughter for a monkey.
> SHYLOCK: Out upon her! Thou torturest me, Tubal. It was my turquoise; I had it of Leah when I was a bachelor; I would not have given it for a wilderness of monkeys.

3.1.93–106

These gathering clouds are, however, wittily interspersed with much ado at Belmont. It seems that Portia has appointments almost daily with her suitors. We first see the Prince of Morocco bite the dust because, after much debating with himself, he went for the golden casket. 'A gentle riddance', says Portia. The Prince of Arragon does no better, so there can be no prizes for guessing that Bassanio chooses the lead casket and wins both lady and fortune. Portia is, as they say, stinking rich and airily offers to pay off Shylock when the news reaches Belmont. She is surprised that the sum in question is only 3000 ducats. She comes across during the first two-thirds of the play as rather an unworldly, passive character. Perhaps she has so much power that she's rather afraid to wield it. We suddenly see what a very remarkable lady she is during the preparation for the trial, as well as during the trial itself. She takes quite a risk by impersonating a lawyer. This trial scene has probably been the basis for all the powerful courtroom scenes in twentieth century dramas. You know that nobody is going to move very much from their allotted formal place and that the force is going to be verbal and intellectual rather than physical. So that when you do actually get a physical confrontation, as when Shylock does go over to perform the excision on Antonio, it should be very shocking indeed. Shylock is, of course, defeated. His fate is sealed and he vanishes from the play. Legal niceties apart, there was never a chance of his winning through anyway. His action is suicidal.

Who is Shylock? I'm probably the wrong person to answer this question since I'm playing Shylock at the moment. My view of him is therefore bound to be subjective. I think I know who Shylock is, but then every actor who has played him would say that. He is a different person to each of us. I believe that the most important point to be resolved about his character is how far he has integrated himself into Venetian society at the beginning of the play. Two things made me aware of this. The first was a long conversation I had with a rabbi, who pointed out the difference between the background and behaviour of Ashkenazi Jews and Sephardic Jews. Shylock is a Sephardic Jew, whose roots would probably have been either in Portugal or Spain. He might well have been a highly educated person who was used to considerable responsibility in, perhaps, the Portuguese court and was removed, fairly gently, by the Catholic administration. He would have had no difficulty in acclimatising himself to the cosmopolitan atmosphere of Venice. The second thing that made me aware of the importance of Shylock's relationship to the local community is the fact that the masque or carnival procession goes past his house. This suggests that he lived on a main thoroughfare or canal, rather than in an obscure ghetto far away from the centre of things. This impression was reinforced by the pictures I looked at of synagogues of this period. They were magnificent places, which bear comparison with Bernini cathedrals. They were places where people of substance obviously centred their social lives, rather than places for hole-in-the-corner worship. So, when playing Shylock, it's important to realise that he certainly thinks that he has integrated himself quite well into Venetian society. He probably has not done so quite as well as he thinks he has, but he does need to feel that he has succeeded. This is probably why he overcomes his natural hesitancy and goes off to dine with Bassanio on that fateful evening when his daughter is stolen away. The more urbane, controlled and confident he is at the beginning of the play, the greater his physical and emotional collapse must be when his daughter leaves him and takes his fortune. The superstructure that he's been allowed to build up as a tolerated alien proves all too flimsy. There is a very devious psychological game called integration which is being played all around us today. Shakespeare shows that he understands the rules of this game in that first scene between Antonio and Shylock. He also succeeds in making Shylock a very understandable person. We learn, for instance, that the ring has sentimental value for him because he 'had it of Leah when I was a batchelor'. He doesn't express any affection for his daughter in the play, but there is this oblique reference to a character we haven't heard of before and don't even see. Shylock is not a likeable man at all, but Shakespeare does make us appreciate his point of view.

ALL'S WELL
THAT ENDS WELL

Barry Took

Barry Took was a writer for comedy programmes such as Round the Horne, *before chairing* Points of View *and* The News Quiz. *Some of this programme was filmed at Burghley House.*

Once upon a time there was a king who was so ill that he promised his daughter's hand in marriage to anyone who could cure him. An apothecary's assistant effected the cure, married the princess, and they all lived happily ever after. *All's Well That Ends Well* tells this traditional piece of folklore with one interesting variation. The king is ill alright, but it's a girl who cures him and asks for his son's hand, well his ward's hand, in marriage. It is duly given but they fail to live happily ever after.

When the play begins the Château of Rousillon is in mourning. The old Count has just died and his son Bertram is off to Paris to become a ward of court to the old and ailing King of France. The Count's physician has also died recently and his daughter Helena is the heroine of the play. She's in love with Bertram but he hardly notices her. After all, she's the local kid he's grown up with and the bright lights of the King's court in Paris beckon. So off he gallops with Parolles, his comical sidekick. Helena follows complete with magic potion bequeathed to her by her late father. She cures the King and, as her reward, is given the pick of the court:

> KING: Fair maid, send forth thine eye. This youthful parcel
> Of noble bachelors stand at my bestowing,
> O'er whom both sovereign power and father's voice
> I have to use. Thy frank election make;
> Thou hast power to choose, and they none to forsake.

2.3.50–4

She asks for Bertram's hand in marriage.

It is probable that Shakespeare based his ideas of life at a feudal court on what he had read or heard. He may also have drawn his characters from eminent Elizabethans such as William Cecil, Lord Burghley, who was responsible for the wards of court, who were wealthy, often aristocratic minors under the guardianship of the state. One of these wards was the Seventeenth Earl of Oxford. Burghley looked after the Earl's affairs from the time the lad was twelve, when his father died, until he was twenty-one and became legally of age. Bertram becomes a ward of the French court when his father dies and some experts believe that there's a strong parallel between the character of Bertram and the Seventeenth Earl of Oxford. They both had an independent turn of mind and were more interested in glory and travel than in settling down to domestic bliss. The young Earl was forced to marry Burghley's own daughter Anne when he was nineteen and she was only fourteen. Although Burghley had to spend money on bringing up his wards, they were the source of a profitable income and contributed handsomely to his great wealth. He could also use them to build up his dynasty. Oxford thought the marriage to Anne was beneath him. For while Burghley was a Lord and a very powerful one too, he was only the first Lord whereas Oxord was the Seventeenth Earl. Oxford may have refused to consummate the marriage because his pride was hurt. Shakespeare recreates a remarkably similar situation in *All's Well:*

> BERTRAM: But follows it, my lord, to bring me down
>   Must answer for your raising? I know her well:
>   She had her breeding at my father's charge.
>   A poor physician's daughter my wife! Disdain
>   Rather corrupt me ever!

2.3.110–4

Bertram reluctantly obeys the King and marries Helena, but leaves before the wedding night and heads off for the Italian wars with Parolles.

Helena is left stranded, but rather than accepting the situation she determines to follow Bertram and, by one means or another, to get him to consummate the marriage. Bernard Shaw once claimed that Helena was the first 'modern woman'. Today I suppose that we would describe her as a '*Guardian* woman' – able, intelligent and determined to work out her destiny in her own way. She's obviously uncomfortable in the traditional woman's role and throughout the play takes events into her own capable hands, first curing the King and later bedding Bertram.

She's also very bright, capable of giving as good as she gets in any verbal skirmish:

> PAROLLES: Are you meditating on virginity?
> HELENA: Ay. You have some stain of soldier in you; let me ask you a question. Man is enemy to virginity; how may we barricade it against him?
> PAROLLES: Keep him out.
> HELENA: But he assails; and our virginity, though valiant in the defence, yet is weak. Unfold to us some warlike resistance.
> PAROLLES: There is none. Man, setting down before you, will undermine you and blow you up.
> HELENA: Bless our poor virginity from underminers and blowers-up! Is there no military policy how virgins might blow up men?
>
> I.I.104–16

This denigration of virginity, together with the gloom of the opening scene, where everyone is in mourning, gives us a very good clue as to when the play was written. Shakespeare clearly could not have written *All's Well* while Queen Elizabeth, a celebrated virgin, was alive and well and living just up the road. I doubt if his feet would have touched the ground before his neck hit the block if he had written lines like 'virginity is peevish, proud, idle, made of self-love, which is the most inhibited sin in the canon' while Gloriana was on the throne. It was just fine, however, for the rough and ready court of James I. I think that we can assume, therefore, that *All's Well* was written after 1603, but not long after. Mourning must have been universal after Elizabeth's death. Toss a coin and it comes down at 1604.

All's Well is described as a 'comedy' but is certainly not the kind of play that we would recognise as a comedy today. It has a couple of funny scenes, to be sure, and there the dialogue struts and swaggers in a fetching and amusing way, but we would not call this comedy. But it isn't a tragedy either, as nobody is killed and, as the title suggests, all comes right in the end. There are some marvellous exchanges and some fascinating characters, but, above all, the play creates its own distinctive mood. Costumes play an important part here. The sombre mourning dress at Rousillon in the first act is followed by the glamour of the French court later on. The Italian scenes in the play tell us everything we need to know about Elizabethan fashion. And what about Parolles, the most extravagantly dressed character in the play? If what you wear speaks volumes, nowhere does it speak louder than in the character of Parolles. His clothes say a great deal about his character, as Lafeu points out:

> I did think thee, for two ordinaries, to be a pretty wise fellow; thou didst make tolerable vent of thy travel; it might pass. Yet the scarfs and bannerets about thee did manifoldly dissuade me from believing thee a vessel of too great a burden. I have now found thee; when I lose thee again I care not; yet art thou good for nothing but taking up; and that thou'rt scarce worth.

2.3.199–205

The Earl of Oxford was no mean dresser. He's credited with introducing Italian fashions, such as embroidered gloves, sweet bags, leather jerkins and costly perfumes, into England. These were, of course, just the accessories. Colourful clothes have always been good for a laugh – just think of teddy boys, mods, rockers and punks. Elizabethan men were no quieter in their dress than young men today. So, to comment on a character's gaudy apparel, it must have been pretty extreme, or extremely pretty. Max Miller and, more recently, Ken Dodd are comedians who deliberately use bright and exaggerated clothing to help with their comic image. There is in Parolles something of the button-holing comedian. Like Miller and Dodd, although he apes his betters, he is at the same time mocking them. When the dignified elder statesman, Lafeu, a Polonius-figure whom some critics suggest is based on Lord Burghley himself, chides Parolles he is chiding all those overdressed dandies in the Jacobean theatres:

> Why dost thou garter up thy arms o' this fashion? Dost make hose of thy sleeves? Do other servants so? Thou wert best set thy lower part where thy nose stands. By mine honour, if I were but two hours younger, I'd beat thee. Methink'st thou art a general offence, and every man should beat thee. I think thou wast created for men to breathe themselves upon thee.

2.3.244–50

Parolles is certainly an overstuffed tailor's dummy, a cad and a coward. He's a sort of sub-Falstaff, a hanger-on who panders to Bertram's vanity. But is he something more? The most telling scene in the play for me is where Parolles is ambushed by his own side, blindfolded and forced to reveal to Bertram and his lieutenants, whom Parolles believes to be the enemy, details of his own side's army, its morale and the character of its commanders. Parolles spills the beans, adding a touch or two of local colour, and when Bertram calls a halt to the farce Parolles realises that he's totally disgraced and revealed for what he is. But in doing so, he's revealed more than his own shortcomings. He's told Bertram and the rest a lot of home truths about themselves. He describes Bertram, very appropriately, as 'a foolish idle boy, but for all that very ruttish'. The young Count hears himself described as 'a dangerous and lascivious boy, who is a whale to virginity, and devours up all the fry it finds'.

After she has been left in the lurch by Bertram, Helena sets out ostensibly on a pilgrimage to Compostella in north-west Spain, although she really goes to Florence to nobble her wandering husband. She does this by what is known as the bed trick. Four poster Elizabethan beds were absolutely ideal for tricks to be performed in. With dim lights and curtains all around it would be very hard to know with whom you were in bed. The whole essence of the bed trick is that Bertram should not know that he's 'sleeping' with his actual legal wife, Helena, and this is arranged as follows. Helena has pursued Bertram to Florence, posing as a pilgrim. When she gets there she finds that Bertram is getting hot under the ruff with one Diana. She convinces Diana's mother that she's Bertram's legal wife, instructs Diana to get Bertram's signet ring in advance of the midnight tryst as a condition of the transaction and to give him Helena's ring in return. Helena will then take Diana's place in bed, no word will be spoken and, well, I'm sure you get the picture. The net result is that Helena becomes pregnant, she has his ring and he hers, and the super-snob Bertram is well on his way to being thoroughly put in his place. He wrote the following words to Helena earlier on in the play:

> When thou canst get the ring upon my finger, which never shall come off, and show me a child begotten of thy body that I am father to, then call me husband; but in such a "then" I write a "never".'

> 3.2.56–8

The bed trick allows Helena to fulfil these conditions at a stroke. Bertram is forced to eat his words. It may not be the best basis for a happy and lasting marriage, but it makes for satisfying drama. The bed trick may seem far fetched, but the Earl of Oxford was apparently the victim of an identical strategem.

All's Well That Ends Well is shot through with fantasy. It is there to be seen rather than analysed. It doesn't read as easily as *Henry V* or *Othello* and that's possibly the reason why it is rarely performed. It may not be a comedy pure and simple, but there is humour in *All's Well* together with some rattling good parts for the actors. The Countess, the King, Lafeu and Diana are all meaty roles. Bertram, possibly the first anti-hero, is an interesting, if difficult, part to play. Helena is a very special person, not quite a female Hamlet, but full of insight and character, wit and presence. Parolles is as good a part as any actor, or audience, could wish for. If the play has a fault, it's that it sits uneasily between reality and fantasy. But, in its better moments, *All's Well That Ends Well* refreshes parts of your mind that other Shakespeare plays cannot reach and for that it deserves our attention.

All's Well
That Ends Well

Sebastian Shaw

Sebastian Shaw played the old Athenian in the BBC
TV *Shakespeare production of* Timon of Athens.
*He has been a member of the Royal Shakespeare
Company since 1966.*

All's Well That Ends Well is one of Shakespeare's three 'problem'
or 'black plays'. The other problem plays, *Measure for Measure* and
Troilus and Cressida, share with *All's Well* a biting cynicism and a
kind of know-all world weariness. Perhaps Shakespeare wrote
these plays during the years when the theatres in London were
closed by the plague and the actors had to keep body and soul
together as best they could in the provinces. Something certainly
seems to have soured him. It may just have been the inconveni-
ence of having to make difficult, tiring and often dangerous
journeys from town to town to play to largely unsophisticated
audiences. It is more likely, however, that it was something more
deeply personal that produced such cynicism. One scholar has
suggested that the young man to whom the greater part of the
Sonnets are addressed was having an affair with the Dark Lady. If
the two people Shakespeare loved most betrayed him, it is no
wonder that he became cynical.

I should declare a particular interest in the play. I rejoined the
Stratford company in 1968 and my first role there was the King
of France in *All's Well*. I hadn't played at Stratford since the 1926
season. We rehearsed six of the plays in six weeks then. It was all
new work for me, but easy enough for the old actors in the company, most of whom played nothing but Shakespeare. There was
then a week of dress rehearsals followed by a week of first nights.
There were two short seasons: the Birthday Festival, followed
by a short tour during which three other plays were added to the
repertoire, before we returned to Stratford for the summer
season. In those days it only lasted eight weeks so we had to cram
a lot into them. There were performances of eight different plays
each week. I was playing Romeo and Prince Hal amongst other

parts. But we were still expected to follow the Stratford tradition and field a cricket side twice a week to play against local teams. It exhausts me to think of it now!

The approach of both actors and directors was more casual in 1926, judging by the time given to rehearsal. The productions were somewhat slapdash and relied too heavily on well-worn traditions. There wasn't time to work out fresh ideas. Acting, like everything else alive in this world, never stands still. What was acceptable to Stratford audiences in 1926 certainly wouldn't be acceptable to audiences today. The style in which we act is largely dependent on the style of present-day behaviour and actors, like audiences, are caught up in the particular relevance of a particular play to a particular time. We recognise in our stage characters remarkable similarities to the people we've met in real life. The world of let's pretend is based on the world of reality. Directing too does not stand still. When Peter Brook directed *A Midsummer Night's Dream* at Stratford some years ago he discovered that, far from being a pretty-pretty fairy play with pretty Mendelssohn music, it had a dark, erotic and sexual side to it. Mothers who had brought their children along to this production for a Christmas treat were indignantly demanding their money back in the interval, while the rest of us were rubbing our eyes at this particular interpretation of that marvellous text. Shakespeare's parallel position as the world's greatest and most often performed playwright is due to his extraordinary relevance to each generation of actors, directors and audiences. The relevance is constantly changing as succeeding generations differ so much from each other, but it is always there.

All's Well, because of it's underlying cynicism doesn't have the popularity of the sunnier comedies such as *As You Like It* and *Twelfth Night,* or of mature, mellow ones such as *The Tempest.* The plot is frankly incredible, but the characters and their inter-relationship are marvellously observed and recognisable so that disbelief can be willingly suspended. We are asked to believe that Helena, an orphan who has been befriended by the charming and elderly Countess Rousillon, is able to cure the King of France's malignant fistula. She has a secret passion for the Countess's son, Bertram, although he is quite unaware of this and treats her as a sister. She finally wins him by that utterly incredible but convenient device known as the 'bed trick'. At the very beginning of the play, Bertram has been called to court to serve the King and is saying goodbye to his mother and Helena. He is to be accompanied by Lafeu, an old, worldly-wise friend of the family, who remembers Helena's father, a famous physician, with great affection. Indeed, just before he and Bertram depart, he urges her to try to 'hold the credit of your father'. Helena is now left alone and declares her love for Bertram in these moving lines:

> O, were that all! I think not on my father;
> And these great tears grace his remembrance more
> Than those I shed for him. What was he like?
> I have forgot him; my imagination
> Carries no favour in't but Bertram's.
> I am undone; there is no living, none,
> If Bertram be away. 'Twere all one
> That I should love a bright particular star
> And think to wed it, he is so above me.
> In his bright radience and collateral light
> Must I be comforted, not in his sphere.
> Th'ambition in my love thus plagues itself:
> The hind that would be mated by the lion
> Must die for love.

1.1.73–86

These reflections are interrupted by Parolles, one of Shakespeare's greatest inventions. He's a boaster, cheat and liar whom the youthful Bertram was unwisely chosen for one of his attendants at court. Parolles quickly establishes himself in the top league of male chauvinist piggery by his remarks on virginity:

> There's little can be said in't; 'tis against the rule of nature. To speak on the part of virginity is to accuse your mothers; which is most infallible disobedience. He that hangs himself is a virgin; virginity murders itself, and should be buried in highways, out of all sanctified limit, as a desperate offendress against nature. Virginity breeds mites, much like a cheese; consumes itself to the very paring, and so dies with feeding his own stomach.

1.1.127–33

Helena is no mean adversary, however, as she's a very quick witted young lady. She's a good example of a charming woman's libber.

The King of France is, not unsurprisingly, melancholy since his disease is extremely painful and apparently incurable. He nevertheless manages to make Bertram cordially welcome at court. Meanwhile, back in the country, the Countess learns of

Helena's love for Bertram and of her resolve to try to cure the King with one of her father's famous remedies. The Countess is often accompanied by a clown called Lavache. He's her servant but, like the fools that turn up in many of the other plays, he is privileged, almost expected, to be disrespectful to his employer. His smart-alec cheekiness must have delighted contemporary audiences. The Countess certainly appears to enjoy it and is able to come up with the occasional quip herself. Lavache is one of the most cynical of Shakespeare's clowns. This is how he refers to his own intended marriage:

> the knaves come to do that for me which I am aweary of. He that ears my land spares my team, and gives me leave to in the crop. If I be his cuckold, he's my drudge. He that comforts my wife is the cherisher of my flesh and blood; he that cherishes my flesh and blood loves my flesh and blood; he that loves my flesh and blood is my friend; ergo, he that kisses my wife is my friend.

1.3.42–8

He goes on to imply that sooner or later all husbands are going to be cuckolded, which doesn't say much for his views, and perhaps Shakespeare's, on the constancy of women. At the court, the King bids farewell to some of the young French lords whom he has sent to win their spurs in the Italian wars between Florence and Siena. Bertram, much to his annoyance, is considered too young to go. Helena arrives to cure the King, although she has to risk death to do so:

> Sweet practiser, thy physic will I try,
> That ministers thine own death if I die.

2.1.184–5

She manages to strike a pretty hard bargain herself:

> Then shalt thou give me with thy kingly hand
> What husband in thy power I will command.

2.1.192–3

I'm not going to take you right through this improbable story, but I am prepared to provide an answer to one question you may have about the play. Yes, Helena does indeed cure the King and he keeps his promise to her. All the young men in the court are lined up for her to choose a husband from:

> Fair maid, send forth thine eye. This youthful parcel
> Of noble bachelors stand at my bestowing,

O'er whom both sovereign power and father's voice
I have to use. Thy frank election make;
Thou hast power to choose, and they none to forsake.

2.3.50–4

Needless to say, she chooses Bertram who reacts badly. After he has been forced to marry her, he claims that 'Although before the solemn priest I have sworn, I will not bed her'. He therefore sets out for the Italian wars with Parolles:

PAROLLES: To th' wars, my boy, to th' wars!
  He wears his honour in a box unseen
  That hugs his kicky-wicky here at home,
  Spending his manly marrow in her arms,
  Which should sustain the bound and high curvet
  Of Mars's fiery steed. To other regions!
  France is a stable; we that dwell in't jades;
  Therefore, to th' war!
BERTRAM: It shall be so; I'll send her to my house,
  Acquaint my mother with my hate to her,
  And wherefore I am fled; write to the King
  That which I durst not speak. His present gift
  Shall furnish me to those Italian fields
  Where noble fellows strike. War is no strife
  To the dark house and the detested wife.

2.3.271–85

Helena goes back to Rousillon and reads an arrogant challenge from Bertram in a letter to his mother:

When thou canst get the ring upon my finger, which never shall come off, and show me a child begotten of thy body that I am father to, then call me husband; but in such a "then" I write a "never".

3.2.56–8

She fulfills the conditions of this challenge to the letter, with more than a bit of help from the famous bed trick, and so finally gets her man. I hope that I may at least have whetted your appetite sufficiently for you to want to find out exactly how Shakespeare revolves the elaborate complexities of the plot in the last part of the play.

One critic has written that in *All's Well That Ends Well* 'there are evidences of haste and superficially not often found in Shakespeare. The verse shows carelessness and is frequently stilted and wooden to such a degree that a few scholars have seen in the play another's handiwork'. Maybe that is how it does appear when you are sitting in your study. As an actor I can only say that it plays like a million dollars. The verse is good to speak and the play remains high on my list of favourite productions.

THE WINTER'S TALE
Stephen Spender

The poet and critic Stephen Spender made this programme at Wilton House.

The Winter's Tale, together with *Cymbeline* and *The Tempest*, is one of Shakespeare's last plays. These plays are not histories, comedies or tragedies. The action in them takes place outside history books and maps. In these last plays, Shakespeare draws upon fragments of time and places and shifts them around like pieces of a game out of which he constructs a world of pure imagination. In the middle of the play, there is a gap of sixteen years, thus enabling the heroine, Perdita, who is a castaway royal baby in the first half, to become in the second half to all appearances a shepherd's daughter of marriageable age. To explain this jump, Shakespeare has Time appear and say that he has skipped sixteen years and that he has no intention of telling us what the characters have been up to in the meantime:

> I, that please some, try all, both joy and terror
> Of good and bad, that makes and unfolds error,
> Now take upon me, in the name of Time,
> To use my wings. Impute it not a crime
> To me or my swift passage that I slide
> O'er sixteen years, and leave the growth untried
> Of that wide gap, since it is in my pow'r
> To o'erthrow law, and in one self-born hour
> To plant and o'erwhelm custom.

4.1.1–9

So here we are in fairyland and the old romances, and yet the first half of the story is of pathological jealousy matching in intensity, realism and power of language that of *Othello*. It's really as though *The Winter's Tale* were two plays: the first at the court of Sicilia and the second in the wild countryside of Bohemia. Each part is about a different order of reality. They are, however, deeply interwoven, perhaps musically and thematically rather than by story-line or plot. The play is in the convention of the masque, in which a spectacle combining song and dance is unified through its use of deep mythological sources.

The play opens with a conversation between two lords. They are talking harmoniously and elegantly about the visit of King Polixenes of Bohemia to his boyhood friend and playmate King Leontes of Sicilia. They talk in prose, in long-drawn-out, measured phrases rather like phrases of notes sustained on violins. I think the musical analogy is rather helpful because although this play seems fragmented, threatening even to fall apart in the middle when considered as action or plot, it has a great symphonic unity like the unity of some symphony by Beethoven, in which different movements correspond to different moods. The characters themselves, although they're very convincing as individuals, also seem like instruments played on by themes. Leontes is played on by his insensate jealousy. His wife Hermione is played on by her love and devotion. Paulina, the great lady at court who defends Hermione against Leontes's unjust charges, is played on by the truth which refuses to be silenced. Perdita is played on by innocence and purity.

After that calm opening scene, there's an ominous change of key. Polixenes, having stayed nine months at the court of Sicilia, is now trying to take his leave. Leontes opposes him in this, insisting that he stays another week. Polixenes refuses to do so. Upon which Leontes asks Hermione to add her voice to his in pressing Polixenes to stay. Hermione does so, with all too fatal success:

HERMIONE: You'll stay?
POLIXENES: No, madam.
HERMIONE: Nay, but you will?
POLIXENES: I may not, verily.
HERMIONE: Verily!
   You put me off with limber vows; but I,
   Though you would seek t' unsphere the stars with oaths,
   Should yet say 'Sir, no going'. Verily,
   You shall not go; a lady's 'verily' is
   As potent as a lord's. Will you go yet?
   Force me to keep you as a prisoner,
   Not like a guest; so you shall pay your fees
   When you depart, and save your thanks.
   How say you?

My prisoner or my guest? By your dread 'verily',
One of them you shall be.
POLIXENES: Your guest, then, madam:

1.2.44–56

This releases the insensate jealousy of Leontes. In what must be one of the most thunderous asides in drama, he breaks into a tirade which, ever expanding in its torrential course, continues for nearly half the play. The rhythms of jealousy, provoked by visions in his mind's eye of the love-making between Hermione and his best friend, break up the blank verse metre:

> Too hot, too hot!
> To mingle friendship far is mingling bloods.
> I have tremor cordis on me; my heart dances,
> But not for joy, not joy. This entertainment
> May a free face put on; derive a liberty
> From heartiness, from bounty, fertile bosom,
> And well become the agent. 'T may, I grant;
> But to be paddling palms and pinching fingers,
> As now they are, and making practis'd smiles
> As in a looking-glass; and then to sigh, as 'twere
> The mort o' th' deer. O, that is entertainment
> My bosom likes not, nor my brows!

1.2.108–119

Leontes wreaks havoc. He puts Hermione on trial, demanding that the court pass sentence of death on her. Having ordered that his newly-born daughter, Perdita, be incinerated on the grounds that she must be a bastard by Polixenes, he relents but only to the extent of ordering his courtier, Antigonus, to take her to some remote region and abandon her there.

The first half of the play seems to come full circle when the emissaries whom Leontes has sent to the Oracle at Delphi return with the Oracle's pronouncement:

> Hermione is chaste; Polixenes blameless; Camillo a true sub-ject; Leontes a jealous tyrant; his innocent babe truly begot-ten; and the King shall live without an heir, if that which is lost be not found.

3.2.130–3

Immediately after this a messenger arrives with the announce-ment that Leontes's young son, the Prince Mamillius, has died, grief-stricken at the sight of his wronged mother's suffering. At this point we may feel that Leontes should drop dead or be killed, but instead of this he survives to put the infernal machinery of tragedy which he has started into reverse:

> Prithee, bring me
> To the dead bodies of my queen and son.
> One grave shall be for both. Upon them shall
> The causes of their death appear, unto
> Our shame perpetual. Once a day I'll visit
> The chapel where they lie; and tears shed there
> Shall be my recreation.

3.2.231–7

The second half of the play is as different from the first as can be imagined. It moves away from the terrifying darkness which Leontes has cast over the court of Sicilia to the sunlit countryside of Bohemia, singing and flowering with the life of simple people and with Spring-time. Amid the surroundings of untouched Nature, we find shepherds and shepherdesses, clowns and the roguish petty thief, Autolycus.

Perdita is being courted by Prince Florizel, son of King Polixenes. Florizel believes her to be a shepherdess. In spite of this, he addresses her as Queen, if only Queen of the Sheep Shearing. King Polixenes, disguised, arrives determined to prevent his son from marrying beneath him. Polixenes's anger with Florizel echoes in a different key the jealous anger of Leontes. The second half of the play reflects back on the first like criticism of it. It's as though Shakespeare were saying that, from the viewpoint of the exuberant pastoral of Bohemian life, the tragedy of Leontes's jealousy is a hurricane which, destructive as its effects were at the time, only ruffles the surface of Nature. It hardly stirred what Gerald Manley Hopkins perhaps meant by 'the dearest freshness deep down things'. Perhaps Shakespeare at the end did not think of tragedy as the final truth about life. Tragedy consists, after all, of making a tremendous, exaggerated fuss about the death of a protagonist who pursues some course of action which is bound to destroy him and will probably destroy a good many other people as well. And, anyway, he and they are going to die whatever happens. The worst tragedy is only a temporary disorder within a vast impassive universe, a spot upon the face of eternity. There are already intimations in the first half of the play that Shakespeare was looking beyond the horrific events connected with the jealousy of Leontes into the depths of nature where there's innocence and peace. For instance, there's a poignant scene between Hermione and the little Prince Mamillius. Hermione draws her son aside from the ladies of the court and asks him to tell her a story:

> HERMIONE: Come, sir, now
> I am for you again. Pray you sit by us,
> And tell's a tale.
> MAMILLIUS: Merry or sad shall't be?
> HERMIONE: As merry as you will.
> MAMILLIUS: A sad tale's best for winter. I have one
> Of sprites and goblins.
> HERMIONE: Let's have that, good sir.
> Come on, sit down; come on, and do your best
> To fright me with your sprites; you're pow'rful at it.
>
> 2.1.21–8

Mamillius is the most innocent character in the play and the only victim, and the purest, of his father's jealousy. But here he seems to be saying that the tragedy which will result in his own death is only a tale of 'sprites and goblins'. Whispering to his mother, he and she seem to be at the centre of some mystery compared with which the frenzy of Leontes is only a nightmare.

In *The Winter's Tale* innocence means a person living in his appearance and behaviour in harmony with his allotted place within the social hierarchy which corresponds to a hierarchy within Nature itself of noble and less noble life. The clowns and shepherds of the Bohemian countryside are uncouth, simple, rude. Autolycus is a petty thief. Nevertheless, they live within a prelapsarian world where there may be naughtiness and mischief but not sin. Perdita combines in her character the simplicity of the shepherds by whom she has been brought up and her royal blood which shows in her appearance and her manners. The idea of royal youths being brought up in humble circumstances without their having knowledge of their rank seems to have appealed to Shakespeare. It occurs in *Cymbeline* as well as in *The Winter's Tale*. The point is not just that they are royal, but that they talk and look and behave like sublime beings and that they instinctively respond to a rank which they have, but of which they have no knowledge, as though to a vocation. Their innocently being their own high nature is what counts:

> PERDITA: It is my father's will I should take on me
> The hostess-ship o' th' day.
> You're welcome, sir.
> Give me those flow'rs there, Dorcas. Reverend sirs,

For you there's rosemary and rue; these keep
Seeming and savour all the winter long.
Grace and remembrance be to you both!
And welcome to our shearing.
POLIXENES: Shepherdess –
A fair one you are – well you fit our ages
With flow'rs of winter.
PERDITA: Sir, the year growing ancient,
Nor yet on summer's death nor on the birth
Of trembling winter, the fairest flow'rs o' th' season
Are our carnations and streak'd gillyvors,
Which some call nature's bastards. Of that kind
Our rustic garden's barren; and I care not
To get slips of them.

4.4.71–85

The innocence of Nature is not just that of childhood and the pastoral life. It can be sublimated in the court. The greatest poet in English of the twentieth century, W. B. Yeats, would have agreed with this. In one of his most famous poems, 'The Second Coming', he writes the line 'the ceremony of innocence is drowned', taking this as a symptom of the decline of our Christian civilisation. By 'the ceremony of innocence' Yeats meant the cultivation by princes of the human affections and the virtues like courage and loyalty, as well as the cultivation of the arts and politeness. In the court of King Leontes 'the ceremony of innocence' had been drowned because Leontes had become a tyrant and he had sacrificed his obligations of love, friendship and loyalty to his passionate, insensate jealousy. Shakespeare shows great interest in the problems of power and kingship in his history plays, but in his last plays I feel that royalty has become a metaphor for the high obligations of people living in their world towards the values of another quite different world which, to him, meant Nature. In our day the concept of royalty may mean very little, but nevertheless the idea that living in our world we are under obligations to the values of another world, different from ours and yet which seems truer to us than the world in which we live, is wonderfully expressed by Marcel Proust in lines which, when I read them, make me think 'this is *The Winter's Tale*':

All that we can say is that everything is arranged in this life as though we entered it carrying the burden of obligations contracted in a former life. There is no reason inherent in the condition of life on this earth that can make us consider ourselves obliged to do good, to be fastidious, to be polite even, nor make the artist consider himself obliged to begin over again a score of times a piece of work, the admiration aroused by which will matter little to his body devoured by worms . . . All these obligations which have not their sanction in our present life seem to belong to a different world founded upon kindness, scrupulosity, self-sacrifice, a world entirely different from this, which we leave in order to be born into this world.

Proust here seems extraordinarily close to *The Winter's Tale.*

THE WINTER'S TALE
Anna Calder-Marshall

Anna Calder-Marshall played Hermione in the BBC
TV *Shakespeare production of* The Winter's Tale.
*Her other Shakespearean parts have included Juliet
and Ophelia.*

'A sad tale's best for winter', says little Prince Mamillius in
this late play of Shakespeare's. The little boy doesn't know that
he is describing the sadness and the tragedy that is about to
sweep the family up. He actually says it very gaily. This line has
for me the same effect as when a child said to me 'it doesn't do to
be too happy, it never lasts'. *The Winter's Tale* is sad, though it
ends happily. It's a sad tale of a jealous king, an unhappy queen,
the death of a prince and a baby abandoned on a sea-shore. Add
to these young love, magic, music, a bear and dancing and you
have an ideal story for a child on a winter's evening.

I think that's why I loved the play when I was young, but it was
the deeper meaning behind it that has made it stay with me. I
first came into contact with it when I was about twelve years old
and at a convent. I had to play Queen Hermione for a drama
examination, so I read the whole play and loved it. It not only
appealed to my imagination, it also disturbed me. I found King
Leontes's anger and the way he treated his wife very disturbing.
Hermione's silence, long suffering and restraint intrigued me.
She didn't speak out like you would if you were a kid and say
'why are you being so beastly to me?' After the adjudicator had
told me that I'd passed, she commented that I was a very 'mature
child'. I wasn't really, I was just playing the part. It was as though
I had a crush on Hermione. I didn't understand what her
strength came from but when I played her it made me feel very
strong and centred. I also found the play religious. I suppose
being at a convent I was very aware of the spiritual side of life. I
didn't see the play as some critics do as improbable and un-
believable. I thought it was very hopeful.

It seems to me now very like a Munch painting called
'Jealousy'. In the background are a man and a woman, who are
painted in a very dream-like manner. You can see through their

clothes to their naked bodies. In the foreground, turned towards us, there's a second man's face. His eyes are wide and wracked with jealousy. It's very much the feeling in the play when Leontes pours out his agonised suspicions to us, whilst his wife and friend laugh gaily in the background. Both the painting and the play are dominated by a jealous man's face. Later on, the play reminds me of a Breughel painting. We see a landscape bustling with activity. The peasant figures are singing, dancing and bringing in the harvest. One man's personal agony isn't that important, it's just one aspect of life. W.H. Auden put his finger on what I mean in a poem called 'Musée des Beaux Arts':

About suffering they were never wrong,
The Old Masters: how well they understood
Its human position; how it takes place
While someone is eating or opening a window or just walking
    dully along;
How, when the aged are reverently, passionately waiting
For the miraculous birth, there always must be
Children who did not specially want it to happen, skating
On a pond at the edge of the wood:
They never forget
That even the dreadful martyrdom must run its course
Anyhow in a corner, some untidy spot
Where the dogs go on with their doggy life and the torturer's
    horse
Scratches its innocent behind on a tree.

In Breughel's *Icarus*, for instance: how everything turns away
Quite leisurely from the disaster; the ploughman may
Have heard the splash, the forsaken cry,
But for him it was not an important failure; the sun shone
As it had to on the white legs disappearing into the green
Water; and the expensive delicate ship that must have seen
Something amazing, a boy falling out of the sky,
Had somewhere to get to and sailed calmly on.

Jealousy can strike on a perfect day.

The court of King Leontes in Sicilia seems to be a very happy place at the beginning of the play. There is the King, his wife Queen Hermione, who's expecting a baby shortly, and their little boy Mamillius, who is a ray of sunshine, 'a gallant child, one that indeed makes old hearts fresh'. The King's boyhood friend, Polixenes, the King of Bohemia, is nearing the end of a nine month stay with the family. Leontes is so devoted to him that he cannot bear to be parted from him. They were, says one of the lords,

> train'd together in their childhoods; and there rooted betwixt them then such an affection which cannot choose but branch now.
>
> 1.1.21–2

Or, as Polixenes himself says,

> We were as twinn'd lambs that did frisk i' th' sun
> And bleat the one at th' other. What we chang'd
> Was innocence for innocence; we knew not
> The doctrine of ill-doing, nor dream'd
> That any did.
>
> 1.2.67–71

There is a fantastic atmosphere, like Christmas. Everybody's having a wonderful time, including the lords and ladies who are highly amused at the banter going backwards and forwards between the two Kings. We've all felt very happy up to now. But suddenly the atmosphere changes. It's as though a dark cloud has obscured the sun. Leontes suddenly turns to us and tells us that he suspects his wife of having an affair with Polixenes. We know that this is crazy, but we watch helpless. From that moment on, the most harmless things that Hermione and Polixenes say or do to each other only serve to confirm Leontes in his worst suspicions. As Hermione and Polixenes leave together, Leontes is left with his son. He finds it hard simply to hug him anymore, since he's no longer sure that Mamillius really is his child. In no time at all he is trying to persuade Camillo, his chief adviser, to poison Polixenes and when the poor bewildered man demurs he reviles him. Leontes then blurts out a list of proofs, which only prove to us how far he's gone:

> Is whispering nothing?
> Is leaning cheek to cheek? Is meeting noses?
> Kissing with inside lip? Stopping the career
> Of laughter with a sigh? – a note infallible
> Of breaking honesty. Horsing foot on foot?
> Skulking in corners? Wishing clocks more swift;
> Hours, minutes; noon, midnight? And all eyes
> Blind with the pin and web but theirs, theirs only,
> That would unseen be wicked – is this nothing?

Why, then the world and all that's in't is nothing;
The covering sky is nothing; Bohemia nothing;
My wife is nothing; nor nothing have these nothings,
If this be nothing.

1.2.284–96

What is terrible yet fascinating about this speech is that com-
pulsion of jealous people to put a bad construction upon the
most innocent behaviour. We, the audience, know that
Hermione has nothing but friendship for Polixenes. We can go
further and say that her real interest in him is that he is her
beloved husband's best friend. It is ironic that, at the very
moment that Leontes is imagining the loosest of conversation
and behaviour from his wife, she is begging to be told about her
husband's childhood. More than that, she wants to hear that in
some way Leontes was the cleverer of the two boys. She asks
whether her husband was the 'verier wag o' th' two'.

Hermione really loves Leontes, but her love can be misinter-
preted. I'm reminded of her in a poem by Robert Browning:

She had a heart, how shall I say?
Too soon made glad, too soon easily impressed.
She liked what'er she looked on,
And her looks went everywhere.

I think that it's important to believe that up to this point it's
been a very happy marriage. Some critics find the suddenness of
Leontes's jealousy hard to take. They find it implausible because
they want something more gradual, like we get in *Othello*. I don't
agree as there is, after all, no shortage of people who are subject
to swift, sudden changes of feeling. I think that Leontes is basic-
ally very insecure. He is what today we would call neurotic, even
mentally sick. Camillo believes that he is ill:

Good my lord, be cur'd
Of this diseas'd opinion, and betimes;
For 'tis most dangerous.

1.2.296–8

Camillo is an honourable man, who is prepared to speak his
mind, but he gets short shrift from Leontes for his pains:

I say thou liest, Camillo, and I hate thee;
Pronounce thee a gross lout, a mindless slave,
Or else a hovering temporizer that
Canst with thine eyes at once see good and evil,

Inclining to them both. Were my wife's liver
Infected as her life, she would not live
The running of one glass.

1.2.300–6

Camillo agrees to poison Polixenes but instead, as soon as
Leontes has left, he warns him of the danger and persuades him
to flee back to the safety of his native Bohemia. Camillo goes to
Bohemia as well, for to have stayed on in Sicilia would have
meant death. He's one of life's born survivors, who always lands
on his feet. He becomes Polixenes's closest friend and adviser.
He is also one of life's doers. Such people of action are often to
be found among the less heroic figures in Shakespeare's plays.
While Hamlet dithers, Fortinbras conquers a country. In this
play, Camillo and Paulina, whom I'll introduce you to later on,
do much more to advance the action in the direction of light than
their masters and mistresses. They are the bricklayers and
plumbers, so to speak, without whom the house would never get
built.

The Queen and her ladies in waiting are playing a game with
Mamillius, unaware that Camillo and Polixenes have fled to
Bohemia. She is happy but tired and tries to get the little boy to
sit down. Into this haven of peace enters Leontes surrounded by
his lords. Polixenes's flight only serves to confirm his worst
suspicions:

Camillo was his help in this, his pander.
There is a plot against my life, my crown;
All's true that is mistrusted. That false villain
Whom I employ'd was pre-employ'd by him;
He has discover'd my design, and I
Remain a pinch'd thing; yea, a very trick
For them to play at will.

2.1.46–52

Leontes then orders the child away from his mother. Little does
she know that she will never see him again. She is then ordered
to prison, accused of adultery and treason. It's terrifying and
more so because of Hermione's resignation:

There's some ill planet reigns.
I must be patient till the heavens look
With an aspect more favourable. Good my lords,
I am not prone to weeping, as our sex
Commonly are – the want of which vain dew

> Perchance shall dry your pities – but I have
> That honourable grief lodg'd here which burns
> Worse than tears drown.

2.1.105–12

She goes off to prison with her ladies in waiting. I find this scene a very elusive thing to get hold of as Hermione's strong and vulnerable at the same time. Shakespeare also seems to have understood that a pregnant woman has the strength of a lioness because she's not just fighting for herself, but for someone else who is totally dependent on her. She's spoken with the tongues of angels but it doesn't save her from prison.

Paulina's valiant efforts on her behalf are to no avail. Paulina is Hermione's closest friend. As soon as she's heard that Hermione has given birth prematurely to a little girl in prison, she offers to take the baby to Leontes in order to soften his heart:

> It is yours.
> And, might we lay th' old proverb to your charge,
> So like you 'tis the worse. Behold, my lords,
> Although the print be little, the whole matter
> And copy of the father – eye, nose , lip,
> The trick of's frown, his forehead; nay, the valley,
> The pretty dimples of his chin and cheek; his smiles;
> The very mould and frame of hand, nail, finger.

2.3.95–102

I have a lot of time for Paulina as she's an admirable woman. Well, she probably talks too much, but she is the only person who confronts Leontes with what he's done and what kind of person he's becoming. Camillo tried, but he had to be more tactful. Paulina has no tact. She's very much a woman of today, dare one say a feminist in the best sense of the word? She's the sort of friend that everyone would like to have when things are going badly. She's loyal and fights like a tiger. She's the kind of woman who would look after battered wives and give the husband hell if he deserved it, as Leontes does.

He humiliates Hermione by bringing her to court for a public trial. She faces death, but this is the least of her anxieties:

> Sir, spare your threats.
> The bug which you would fright me with I seek.
> To me can life be no commodity.
> The crown and comfort of my life, your favour,
> I do give lost, for I do feel it gone,

But know not how it went; my second joy
And first fruits of my body, from his presence
I am barr'd, like one infectious; my third comfort,
Starr'd most unluckily, is from my breast-
The innocent milk in it most innocent mouth–
Hal'd out to murder; myself on every post
Proclaim'd a strumpet; with immodest hatred
The child-bed privilege denied, which 'longs
To women of all fashion; lastly, hurried
Here to this place, i' th' open air, before
I have got strength of limit.

3.2.89–104

What a marvellous picture you get from this speech of the life
that Hermione's led in prison and the state it has left her in.
She's just given birth prematurely to a baby, which has been
taken away from her. She hasn't seen her son. She's weak, yet
here she is, the Queen, in front of the court in the open air being
accused of being a strumpet. She is strong enough, however, to
demand to be tried by the Oracle at Delphi, which was regarded
as the ultimate and final arbiter of the truth. Leontes agrees to
accept the Oracle's verdict, until it finds in favour of Hermione:

LEONTES: There is no truth at all i' th' oracle.
    The sessions shall proceed. This is mere falsehood.
SERVANT: My lord the King, the King!
LEONTES: What is the business?
SERVANT: O sir, I shall be hated to report it:
    The Prince your son, with mere conceit and fear
    Of the Queen's speed, is gone.
LEONTES: How! Gone?
SERVANT: Is dead.
LEONTES: Apollo's angry; and the heavens themselves
    Do strike at my injustice.

3.2.139–144

Hermione collapses and is carried out of court. Leontes admits
that he has 'too much believ'd mine own suspicion'. Paulina
rushes back in at this moment of truth for Leontes and lashes
him with her tongue. This time, however, he is prepared to listen
to her as he realises that he deserves 'all tongues to talk their
bitt'rest'. The change from jealousy and vindictiveness to
humility and a desire for redemption is as sudden now as the
onset of his madness was at the beginning and underlines a basic

instability in the man's character. I can't help thinking that Leontes has never grown up. Perhaps his jealousy of Polixenes stems from a childhood envy which he had never got over. This would explain the seeming unreasonableness of his passion. It is childish, therefore not totally unsympathetic. Leontes resolves to lead a life of repentence and to visit every day the chapel where Hermione and Mamillius will be buried.

But what hope has he of recovering his little daughter, whom he himself decreed should be abandoned in a strange place? She has in fact been left on the coast of Bohemia. Antigonus places a casket of gold and a necklace beside her in the vain belief that they will help her and then reluctantly departs as a storm begins to rage. His departure is marked by what is probably the most famous stage direction in all Shakespeare's plays, 'exit, pursued by a bear'. Yes, a bear. It would probably have been a real, if tame one in Shakespeare's time. What a difference this bear makes, for the mood changes from one of tragedy to comedy. We are introduced to one delightful character after another. There's an old Shepherd and his son, the Clown, who has seen Antigonus being eaten by the bear. But somehow we hear the news without being upset. All the crew of the boat bringing Antigonus and the babe to the coast of Bohemia have been drowned, so no one remains alive who knows the true identity of the baby.

The appearance of Father Time is just as startling as that of the bear. We are whizzed forward sixteen years by this benign gentleman, where we discover that the baby has grown into the beautiful Perdita, the Queen of the harvest feast and the daughter of the old Shepherd who found her. She doesn't of course know yet that she is the daughter of a king, but she is being courted by Florizel, who is the son of a king who happens to be Polixenes. Their young love is innocent, gentle and touching. After storm and catastrophe we have passed into a land of rural wholeness, which is more like Warwickshire than Bohemia. We have moved from a winter's tale to a summer's tale. There is song and dancing and the arrival of a mischievous tinker called Autolycus. This happy scene doesn't last forever. The young people have a setback when Polixenes appears on the scene. He is definitely unamused by his young son's attachment to a mere shepherdess. He loses his temper and lashes the two young people with his tongue, forbidding them on pain of death to see one another. We hear echoes of Leontes here. But young love is not so easily thwarted, especially when it gains an ally in Camillo, the King's closest friend and adviser. He offers to help the lovers escape to the court of Leontes. He has his own motives for doing this, since he yearns to see his old country and master again. The young people's problems are not over yet, but I'll leave you to find out what happens to them.

I hope I've not made the play sound too disjointed or too tragic. It's not a tragedy. Emotionally it goes from A to Z. The action takes place in two different countries and spans two generations. The differences and varieties are those of life itself and what one is left with most powerfully is that age-old theme of poets and artists, 'love conquers all'. But not in a facile way, as I think that Shakespeare believed in this theme very deeply. He died only a few years after writing *The Winter's Tale*, which expresses his strong feeling for the goodness and power of youth and childhood, not just its wholeness, but its power to do good to older people like himself. As Polixenes says, speaking of his own young son,

> He's all my exercise, my mirth, my matter;
> Now my sworn friend, and then mine enemy;
> My parasite, my soldier, statesman, all.
> He makes a July's day short as December,
> And with his varying childness cures in me
> Thoughts that would thick my blood.

1.2.166–71

Has anyone ever put into better words the benefits of parenthood? In the end, *The Winter's Tale*, for all its darker elements, is about the triumph of youth, love, gentleness and faith. It looks forward hopefully to life.

TIMON OF ATHENS

Malcolm Muggeridge

Malcolm Muggeridge worked as a journalist on The Manchester Guardian, The Evening Standard, The Daily Telegraph *and* Punch. *He is a well-known broadcaster on religion and contemporary social attitudes. He made this programme at his home at Robertsbridge.*

We know very little about *Timon of Athens*. It has only been produced very rarely so that very few people have seen it. As a matter of fact, I haven't seen it myself. There are no long, exciting parts in it to attract the attention of famous or aspiring actors and no parts for women at all. It's also a hard read. The truth is that, but for a tenuous connection with Shakespeare, it would probably have got forgotten like many another Elizabethan play. Let me say straightaway, however, that there are lines in it saying a tremendous lot in a very few words that only Shakespeare can write. One of them has echoed in my mind ever since I read the play years ago: 'Men shut their doors against a setting sun'. It evokes marvellously the circumstances of fallen greatness.

I'm going to assume that some obscure Elizabethan writer made a rough sketch for a play about Timon of Athens. The story-line would have run as follows. Timon was a rich nobleman, who was enormously popular. He was charming, attractive and generous. He had hosts of friends and was constantly giving people presents or helping them out of difficulties. But he suddenly finds himself penniless and deeply in debt. He sends to all his ostensible friends for help and not one single one of them responds. Then this normally so amiable gentleman falls into a high rage and invites them all together for one more dinner. He gathers them at the table and begins the proceedings by remarking 'Uncover, dogs, and lap'. When they do uncover, they find the plates which should have held delicious food have only hot water in them. The whole thing ends in chaos and confusion and Timon, despairing of the human race, retires into the country. Whilst digging for roots to eat, he ironically discovers rich stores of gold.

Given that the story-line of *Timon of Athens* was so very much up Shakespeare's street, it seems extraordinary that he should have contented himself with just tinkering about with the script instead of re-writing the play as he had done on previous occasions. I think that the explanation lies in the fact, which came as a surprise to me, that *Timon of Athens* was not produced at the Globe, or indeed anywhere else in Shakespeare's lifetime. I can quite understand that writing a play that was not going to be produced would be for me like writing an article or a book that was not going to be published. Shakespeare was not, after all, in any sense a man of letters as we see it. He was a man of the theatre. He began as an actor, not a writer, and his days were spent in the Globe Theatre editing scripts, lurking in the wings to scribble out some piece that was needed to fill a gap or to provide a bit of comic relief when the tension was proving too strong. His life consisted of the turmoil in front, on and behind the stage. It could not have been more different from the life of a Bernard Shaw or Sir James Barrie, sitting at their desks and writing their plays as the spirit moved them. Shakespeare was a man of the theatre, but he didn't like it. His references to acting and the theatre in his plays are uniformly contemptuous. As soon as he could, he got out of the place and went back to Stratford. He bought a coat of arms, settled down as a country gentleman and never wrote another word. He didn't even prepare his plays for publication. But it's rather marvellous to think that those words produced in those circumstances at the Globe Theatre are among the most beautiful and sometimes the most hilarious ever written in the English language. A reflection that I, as an old superannuated journalist who for the last fifty years has also been writing words under stress as Shakespeare did, find highly pleasing.

The mood of *Timon of Athens* is sombre throughout. There's not a single laugh in it which is rare with Shakespeare. It's all passion and rhetoric. Shakespeare's own mood seems to have rather coincided with that of the play, as though he was going through one of those despairing phases that great artists and mystics are subject to, called in the case of mystics 'the dark night of the soul'. I was delighted to see that the eminent critic, E.K. Chambers, takes a similar view, though admitting that it's a subjective one. 'Shakespeare', he writes, 'dealt with *Timon* under conditions of mental and perhaps physical stress which led to a breakdown'. He goes on, 'In any case, he seems to have abandoned the play and never to have taken it up again'. I know it's a hazardous thing to play around with dates where Shakespeare is concerned, but I don't think that it would be unreasonable to suppose that he worked on *Timon* between completing *King Lear* and tackling *Macbeth*. There is, of course, a considerable parallelism between Lear and Timon. Lear gave away his kingdom to his daughters and Timon gave away his fortune to his friends. They both discovered that affection based on largesse is very fragile and that when the largesse comes to an end the affection is likely to as well. This discovery reduces Timon to a state of gibbering rage, whereas in Lear's case it leads him eventually to see through the fantasy of power and into the reality of love. *Macbeth* is, of course, all about power. Macbeth himself pursues power and is destroyed thereby, coming to see life in terms that would have delighted Timon.

Timon, like Macbeth, is obsessed with power, but power in terms of money. At the beginning of the play he showers his largesse on one of his servants, Lucilius, who has fallen in love with a rich Athenian girl:

OLD ATHENIAN: One only daughter have I, no kin else,
  On whom I may confer what I have got.
  The maid is fair, o' th' youngest for a bride,
  And I have bred her at my dearest cost
  In qualities of the best. This man of thine
  Attempts her love; I prithee, noble lord,
  Join with me to forbid him her resort;
  Myself have spoke in vain.
TIMON: The man is honest.
OLD ATHENIAN: Therefore he will be, Timon.
  His honesty rewards him in itself;
  It must not bear my daughter.
TIMON: Does she love him?
OLD ATHENIAN: She is young and apt:
  Our own precedent passions do instruct us
  What levity's in youth.
TIMON: Love you the maid?
LUCILIUS: Ay, my good lord, and she accepts of it.
OLD ATHENIAN: If in her marriage my consent be missing,
  I call the gods to witness I will choose
  Mine heir from forth the beggars of the world,
  And dispossess her all.
TIMON: How shall she be endow'd,
  If she be mated with an equal husband?
OLD ATHENIAN: Three talents on the present; in future, all.

TIMON: This gentleman of mind that serv'd me long;
    To build his fortune I will strain a little,
    For 'tis a bond in men. Give him thy daughter:
    What you bestow, in him I'll counterpoise,
    And make him weigh with her.

1.1.124–49

In this particular case, anyway, Timon really did seem to be trying to ensure that the course of true love ran smoothly. In general, however, he remained preoccupied with this operation of using money to buy friendship and affection. It's by no means uncommon. Along the murky corridors of power which journalists have to frequent, we see a great deal of it. A good example in my lifetime was the late Lord Beaverbrook who used his great fortune to buy power. The most extraordinary example of it on a worldwide scale that I've ever come across was in Washington after the Second World War. It's now largely forgotten, but at that time America was really richer and more powerful than all the rest of the world and could have done anything they wanted to. But they followed Timon and simply handed out dollars on all sides with a view to making themselves loved. All they achieved was to intensify anti-Americanism everywhere.

It's very easy to be righteously indignant on this theme. I was thinking about it at Christmas time this year and suddenly it occurred to me that, when I was working out the distribution of my own little Christmas boxes, I too, like Timon, was thinking of the usefulness to me rather than the pleasure it would give to the recipient. Timon started off believing in the genuineness of his own generosity, which was why he was so shocked to find that the beneficiaries of his generosity failed to respond to his calls for help. They all make their excuses:

LUCULLUS: Thy lord's a bountiful gentleman; but thou art wise, and thou know'st well enough, although thou com'st to me, that this is no time to lend money, especially upon bare friendship without security. Here's three solidares for thee. Good boy, wink at me, and say thou saw'st me not. Fare thee well.

3.1.39–44

Timon of Athens is essentially a play about money. So, for that matter, at a very low level is life itself. Judas sold Christ to his enemies for thirty pieces of silver. Governments sell weapons of destruction to other governments. Lenin remarked once that the Bolsheviks should co-operate with capitalists as a rope co-operates with a man about to be hanged. 'Where are we going to get the rope?', someone asked him. He replied 'they'll sell it to us'. This prophecy has proved to be correct. In fact it has quite often been given to them, gratis. In every vision of the Kingdom of Heaven on earth, up to and including Marx's, money is abolished. Marx indeed found the account of the role of money in *Timon of Athens* very much to his taste:

> Shakespeare stresses especially two properties of money – one, it's the visible divinity; two, it's the common whore, the common pimp of people and nations. Money is the pimp between man's need and the object, between his life and his means of life.

Yet money goes marching on. It's the Devil's sacrament: 'This is my money; spend this in remembrance of me'.

Shakespeare, of course, knew all about money. It was the means whereby he escaped from the Globe Theatre and also, perhaps, the means whereby he had to suffer excruciating boredom in Stratford. He shows us Timon first in the munificence of his affluence, then penniless and friendless and finally rich again. Money is presented as the root of all evil:

> Gold? Yellow, glittering, precious gold? No, gods,
> I am no idle votarist. Roots, you clear heavens!
> Thus much of this will make black white, foul fair,
> Wrong right, base noble, old young, coward valiant.
> Ha, you gods! why this? What, this, you gods? Why, this
> Will lug your priests and servants from your sides,
> Pluck stout men's pillows from below their heads –
> This yellow slave
> Will knit and break religions, bless th' accurs'd,
> Make the hoar leprosy ador'd, place thieves
> And give them title, knee, and approbation,
> With senators on the bench. This it is
> That makes the wappen'd widow wed again–
> She whom the spital-house and ulcerous sores
> Would cast the gorge at this embalms and spices
> To th' April day again. Come, damn'd earth,
> Thou common whore of mankind, that puts odds
> Among the rout of nations, I will make thee
> Do thy right nature.

4.3.26–44

When the sycophants gather round him, having heard of his newfound wealth, Timon pelts them with stones. The only largesse he distributes is to whores to encourage them to spread disease both spiritual and physical:

> Consumptions sow
> In hollow bones of man; strike their sharp shins,
> And mar men's spurring. Crack the lawyer's voice,
> That he may never more false title plead,
> Nor sound his quillets shrilly. Hoar the flamen,
> That scolds against the quality of flesh
> And not believes himself. Down with the nose,
> Down with it flat, take the bridge quite away
> Of him that, his particular to foresee,
> Smells from the general weal. Make curl'd pate ruffians bald,
> And let the unscarr'd braggarts of the war
> Derive some pain from you. Plague all,
> That your activity may defeat and quell
> The source of all erection. There's more gold.
> Do you damn others, and let this damn you,
> And ditches grave you all!

4.3.150–65

Venereal disease among the Elizabethans was, in the most literal sense of the word, a very sore point. After his exile from Athens, Timon wants anarchy as well as lechery to thrive:

> Obedience, fail in children! Slaves and fools,
> Pluck the grave wrinkled Senate from the bench
> And minister in their steads. To general filths
> Convert, o' th' instant, green virginity.
> Do't in your parents' eyes. Bankrupts, hold fast;
> Rather than render back, out with your knives
> And cut your trusters' throats. Bound servants, steal:
> Large-handed robbers your grave masters are,
> And pill by law. Maid, to thy master's bed:
> Thy mistress is o' th' brothel. Son of sixteen,
> Pluck the lin'd crutch from thy old limping sire ,
> With it beat out his brains.

4.1.4–15

I must say to me it reads very like a preview of what we call the permissive society. *Timon of Athens*, then, ends in mere despair and fury, perhaps reflecting such a mood in Shakespeare himself, some sort of breakdown even. There's no Falstaff to offset the rhetoric of passion, no intimation of love apart from a passing reference. It's a black tragedy, if ever there was one.

Timon of Athens

Richard Pasco

Richard Pasco played Jaques in As You Like It *and Brutus in* Julius Caesar *in the* BBC TV *Shakespeare productions. He is a member of the Royal Shakespeare Company, where, amongst other roles, he alternated the parts of Richard II and Bolingbroke with Ian Richardson.*

I had the pleasure of being invited to return to the Royal Shakespeare Company in the summer of 1980 to portray Timon of Athens. The part had attracted me since I had been involved as a small-part actor in Sir Tyrone Guthrie's production in 1952 at the Old Vic with the late Andre Morell in the title role. The stage was filled with Guthrie's swirling stage-craft and genius, which seemed to make Timon's banqueting hall into a very heavily populated palace fill with courtiers, senators and masquers. But I was now to play the part in a production at the Royal Shakespeare Company's small stage theatre, the Other Place, with a cast of only fourteen or so actors. This posed a real problem for both the cast and Ron Daniels, the director. I played my first leading Shakespearean role in 1954 in Sir Barry Jackson's company at the old Birmingham Repertory Theatre. The part was Pericles, another of Shakespeare's lesser known and rarely performed works, which I had seen directed brilliantly by Ron Daniels at the Other Place with Peter McEnery in the title role. So I had unusual confidence in my director and welcomed the idea of tackling 'this still-born twin of Lear' in an intimate situation which would enhance the closer interpretation of the text to the audience. The play has been described by various critics over the years as 'unsatisfactory', 'unwieldy', 'unfinished' and so on. But for me it is a grossly neglected masterpiece, which explores dramatically man's inhumanity to man and the outward manifestations of the human psyche under stress. It deals with disillusionment, despair and grief, all of which produce a total weariness of body and spirit.

Scholars argue about exactly where *Timon* belongs in the Shakespearean canon. Suffice it to say here that it's almost certainly a late play, written after *King Lear* and probably around the same time as *The Winter's Tale* and *The Tempest*. The scene is set in Athens and the woods nearby. The principal characters, apart from Timon, are the soldier Alcibiades, the philosopher Apemantus and the faithful steward Flavius. We see the rest collectively as faces in a crowd. The only women who appear in the play are the masquers at Timon's first banquet and Alcibiades's mistresses, Phrynia and Timandra. The plot is probably one of the simplest of all Shakespeare's to follow. Timon, a leading Senator and wealthy lord, spends money like water on anyone in need. He offers gifts, loans, the payment of debts and extravagant entertainment to all and sundry. This profligacy leads to bankruptcy. When Timon turns to his supposed friends for help they all refuse him. The pain and disillusionment that follow are the crux of the whole of the second half of the play.

The character of Timon of Athens is at once a mystery. Shakespeare gives us no hint of his background or his forebears. We know something at least of the character of the leading protagonist in most of the great tragedies: Hamlet's life at Elsinore, Lear's court and his three daughters, Julius Caesar and the state of Rome. But we know nothing of Timon. We don't even know whether he acquired his vast wealth and lands by inheritance or gift. We know nothing of his family. He is, of all Shakespeare's major figures, the most isolated. Timon is certainly revered and adulated at the beginning of the play. The air is filled with the blandishments of Poet, Painter, Jeweller and Senator alike. It is possible that he has been a great benefactor to the state, or indeed a soldier of some reknown. He himself believes that he has done the state some service:

> Go you, sir, to the senators,
> Of whom, even to the state's best health, I have
> Deserv'd this hearing. Bid 'em send o' th' instant
> A thousand talents to me.

> 2.2.196–9

This is confirmed later on by Alcibiades:

> I have heard, and griev'd,
> How cursed Athens, mindless of thy worth,
> Forgetting thy great deeds, when neighbour states,
> But for thy sword and fortune, trod upon them –

> 4.3.92–5

We can, however, only surmise about the exact nature of this service.

The whole structure of the play is created around Timon's character. There is neither conflict between hero and heroine, nor hero and villain. The conflict lies rather in Timon's inner soul and his response to the betrayal and insults of his friends. It is easy to dismiss Timon's unending generosity as misguided or downright foolish, but his belief in the gift of friendship does come from the heart:

> O, no doubt, my good friends, but the gods themselves have provided that I shall have much help from you. How had you been my friends else? Why have you that charitable title from thousands, did you not chiefly belong to my heart? . . . We are born to do benefits; and what better or properer can we call our own than the riches of our friends? O, what a precious comfort 'tis to have so many like brothers commanding one another's fortunes!
>
> 1.2.84–100

That fascinating character Apemantus, a professional cynic who is surely a cousin of Jaques and Thersites, suggests that Timon's friends are merely flatterers in a series of asides to the audience as well as to Timon's face:

> I scorn thy meat; 'twould choke me, for I should ne'er flatter thee. O you gods, what a number of men eats Timon, and he sees 'em not! It grieves me to see so many dip their meat in one man's blood; and all the madness is, he cheers them up too.
>
> 1.2.37–41

Timon's dispensation of largesse is certainly excessive: 'Methinks I could deal kingdoms to my friends/And ne'er be weary'. But his main characteristic is that he is a man with a feeling of great compassion towards his fellow human beings. He is at once highly sensitive and greatly vulnerable.

His steward, Flavius, continually warns him that his assets are nil. This faithful servant confronts his master, after he has come back from a day's hunting with Alcibiades, with the fact that he is totally bankrupt. Timon is convinced, however, that he is still 'wealthy in my friends' and so dispatches his servants to borrow money from them. Not one of these friends responds to Timon's pleas and so the servants return home empty-handed. Alcibiades, perhaps his sincerest friend, has by now disappeared from the main stream of the play. There is a vital scene in the Senate where his pleas for mercy for a fellow soldier are rejected, resulting in the death of the soldier and his own banishment. We do not see him again until he meets Timon by chance in the second half of the play. Timon is therefore alone, save for his steward and the servants who prepare the dishes of lukewarm water and stones which he hurls at his fellow senators in the second banquet scene of the play. This public demonstration of contempt is preceded by Timon's prayer to the gods. When delivering this grace in the presence of the unctuous senators, Timon reveals the beginnings of his mental breakdown. The tragedy of betrayal has unbalanced his noble innocence:

> Make the meat be beloved more than the man that gives it. Let no assembley of twenty be without a score of villains. If there sit twelve women at a table, let a dozen of them—be as they are   For these my present friends, as they are to me nothing, so in nothing bless them, and to nothing are they welcome.

3.6.80–84

There follows the disintegration of the supposed banquet and the senators retire bemused, resentful and wet.

Timon delivers his first great soliloquy as he looks back at the walls of Athens and condemns the city and all its inhabitants to ineffable ruin. The speech is quite equal in its ferocity and anger to anything that Shakespeare wrote for Lear on the blasted heath. It is filled with the kind of cosmic doom that can leave an audience feeling very uneasy indeed. Timon retreats to the woods, although one feels that they are never far away from the sea. It's a barren coast filled, almost like Prospero's island, with strange noises, wild beasts and birds of prey. Timon has never been able to make any genuine human contact. His character is revealed by misfortune but not transformed by it. Shakespeare's supreme sense of irony reveals itself when Timon is desperately searching for food in the wilderness. Whilst digging frantically for roots, he discovers, quite by chance, a hoard of gold. As soon as he renounces gold, he finds an abundance of it. His speeches against gold are very applicable to our own acquisitive society:

> This yellow slave
> Will knit and break religions, bless th' accurs'd,
> Make the hoar leprosy ador'd, place thieves
> And give them title, knee, and approbation,
> With senators on the bench.

4.3.33–7

His anger and frustration could easily be vented against us today as we sit and watch the television news almost like troglodytes. I have seen, within the same bulletin, scenes of thousands of innocent children on the point of starvation followed immediately by pictures of sleek, highly tuned Olympic athletes. These were in turn followed by other scenes of man's inhumanity to man in so many parts of our world: scenes of war, torture, pillage, injustice, prejudice and all-pervading violence. Timon realises that this is the state of his world. His cry to Apemantus, 'What wouldst thou do with the world, Apemantus, if it lay in thy power?', is the clarion call of man's helplessness. Any critic who says that Timon's character is predictable and doesn't mature has surely never had more than a cursory glance at the text, or even begun to probe Shakespeare's powerful expression of man's bitterness and anger.

Leigh Hunt said of Alicibiades's meeting with Timon in the wilderness that it is 'the meeting of hope with despair'. It is interesting not only because of Timon's rejection of Alicibiades, but also because it is the only time that there are any illusions to sex in the play. Timon sees it in terms of disease and corruption. He bids the whores, Phrynia and Timandra, to 'spread disease to youth and mankind alike' as he fills their aprons with gold. He refers continually to venereal disease and the pain and corruption which will result from the war Alcibiades is about to unleash on Athens. Apemantus is the next person to find Timon. The cynic has made a special trip to see whether it was true that Timon now affected 'my manners and dost use them'. Shakespeare gives Apemantus one of the most revealing comments about Timon in the whole play: 'the middle of humanity thou never knewest, but the extremity of both ends'. Apemantus's cynicism is counterpointed to Timon's desperation. The churlish philosopher maintains that, if the world lay in his power, he would give it to the beasts as they would at least rid it of men. Timon follows this with one of his supreme denunciations:

A beastly ambition, which the gods grant thee t' attain to! If thou wert the lion, the fox would beguile thee; if thou wert the lamb, the fox would eat thee; if thou wert the fox, the lion would suspect thee, when, peradventure thou wert accus'd by the ass. If thou wert the ass, thy dulness would torment thee; and still thou liv'dst but as a breakfast to the wolf. If thou wert the wolf, they greediness would afflict thee, and oft thou shouldst hazard thy life for thy dinner. Wert thou the unicorn,

pride and wrath would confound thee, and make thine own
self the conquest of thy fury. . . . What beast couldst thou be
that were not subject to a beast? And what beast art thou
already, that seest not thy loss in transformation!

4.3.324–343

This scene with Apemantus ends with them both hurling abuse
at each other.

Timon's invocation to the gold scattered at his feet is for it to
destroy mankind:

> thou visible god,
> That sold'rest close impossibilities,
> And mak'st them kiss! thou speak'st with every tongue
> To every purpose! O thou touch of hearts!
> Think thy slave man rebels, and by thy virtue
> Set them into confounding odds, that beasts
> May have the world in empire!

4.3.384–90

Some bandits and thieves appear and Timon gladly dispenses
gold to them as he bids them 'Do villainy, do'. Timon begins a
period of transition. The dawning realisation of inner despair
leads to a kind of spiritual abnegation. His faithful steward reappears and attempts to stay and comfort him. Timon banishes
the steward as well, after proffering handfuls of gold at him with
the injunction:

> Hate all, curse all, show charity to none,
> But let the famish'd flesh slide from the bone
> Ere thou relieve the beggar. Give to dogs
> What thou deniest to men; let prisons swallow 'em,
> Debts wither 'em to nothing. Be men like blasted woods,
> And may diseases lick up their false bloods!
> And so, farewell and thrive.

4.3.527–33

By the time that the steward reappears with two of the Senators,
who try to appeal to Timon to return to Athens to protect them
from the onslaught of Alicibiades's army, we know that Timon
has passed beyond worldly hate and misanthropy to an almost
trance-like willingness for death:

> Why, I was writing of my epitaph;
> It will be seen to-morrow. My long sickness
> Of health and living now begins to mend,

And nothing brings me all things. Go, live still;
Be Alcibiades your plague, you his,
And last so long enough!

5.1.183–8

Timon's body is found 'Entomb'd upon the very hem o' th' sea',
but we are left uncertain as to how he dies. Shakespeare just
writes 'Exit Timon into his cave'. It is remarkable that, of all
Shakespeare's tragic heroes, he is the only one to walk from the
stage instead of being carried from it. Does he drown in the sea
or starve in his cave? Or on the sea-shore? Is his death by natural
causes, or, in the final despair by his own hand? We do not know
what Shakespeare intended:

Lips, let sour words go by and language end:
What is amiss, plague and infection mend!
Graves only be men's works and death their gain!
Sun, hide thy beams. Timon hath done his reign.

5.1.218–21

ANTONY AND CLEOPATRA
Anna Raeburn

The journalist and broadcaster Anna Raeburn made some of this programme on location in the City of London.

*A*ntony and Cleopatra presents us with the idyllic picture of a great and powerful love being shared by two people at the height of their fame and glory. Their wealth and power makes it possible for them to build a private world. As long as they can have that private world and maintain it without interference from the outside, all will be well. Antony and Cleopatra have this world, but it imposes its own limitations which force them to chafe. Ironically they personify the limitations of that world, each for the other. The real world intervenes and reminds them constantly that they come from opposing cultures and cannot escape their respective destinies. As the drama develops, the uneasy murmurings build to a roar climaxing in Cleopatra's death and simultaneously we see the whole story in clearer and clearer focus until all the unfortunate little lines and shadows are revealed.

Antony and Cleopatra is an epic love story and these lovers wish to see themselves totally outside the responsibilities of their past and present. We can admire them or despise them. We can find them wilful and even absurd, but I think such a passion has its appeal for all of us. They are involved in a situation with which we can all at least identify to some extent. Love is a deceptively simple word which is used to cover a vast variety of emotions. It can be spiritual or venial. It can inspire great sacrifice or simply become an excuse for meanness and degradation. A great love like Antony's for Cleopatra is infinitely variable and what this play is really about is the fragility of human beings when they place themselves totally at risk:

ANTONY: Let Rome in Tiber melt, and the wide arch
    Of the rang'd empire fall! Here is my space.
    Kingdom's are clay; our dungy earth alike

Feeds beast as man. The nobleness of life
Is to do thus, when such a mutual pair
And such a twain can do't, in which I bind,
On pain of punishment, the world to weet
We stand up peerless.

I.I.33–40

Shakespeare has endured as a writer because his observations do not date. Language changes, people come up with different interpretations of characters and plays, but he's always worthwhile making the effort to understand. His perception of heroes is just as applicable to much more ordinary people. His language is, of course, different in either case. Here he is writing about people who were already legendary and he writes lines which are dense with meaning and employ evocative images, yet it is a language for the human as well as the heroic.

Nowadays it's hard to believe in heroes and there's little opportunity for men like Antony to bestride the world or for women like Cleopatra to dazzle the eye and haunt the imagination. Yet there are still contexts in which an Antony or a Cleopatra could exist. Imagine Antony as a captain of industry or the chairman of a multinational. His rowing blue secured him patronage and now, with diligence and the right amount of political deviousness, he's climbed to the top. Is he perhaps one of those fortunate people who are always in the right place at the right time? He certainly does all the right things. He makes a suitable marriage, has two lovely daughters and a house by the river. He's at the top of his profession. You've got to admire Antony, a natural leader with the common touch. If he seems a little pompous, even arrogant sometimes, that's only the natural rough edge of his exemplary virility. Yet his temples are, on closer inspection, more grey than greying. Is good living finally beginning to blur the outline? He's finding it increasingly difficult to be the life and soul of the party, though he still desperately wants to be accepted as one of the boys. And the job? It runs itself. There was a time when he cherished political ambitions, but that's past. He's still consulted, of course, as one of the inner sanctum, but destined for nothing more. Yet he's still a commanding figure who inspires great respect and loyalty. Why, then, does he feel increasingly that it's all tarnished and that life is passing him by? Is he a victim of what we call the mid-life crisis, the male menopause? If he is, the story's an old one. He may well go off the rails and somewhere the other woman is waiting, the Cleopatra of the story. As soon as he steps out of line, the ranks close against him. The boss is bound to disapprove if you go completely native:

> OCTAVIUS: Let's grant it not
> Amiss to tumble on the bed of Ptolemy,
> To give a kingdom for a mirth, to sit
> And keep the turn of tippling with a slave,
> To reel the streets at noon, and stand the buffet
> With knaves that smell of sweat. Say this becomes him—
> As his composure must be rare indeed
> Whom these things cannot blemish – yet must Antony
> No way excuse his foils when we do bear
> So great weight in his lightness. If he fill'd
> His vacancy with his voluptuousness,
> Full surfeits and the dryness of his bones
> Call on him for't! But to confound such time
> That drums him from his sport and speaks as loud
> As his own state and ours – 'tis to be chid
> As we rate boys who, being mature in knowledge,
> Pawn their experience to their present pleasure,
> And so rebel to judgement.

> 1.4.16–33

It's as if Antony looks back down the whole of his life and finds it without savour. His love for Cleopatra makes him want to live again. For him she is part mother, part mistress, wholly enchantress. To cast her off would be to admit the chaos of his innermost being and he can't face that. Few people at forty plus can, or are willing to. He clings to her as the only alternative he can find to what he has lacked in all the preceding years.

Antony needs to escape. He needs a grand passion, indeed he decides to have one and believes he has found it in Cleopatra. He dedicates himself to it: deserting his wife Fulvia and Rome, quarrelling with Caesar and alienating himself from his friends and his men. He wants to count the world well lost for love, to believe that his love for Cleopatra and hers for him will sustain him in the face of anything. When Fulvia dies, Rome intervenes briefly and lures him away from Egypt. It is almost a relief for him. He's something of a puritan in spite of his love of the flesh-pots, and Cleopatra has always known that she can only bind him to her if she can keep him with her in Egypt. Part of her spell is a desperation not dissimilar to his own. She is not young. She has invested heavily in their love, believing it to be epic and all-consuming. Is this her immortality?

CLEOPATRA: Can Fulvia die?
ANTONY: She's dead, my Queen.
    Look here, and at thy sovereign leisure read
    The garboils she awak'd. At the last, best.
    See when and where she died.
CLEOPATRA: O most false love!
    Where be the sacred vials thou shouldst fill
    With sorrowful water? Now I see, I see,
    In Fulvia's death how mine receiv'd shall be.

1.3.58–65

The aspect of Shakespeare's play which comes over least clearly in the writing is that the action takes place over a period of ten years. No infatuation of the kind associated with a crisis or turning point in life would last that long of itself. There is a desperation between Antony and Cleopatra and their relationship is more to do with obsession than affection. The western romantic tradition has only ever accepted unsuitable love providing it ends in death – a tremendously wasteful concept as far as I am concerned. Cleopatra has been called a compound of contradictions. A large part of her charm lay in her 'infinite variety'. She could be all queen one minute, all courtesan the next, at first imperious and then amazingly childish and child-like. It's probably fair to say that she's the antithesis of any Roman matron that Antony had ever known – wonderful to behold, but probably hell to live with. She had already captivated Julius Caesar and Pompey and she represented a dark, mysterious world that the Romans were afraid might one day overtake them. She has all the magic and mystery of the great stars of the silent screen such as Theda Bara and Claudette Colbert, when the cinema was in its infancy and nobody quite understood the miracle of the movie. Like these stars, Cleopatra was mercurial, passionate, sensuous and, for those who worshipped her, just a little untouchable and aloof.

Although Cleopatra belongs in the cinema, films could never have done her justice. She lives in report, as, for instance, in Plutarch's description of her on her barge on the river Cydnus:

The poop whereof was of gold, the sails of purple and owres of silver, which kept stroke in rowing after the sound of the music of flutes, howboyes, citherns, viols, and other such instruments as they played on in the barge. And now for the person of herselfe: she was layd under a pavillion of cloth of gold of tissue, apparrelled and attired like the Goddess Venus, commonly drawen in picture: and hard by her, on either hand of her, prettie fair boys, apparrelled as painters doe set forth God Cupid, with little fans in their hands, with the which they fanned the wind upon her.

The stuff of which dreams are made and hard to improve upon, and Shakespeare, clever fellow, didn't try. As always, he took exactly what he needed from his source and fashioned a wonderful image of colour and light, silken and lyrical. We, the onlookers, ask whether Cleopatra was beautiful and Enobarbus replies:

> The barge she sat in, like a burnish'd throne,
> Burn'd on the water. The poop was beaten gold;
> Purple the sails, and so perfumed that
> The winds were love-sick with them; the oars were silver,
> Which to the tune of flutes kept stroke, and made
> The water which they beat to follow faster,
> As amorous of their strokes. For her own person,
> It beggar'd all description. She did lie
> In her pavilion, cloth-of-gold, of tissue,
> O'erpicturing that Venus where we see
> The fancy out-work nature. On each side her
> Stood pretty dimpled boys, like smiling Cupids,
> With divers-colour'd fans, whose wind did seem
> To glow the delicate cheeks which they did cool,
> And what they undid did.

2.2.195–209

Enobarbus watches everything and comments on it like a Greek chorus. This plain-spoken man has more subtlety and insight into human nature than Antony and Cleopatra put together. It is he who watches while Antony goes to meet Caesar to clear the air and himself of blame for the insurrection raised by his brother and his late wife, Fulvia. Enobarbus is watching again when Antony contracts an expedient marriage to Caesar's sister, Octavia. For a moment Enobarbus hopes that Antony will break away from Egypt and be himself again. But even as he hopes, he knows in his heart of hearts that the pull of Cleopatra is too strong and that Antony will return to her, Octavia will be insulted, Caesar angered and that trouble will follow.

Antony takes his stand against Caesar, Rome and everything

ANNA RAEBURN

he once believed in on the sea of Actium. He needs to believe
that he's still the golden boy who can do anything and Cleopatra
encourages him in this belief. They're just like elderly children
playing 'Who's the king of the castle?', but they forget that the
ships, the soldiers and the risks are all real. The decision to fight
is fatal. Suddenly, in the midst of the battle, Cleopatra's barge
turns and leaves the scene. To the shame and disillusion of his
men, Antony follows her. The valiant general has broken faith
with himself and them and is now seen as a strumpet's fool.
What compelled him to this fateful and uncharacteristic
decision? He can't explain it even to himself. He acted blindly.
He rails at Cleopatra, but honesty compels him to admit that the
responsibility is his and his alone. No matter how much he loves
her, with this one decision he has made an irrevocable break with
the past. Honour, reputation and self-respect are all sacrificed.
Now he really is hers and hers alone. But Cleopatra loved the old
Antony, the noble Roman, the conquering hero, and it is
essential to her love that they maintain their images of power and
fame. So Antony roars himself back into the role of warrior once
again and Enobarbus watches, only too aware that it's all bluff, of
no more substance than a small boy shouting in the dark:

> ANTONY: Caesar sits down in Alexandria, where
> I will oppose his fate. Our force by land
> Hath nobly held; our sever'd navy too
> Have knit again, and fleet, threat'ning most sea-like.
> Where hast thou been, my heart? Doest thou hear, lady?
> If from the field I shall return once more
> To kiss these lips, I will appear in blood.
> I and my sword will earn our chronicle.
> There's hope in't yet.
> CLEOPATRA: That's my brave lord!

> 3.13.168–76

Yet, in the midst of all his bluster, Antony knows that he is
doomed. Fortune has turned against him. As he dons his armour
for the forthcoming battle, he is told that Enobarbus has
deserted him. I don't hear any surprise or recrimination in his
reception of the news, only forgiveness and resignation. It is yet
another omen for the future.

An initial success in battle makes the lovers expansive again,
but not for long. The fleet is routed and Antony blames his
Egypt for having sold him to Caesar. Cleopatra plays her trump
card. She pretends to kill herself and is reported to have called

Antony's name with her dying breath. Both the Romans and the Egyptians had a profound respect for death and particularly suicide as a positive act. Antony hears the news as cleansing and noble. Now at last he's free to love Cleopatra again and he dreams of being reunited with her where the cares and troubles of the world cannot intrude upon them. In death, he says, there is triumph; in life, only disappointment. He longs to see Cleopatra again and so summons Eros to kill him, but Eros declines – the final irony of love refusing to put the great lover out of his misery. And so Antony must take the final responsibility and he falls upon his sword in true Roman fashion. Dying, Antony is taken to the monument where Cleopatra and her women have taken refuge and here the lovers share the most naked exchange of the play. They have so far dominated their worlds that it is only in facing something more powerful than themselves, in this case the inexorability of death, that they are at last free to act as human beings:

> CLEOPATRA: Noblest of men, woo't die?
> Hast thou no care of me? Shall I abide
> In this dull world, which in thy absence is
> No better than a sty? O, see, my women,
> The crown o' th' earth doth melt. My lord!
> O, wither'd is the garland of the war,
> The soldier's pole is fall'n! Young boys and girls
> Are level now with men. The odds is gone,
> And there is nothing left remarkable
> Beneath the visiting moon.

4.15.59–68

In some ways the play is very moral. It teaches that you cannot escape from the person you are, even if that is other than the person you wish to be, and that you cannot escape that knowledge for long. It teaches that the price of passion is often death, sometimes dishonour, almost certainly disillusion; that nobody is exempt from the price of passion, not the mightiest, the richest or the most wise. A man of forty is no stronger than a boy of fourteen if he thinks he has met the woman of his dreams, and a woman of forty will resort to all kinds of charm and trickery if she believes it will bind her true love to her side. If this seems little to get out of a great play perhaps its greatness lies in the truth of its perceptions. Antony and Cleopatra may be ridiculous to us, but to each other they were the magnificent animals, larger than life, that nobody else wanted them to be.

Antony and Cleopatra
Barbara Jefford

Besides Cleopatra, Barbara Jefford's other Shake-
spearean parts have included Isabella, Rosalind,
Portia, Viola, Ophelia, Katherina and Mistress
Quickly.

Age cannot wither her, nor custom stale
Her infinite variety. Other women cloy
The appetites they feed, but she makes hungry
Where most she satisfies; . . . .

2.2.239–42

*A*ntony and Cleopatra has the broadest canvas of all Shakespeare's plays. It involves a huge empire and its scenes take place
from one end of the Mediterranean to the other. They switch
with cinematic speed from Alexandria to Rome, from Athens to
Actium, from palace to palace and from battlefield to battlefield.
The play deals with the sprawling political and military contest
with the highest stakes imaginable, the rulership of the civilised
world. Shakespeare used Sir Thomas North's translation of
Plutarch's *Lives of the Noble Grecians and Romans* as his source
and out of this historical account extracted a magnificent
tragedy. Despite the vastness of its background and its wealth of
historical detail, the play is essentially the tragedy of two lovers.
It is one of the greatest love stories, although also one of the
strangest. For it contains no private love scenes. Instead we see
the two lovers arguing in public, showing-off in public, meeting
in public after battles, clinging together in despair, behaving
irresponsibly and, finally, dying their very public deaths. Yet it is
still a love story.

I first came into contact with the play as a student in Bristol at
the age of fifteen and since then have had the good fortune to
play Cleopatra in three different productions. The first was at
the Oxford Playhouse in 1965, opposite my husband, John
Turner, and directed by Frank Hauser. Frank is a wonderful
director to work with and my line on the part was formed during

his rehearsals and hasn't changed much, although I hope that my ability to cope with the technical problems of playing it has improved. Then there was a production at the Nottingham Playhouse in 1966, again opposite my husband who was also playing Antony in *Julius Caesar*. The third time round was at the Old Vic, my favourite theatre. John and I were playing in Dryden's version of the story *All for Love* in repertoire with Toby Robertson's production of *Antony and Cleopatra*. It was a marvellous experience to do both plays, particularly on the same day.

One of the most important qualities about Cleopatra is that she is foreign and exotic. She was a foreigner to the Egyptians as well as to the Romans, as she was a Macedonian Greek, descended from one of Alexander the Great's generals. She is a strange, temperamental creature, whose capricious behaviour and volatile moods both confuse and fascinate everyone in the play. Her beauty should be dark and Mediterranean. It would have been unfashionable to the Elizabethans and not usually presented for admiration on their stages. It is interesting that the young man who first played her apparently also played Mistress Quickly and Juliet's Nurse. The part therefore makes different demands from those normally associated with 'leading ladies'. Cleopatra has to be exotic, but she also has to be something of a comedienne. She is also a Queen and a particularly tragic one. Her character is in fact a mass of contradictions: she's capricious and resolute, comic and terrifying, tender and cruel, coarse and lyrical. She's thus the biggest challenge any actress could be presented with.

Her lover Antony, although cast in a different mould temperamentally, shares with her this kind of larger than life personality. He's a heroic figure, who is an honoured and respected military leader and member of the Roman Triumvirate. He is a charismatic general as well as an able technician and tactician. He was always a man of huge appetites, but his behaviour after his alliance with Cleopatra set new standards even for that age and the scandal reverberated round the empire. We get the Roman view of their antics from Philo at the very beginning of the play:

Nay, but this dotage of our general's
O'erflows the measure. Those his goodly eyes,
That o'er the files and musters of the war
Have glow'd like plated Mars, now bend, now turn,
The office and devotion of their view
Upon a tawny front. His captain's heart,

Which in the scuffles of great fights hath burst
The buckles on his breast, reneges all temper,
And is become the bellows and the fan
To cool a gipsy's lust. Look where they come!
Take but good note, and you shall see in him
The triple pillar of the world transform'd
Into a strumpet's fool. Behold and see.

I.I.I–I3

This is probably the start of one of their 'gaudy nights'. It is very much a public scene. Cleopatra demands that Antony should publicly tell her how much he loves her. It's not a romantic scene and the imagery is extravagant rather than tender. Their gestures are also extravagant. Cleopatra describes later on in the play how she 'put my tires and mantles on him, whilst/I wore his sword Philippan'. On stage we tried to give a visual illustration of this extravagant behaviour by exchanging our outer garments. Reports of these 'gaudy nights' lead to Octavius's complaints about Antony. The shock to the Romans of this behaviour can be assessed if we imagine reports of the Duke of Edinburgh on a royal tour being seen on the streets of Delhi early one morning blind drunk and dressed in a sari.

When the messengers from Rome suddenly arrive, it's like a bucket of cold water being thrown over the mischievous party spirit. Cleopatra, sensing that Antony may be called away, embarks on a typically dazzling display of her manipulative techniques over him. She taunts him, but urges him to 'hear the ambassadors' rather than trying to persuade him not to as a less astute woman might have done. She takes him to the edge of anger but finally has her way completely. The messengers are brushed aside and the lovers head for yet another night on the town: 'To-night we'll wander through the streets and note/The qualities of people'. For Antony this is only a postponement of the moment when he has to face up to his duty. His wife Fulvia is dead after being involved with his brother in an armed rebellion. The other piece of bad news is that Pompey, the son of Pompey the Great, is threatening the security of Rome. Antony the Roman commander begins to take over from Antony the libertine, Hercules and plated Mars from Dionysius. Despite Cleopatra's desperate attempts to stop him, he leaves to face up to his responsibilities. At the moment of their parting, Cleopatra switches from the taunting, provoking tactics

that usually work so well to being a loving, dignified and understanding Queen:

> Your honour calls you hence;
> Therefore be deaf to my unpitied folly,
> And all the gods go with you! upon your sword
> Sit laurel victory, and smooth success
> Be strew'd before your feet!

1.3.97–101

This binds him to her with a sort of golden cord that will draw
him back to her emotionally however far away he strays.

So Antony leaves Alexandria and the play leaps ahead of him
to Rome, where we meet Octavius and Lepidus, before returning to Egypt for what is usually called the Mandragora scene
with Cleopatra languishing extravagantly after her lover's
departure. I have the feeling she scarcely ever got properly
dressed whilst Antony was away. We based the costumes at the
Old Vic on Tiepolo paintings so I was in the wonderful desha-
bille that you often see his ladies and goddesses disporting themselves in, lolling on cushions and saying:

> O Charmian,
> Where think'st thou he is now? Stands he or sits he?
> Or does he walk? or is he on his horse?
> O happy horse, to bear the weight of Antony!
> Do bravely, horse, for wot'st thou whom thou mov'st?
> The demi-Atlas of this earth, the arm
> And burgonet of men. He's speaking now,
> Or murmuring 'Where's my serpent of old Nile?'
> For so he calls me. Now I feed myself
> With most delicious poison. Think on me,
> That am with Phoebus' amorous pinches black,
> And wrinkled deep in time?

1.5.18–29

We are next introduced to Pompey in Messina and quickly see
what an empty shell this bearer of a great name is. Then we go
back to Rome and the meeting of the Triumvirate, where we see
the differences in temperament that divide Antony and Octavius.
Antony is relaxed, magnanimous, assured and humorous with
the easy strength of someone with such a massive reputation that
he doesn't have to try too hard. Octavius, at this time still untried
in command, seeks refuge in being reproving, priggish and almost
schoolmasterish. There's a splendid contrast between Antony,

BARBARA JEFFORD

the magnificent, likeable 'one man band' with his informal,
irreverent followers such as Enobarbus, and Octavius, an organised delegator of authority who always finds the right man for
the right job. Octavius seems relatively callow, but don't be
fooled by him. He has the cleverness, ambition and the will to do
something about it. He's the sort of man who takes work home at
weekends. I suspect that Antony senses that this ambitious young
man will eventually try to overshadow him and perhaps that is
why he's so ready to agree to a political marriage between himself and Octavius's sister, Octavia. Meanwhile, the others in
Octavius's train are panting to know the truth behind the
rumours from Alexandria. Enobarbus, the archetypal knowing
old soldier from a notorious posting launches into that glorious
evocation of the aura of glamour, mystery and excitement which
surrounds Cleopatra with the simple preamble 'I will tell you':

> The barge she sat in, like a burnish'd throne,
> Burn'd on the water. The poop was beaten gold;
> Purple the sails, and so perfumed that
> The winds were love-sick with them; the oars were silver,
> Which to the tune of flutes kept stroke, and made
> The water which they beat to follow faster,
> As amorous of their strokes. For her own person,
> It beggar'd all description. She did lie
> In her pavilion, cloth-of-gold, of tissue,
> O'erpicturing that Venus where we see
> The fancy out-work nature. On each side her
> Stood pretty dimpled boys, like smiling Cupids,
> With divers-colour'd fans, whose wind did seem
> To glow the delicate cheeks which they did cool
> And what they undid did.

2.2.195–209

It is Octavius who precipitates the action from here on in. He
organises the rout and destruction of Pompey efficiently and
ruthlessly. He then removes Lepidus on what seem to be
dubious charges of conspiracy. Antony, at a safe distance in
Athens, sees himself as the next target and so returns to Cleopatra. They declare UDI and consolidate their corner of the
empire with various alliances. Yet Octavius bears down implac-
ably upon them. As the play begins to move at lightning pace we
see how Antony, despite having the great advantage in land
power, is determined to fight at sea. Cleopatra contributes sixty
ships and graces the event with her own presence. The battle at

Actium is the turning point. It is a momentual defeat and a momentual error of judgement by Antony. His soldiers are appalled by the way in which Cleopatra leaves during the height of the battle and is followed by her lover: 'I never saw an action of such shame'. They realise only too well that 'our leader's led,/And we are women's men'. Antony, away from Cleopatra, can think and act calmly and clearly, but in her arms he is over-whelmed by her mood to his eventual destruction. This would be a new experience for him. He had had many other affaires, but had always been in charge. Now he is in thrall to Cleopatra. This is his fatal flaw. It eventually destroys him and is his tragedy.

The strange chemistry that draws them together is fatal for Cleopatra as well. She is a highly intelligent, politically aware woman, who has been on the throne since the age of eighteen. She has eased her way through the dangerous shoals and reefs of an unstable age to the point where there is the possibility of her establishing with Antony a Greco-Roman monarchy, which would rule the entire Roman world. She was also a brilliant linguist, the first of the Ptolomies to learn to speak Egyptian. She would also speak to Parthians, Syrians, Medes, Jews and Arabs in their own languages. Plutarch tells us that she rarely needed an interpreter when conducting business of state. She and Antony would have been quite a political combination. They were indeed quite a combination, but in the wrong way. They had the worst possible effect on each other, behaving like demi-gods in a political climate that had no room for such physical and mental indulgence. They loved each other and ruined each other.

It's now a greatly diminished Antony whom we see treating the winning of a minor skirmish on land as if it were a great battle. The language is, as usual, grandiloquent, but it is now tinged with a consciousness of his age:

> Mine nightingale,
> We have beat them to their beds. What, girl! though grey
> Do something mingle with our younger brown, yet ha' we
> A brain that nourishes our nerves, and can
> Get goal for goal of youth.

4.8.19–23

I used to love playing this scene, leaping into Antony's arms and being hurled into the air. What a triumph they would have had in Rome if they had won. Antony's days of triumph are, however, in the past. The last encounter with Octavius sees the Egyptian navy deserting him to join the Romans. When he returns from the battle he is demented with rage against the Fates, his forces and, above all, Cleopatra, whom he feels has betrayed him. She really is in fear of her life when she flees to the monument and sends word that she is dead. This impulsive, emotional reaction is designed to prevent the enraged Antony from following her. She immediately thinks better of it, but by then it is too late. Antony has followed his Roman instincts and attempted to kill himself in order to join Cleopatra 'where souls do couch on flowers'. Fortunately for generations of playgoers, he does not succeed and survives to die in Cleopatra's arms. The great fallen giant strives to keep enough breath in his body to give his protective advice, pathetically mistaken as it happens, and she tenderly echoes her first mocking scenes with him by gently chiding him: 'Noblest of men, won't die?/Hast thou no care of me?' Antony's last moment in our production showed him, with a ghost of the laughter she could usually provoke him, trying to raise a hand to caress her face.

Cleopatra is then alone, and being alone, rises to heights not achieved in any other Shakespeare play. The last scenes of *Antony and Cleopatra* are superb. Cleopatra is determined to join Antony in death 'after the high Roman fashion', but with a last piece of play-acting convinces Octavius that she is keeping treasure from him and that she intends to stay alive. She thus buys herself all the time she needs to be arrayed 'like a Queen' and to die nobly. Her last speech is incomplete. I always imagine her seeing her lover as the asp's poison starts to work, seeing him before her as he was in his prime, laughing, glorious, making all around look commonplace, holding out his mighty arms to fold her in. 'O Antony!', she says, 'What should I stay'. And she joins him in those Elysian fields, where the other spirits gaze in envy. The writing throughout this last passage of the play is masterly. The sheer musicality of it is breathtaking. It demands from the actress a quality that Ralph Richardson calls 'the bowing' and reminds me of one of the last quartets of Beethoven in its compressed passion and lyricism. I think it is the greatest work of the greatest of poets.

FURTHER READING

I have compiled a reading list on the plays covered in each year of the *Shakespeare in Perspective* programmes. This is then distributed to those who write into the BBC for it. I don't want to duplicate those lists here, particularly in view of what I and many of the contributors have said about the importance of Shakespeare in performance. I would like instead to offer a much more selective list of some of the books that Victor Poole and I have found helpful when thinking about the plays. Like the other views expressed in this volume, this list is very much a personal choice. It contains some of the books on Shakespeare that I would take to my desert island, along with the complete works.

A. P. ROSSITER *Angel with Horns and Other Shakespeare Lectures* (Longmans, 1970, paperback)

PETER SACCIO *Shakespeare's English Kings: History, Chronicle and Drama* (Oxford University Press, 1977, paperback). Provides essential background material on the histories

JOHN WILDERS *The Lost Garden: A View of Shakespeare's English and Roman History Plays* (Macmillan, 1978, paperback)

MICHAEL LONG *The Unnatural Scene: A Study in Shakespearean Tragedy* (Methuen, 1976, paperback)

C. L. BARBER *Shakespeare's Festive Comedy: A Study of Dramatic Form in Relation to Social Custom* (Princeton University Press, 1972, paperback)

ARNOLD KETTLE (ED.) *Shakespeare in a Changing World* (Lawrence and Wishart, 1964)

LESLIE FIEDLER *The Stranger in Shakespeare* (Paladin, 1974, paperback) lively, polemical and topical

JAN KOTT *Shakespeare our Contemporary* (Methuen, 1967, paperback) one of the most influential recent studies

SAMUEL SCHOENBAWM *William Shakespeare: A Compact Documentary Life* (Oxford University Press, 1978, paperback) well illustrated, scholarly but entertaining biography

ANNE RIGHTER *Shakespeare and the Idea of the Play* (Chatto and Windus, 1962, and subsequently in paperback by Penguins)

JOHN RUSSELL BROWN *Free Shakespeare* (Heineman, 1977, paperback) lively polemic on the need to put Shakespeare back in the theatre

ALFRED HARBAGE *Shakespeare's Audience* Columbia University Press, 1961, paperback)

NICHOLAS BROOKE *Shakespeare's Early Tragedies* (Methuen, 1973, paperback)

NORTHROP FRYE *A Natural Perspective: The Development of Shakespearean Comedy and Romance* (Harcourt, Brace & World, inc., 1965, paperback)

Some of these accounts are aimed at university students, although I believe that they are all reasonably accessible to a wider audience. It is often better, however, to find out something about a particular play from the various anthologies and series available before going to the more specialist studies:

BBC TV *Shakespeare Editions of the Plays*
These contain a short discussion of the play by John Wilders, as well as an account by Henry Fenwick of some of the ideas which informed the production.

Edward Arnold Studies in English Literature
This series of short paperback introductions now covers most of Shakespeare's plays.

Penguin Shakespeare Library Anthologies
Anthologies of modern criticism on the tragedies, histories and comedies.

Stratford-Upon-Avon Studies (Edward Arnold)
A number of volumes of critical essays on Shakespeare and Elizabethan and Jacobean theatre. Arranged thematically or chronologically.

Macmillan Casebook Series
Anthologies of critical opinions on most of the major plays.

Shakespeare Survey (Cambridge University Press)
Annual publication of essays, often grouped around a particular play or theme, together with book and theatre reviews. Some of the essays have been reprinted in book form, eg. ed. K. Muir and S. Wells, *Aspects of Hamlet* (Cambridge University Press, 1979, paperback)

Useful reference books include two by Stanley Wells, *Shakespeare: An Illustrated Dictionary* (Oxford University Press, 1978, paperback) and *Shakespeare: Select Bibliographical Guides* (Oxford University Press, 1973, paperback)